SUCHE WERKIS TO WERCHE

SUCHE WERKIS TO WERCHE

Essays on *Piers Plowman*

In Honor of David C. Fowler

Edited by Míceál F. Vaughan

East Lansing

COLLEAGUES PRESS

1993

MEDIEVAL TEXTS AND STUDIES 15

ISBN 0–937191–36–1
Library of Congress Catalog Card Number 93–72663
British Library Cataloguing-in-Publication data available
Copyright 1993 by Colleagues Press Inc.

Published by Colleagues Press Inc.
Post Office Box 4007
East Lansing, MI 48826

Distribution outside North America
Boydell and Brewer Ltd.
Post Office Box 9
Woodbridge, Suffolk IP12 3DF
England

PREFACE

DETERMINING EXACTLY WHEN, and how, to honor the career of a distinguished colleague never proves an easy task. It is made no easier when that colleague is David Fowler, who has combined a long career of teaching and service at the University of Washington with distinguished research and publication in a number of distinct areas of medieval English culture: his dissertation editing the A-Version *Vita* of *Piers Plowman* and a subsequent book examining the literary relations between the A- and B-Versions; a monograph on Chrétien de Troyes; a literary history of the popular ballad; two books dealing with the Bible and biblical tradition in Old and Middle English literature; and three books on John Trevisa (two biographical studies and an edition of his translation of Aegidius Romanus's *De Regimine Principum*). Those who know David well know how these variegated plants interdepend in the ecology of his uniquely fertile half-acre.

Originally intended to honor David's retirement from classroom teaching at the University he had served for more than forty years, this book now instead celebrates the productive continuation of his scholarly career. While researching his dissertation at the University of Chicago, David inaugurated his scholarly publications with a letter in the *Times Literary Supplement* querying the location of the Ingilby MS, a manuscript most famous perhaps for its eighty-seven lines from the problematic "Passus Twelve" of *Piers Plowman* A. His subsequent publications — fully detailed in the bibliography provided by Paul Remley later in this book — asked a number of less easily answered questions. The answers David himself presented were delivered in a firm, authoritative voice, a voice he invokes only in scholarly disputation. There, his energetic beliefs assume a rhetorical force and assertiveness which complement the gentle and humane civility that graces his generous exchanges with students, colleagues, and friends.

Forty-five years after his first appearance in print, it is appropriate to celebrate the sustained accomplishments of this scholar and gentleman with a small book of essays on his beloved *Piers Plowman*. With it we acknowledge David Fowler's contributions to the rich and continuing discussions and debates which surround that subject, and these efforts by fellow-laborers in that large and productive vineyard will, we know, be generously received by David. We hope they may also contribute to our collaborative efforts at understanding the varied texts we call by the singular name *Piers Plowman*.

CONTENTS

ABBREVIATIONS

CEMERS   Center for Medieval and Early Renaissance Studies (Binghamton, NY)

EETS   Early English Text Society (OS = Original Series; ES = Extra Series; SS = Supplementary Series)

JEGP   *Journal of English and Germanic Philology*

MS(S)   Manuscript(s)

PL   J. P. Migne, *Patrologiae Cursus Completus . . . Series Latina*

PMLA   *Publications of the Modern Language Association*

RES   *Review of English Studies*

SUCHE WERKIS TO WERCHE

The Figure of Repentance in *Piers Plowman*

JOHN A. ALFORD

B ECAUSE CRITICAL DISCUSSION of the confessional drama in *Piers Plowman* B V. 60–505 has focused almost exclusively on the poet's vivid portraits of the Seven Deadly Sins, many readers may be surprised to learn that the central role belongs to Repentance.[1] None of the Sins is given so many lines (more than a hundred). Like countless other allegorical virtues,[2] Repentance suffers from a lack of imaginative appeal. The Seven Deadly Sins are described in concrete language ("Enuye . . . pale as a pelet," "Coueitise . . . bitelbrowed and baberlipped," "Sleuþe al bislabered wiþ two slymy eiȝen"); they have friends named Betty Brewster and Robin Roper; they congregate in kitchens, taverns, markets; they all have stories to tell. By contrast, throughout the entire scene, Repentance remains a faceless personification, little more in fact than a voice. We *see* the Sins; we only hear Repentance.

---

[1] Because this essay was written expressly for a volume in honor of David C. Fowler, I would like to acknowledge the force of his example in approaching each version of *Piers Plowman* as a discrete poem in its own right, an example well illustrated in his book *Piers the Plowman: Literary Relations of the A and B Texts* (Seattle: University of Washington Press, 1961). Whether these versions were the product of one author, as I assume here, or of several, as Fowler maintains, has no bearing on my conclusions. Throughout the essay the editions cited are, for the A-Text, George Kane, ed. (London: Athlone, 1960); for the B-Text, George Kane and E. Talbot Donaldson, eds. (London: Athlone, 1975); for the C-Text, Derek Pearsall, ed. (Berkeley and Los Angeles: University of California Press, 1979). Editorial brackets have not been retained.

[2] For example, Mercy in the play *Mankind*, who has more lines by far than any of the more colorful — and more memorable — rascals who oppose him.

However dull the figure of Repentance may seem, his prominence in the confession scene demands an explanation, especially in
the light of his previous existence. No reader coming directly from
the A-Text to the B-Text can fail to notice that Repentance is virtually a new creation. In the earlier version he begins his life as an
emotional response to Conscience's sermon on the field,

> Þanne ran repentaunce and reherside his teme
> And made wil to wepe watir wiþ his eiȝen
>   (A v. 43–44),

and then spends himself in a single breath, "ȝis, redily . . . Sorewe
for synne sauiþ wel manye" (A v.103–4). Present in only four lines of
the A-Text, Repentance is one of the myriad "low-intensity" personifications that spring like mayflies from the abstract nouns of the
poem and then, just as quickly, disappear forever.[3] In the revised
confessions, however, Repentance emerges as the focal character. It
is not simply that he has the most lines. His enlarged presence
qualitatively changes the scene. The personification now frames the
entire action: Repentance gives rise to the confessions in the first
place, sustains them throughout by intermittent questions and ex-
hortations, and closes the scene with a long, formal prayer. Even
when Repentance is not speaking his presence is acknowledged —
most subtly in the altered language and decorum of the Sins, most
obviously in their responses to direct questions like those put to
Coveitise:

> "Repentedestow euere," quod Repentaunce, "or restitucion madest? . . .
> Vsedestow euere vsurie? . . .
> Lentestow euere lordes for loue of hire mayntenaunce? . . .
> Hastow pite on pouere men þat for pure nede borwe? . . .
> Artow manlich among þi neȝebores of þi mete and drynke?"
>   (B v. 230–57)

Just when Coveitise seems to think that he has finished his confession (and in the A-Text he *has*), the questions begin. And the more

---

[3]The description of Repentance as "low-intensity" belongs to Elizabeth D. Kirk,
The Dream Thought of Piers Plowman (New Haven: Yale University Press, 1972), 47.

deeply Repentance probes, the more sin he uncovers.[4] The effect is not only to underscore a point made repeatedly in penitential manuals — that confession should be thorough — but also to recast the entire scene as a series of exchanges between penitents and priest-confessor. The expansion of Repentance transforms a sequence of monologues, or "murals" in one critic's apt description (Kirk 64), into something genuinely dramatic.

What drove the poet's revision of the scene, however, was probably more doctrinal than rhetorical. The sacrament of penance is cast in a wholly new light. When Robert Adams says that in the confession scene "the emphasis falls not on the objective ritual of penance but on the psychological reality of repentance,"[5] it is clear that he has the *revised* versions in mind. True repentance or contrition, as evidenced by a willingness to give back all the benefits of sin (restitution), becomes the touchstone of a valid confession. This emphasis on motive is carried through the rest of the poem. Indeed, the foregrounding of Repentance is perhaps the earliest hint of the B and C revisions' massive shift toward a more psychological view of Christian perfection. The original imperatives remain — to obey the law, to observe the Commandments, to fulfill the obligations of one's estate — but the ethical test of such conduct is increasingly the disposition of the will.[6] Trajan's pronouncement may be taken as a blunt summary of this new, or at least more manifest, perspective: "Lawe wiþouten loue . . . ley þer a bene!" (B XI.171).

In the following pages my focus will be primarily on the doctrinal implications of Repentance's expanded role — first, its meaning in relation to the sacrament of penance (including restitution); next, its meaning in relation to the sinners making their confessions (particu-

---

[4]In his note to this passage in the C-Text (119), Pearsall points out, "Repentance's questions have the sharpness and precision recommended to the confessor by penitential manuals (e.g. Mirk, *Instructions* 1293)." The action is repeated, in a sense, in the Haukyn episode: the longer Conscience and Will examine Haukyn's coat, the more they see how "it was moled in many places wiþ manye sondry plottes, / Of pride here a plot, and þere a plot of vnbuxom speche," etc. (B XIII.274 ff.).

[5]"Langland's Theology," *A Companion to Piers Plowman*, ed. John A. Alford (Berkeley: University of California Press, 1988), 101.

[6]See, for example, John Bowers, *The Crisis of Will in Piers Plowman* (Washington, D. C.: The Catholic University of America Press, 1986). That the poet's "revisions suggest a growing preoccupation with the powers and limitations of the will" (42) is a point to which Bowers returns often.

larly Robert the Robber); and finally its meaning in relation to the larger purpose of the poem.[7]

I

It has long been acknowledged that the sacrament of penance — comprising the three steps of *contritio cordis*, *confessio oris*, and *satisfactio operis* — is the underlying schema of the second vision of *Piers Plowman*. "In this vision," as James Simpson notes, "Reason provokes *contrition* through his sermon; Repentance hears the *confessions* of the contrite sinners; and in hope of absolute pardon, the sinners make *satisfaction* through their pilgrimage."[8] Although this description holds for all three versions of the poem, only in B and C is the pattern fully developed. In A the emphasis is on the outward signs of the sacrament, oral confession and satisfaction of works (penance); the vital impulse of contrition figures minimally, and the word itself (of which there are twenty-eight occurrences in B[9]) not at all.

What is contrition? The A-Text raises the question only to frustrate any attempt to answer it. Although Repentance initially seems to stand for the contrition felt by the folk on the field — "þanne ran repentance . . . And made wil to wepe watir" — it is not long before we see a clear distinction between this personification of penitential sorrow and the "sorwe" expressed by some of the penitents themselves. Repentance's only words in the A-Text — "ʒis, redily . . . Sorewe for synne sauiþ wel manye" — get the following response:

---

[7]Questions arising from the allegorical nature of Repentance — such as how one figure can represent both the contrition of those who confess and the priest who hears their confessions — must be postponed. For the time being, J. A. Burrow's comment will suffice: " '[C]onfessing to Repentance,' unlike 'listening to Reason' [who has just preached], makes little sense when one tries to convert it into literal terms. But the general point of the episode is quite clear. Once a man has taken thought and recognised his imperfections, he must then repent and confess" ("The Action of Langland's Second Vision," *Essays in Criticism* 15 [1965]: 251; repr. in Robert J. Blanch, ed., *Style and Symbolism in Piers Plowman* [Knoxville: University of Tennessee Press, 1969], 213).

[8]*Piers Plowman: An Introduction to the B-text* (London: Longman, 1990), 64.

[9]These are as follows: *Contricio*, IV.36, XI.81, XIV.17; *contritum*, XIII.58, XV.194; *contrit*, XIV.90; *contricion*, XI.81, XI.135, XII.175, XII.177, XII.181, XIV.16, XIV.83, XIV.85, XIV.88, XIV.93, XIV.282, XIV.286, XIX.331, XIX.346, XX.213, XX.316, XX.333, XX.357, XX.363, XX.369, XX.371, XX.376.

"I am sory," quaþ enuye, "I am but selde oþere,
And þat makiþ me so mat for I ne may me venge."
(A v.104–5)

No doubt, Envy *is* "sory," for sorrow is the very essence of this particular sin. As Aquinas observes, "[S]ome sins are committed through sorrow, e.g. sloth and envy."[10] The point is made repeatedly in vernacular penitential treatises. *Handlyng Synne* notes, "þe man þat ys ful of enuye, / He ys euer sorowful,"[11] and Chaucer's Parson comments, "For wel unnethe is ther any synne that it ne hath som delit in itself, save oonly Envye, that evere hath in itself angwissh and sorwe."[12] As for sloth, its Latin name is *tristitia* (sorrow) as well as *acedia*;[13] and the Parson's characterization of the sin as "hevy, thogtful, and wraw . . . the angwissh of troubled herte" (677–78) is close to that of envy. Thus when we read that "Sleuþe for sorewe fil doun a swowe" (A v.213), we cannot be certain that this is not, once again, the habitual sorrow of the sin itself, the sorrow of despair against which Vigilate warns Sloth immediately after, "war þe for wanhope wile þe betraye" (A v.216). Nowhere is the deflation or ironic extension of penitential language more evident, however, than in the confession of Glutton (A v.146–212).[14] On his way to church in order "hise coupe to shewe," Glutton ends up instead at the tavern; the entire scene then develops (in a manner reminiscent of goliardic parodies) as a grossly comic substitution for the sacramental observance Glutton has put off. Glutton's attention is diverted from his "coupe" to his "cuppe"; he participates in a game in which the cloak of a cobbler named "Clement" is used for "amendis," while "whoso repentiþ [i.e., reneges] raþest shulde rise aftir" and make satisfaction

---

[10]*Summa Theologica*, Part 3, Supplement, ques. 2, art. 3; trans. Fathers of the English Dominican Province, 2nd rev. ed. (London: Burns Oates and Washbourne, 1928), 18:108. All subsequent citations in English from the *Summa Theologica* are from this translation.

[11]*Robert of Brunne's "Handlyng Synne"*, ed. F. J. Furnivall, part 1, EETS OS 119 (London: Kegan Paul, Trench, Trübner, 1901), 133 (lines 3919–20).

[12]*The Canterbury Tales*, X 490, in *The Riverside Chaucer*, gen. ed. Larry D. Benson (Boston: Houghton Mifflin, 1987), 303. All subsequent citations of Chaucer are from this edition.

[13]See Siegfried Wenzel, *The Sin of Sloth: Acedia in Medieval Thought and Literature* (Chapel Hill: University of North Carolina Press, 1967), 25 et seq.

[14]Glutton's confession as a parody of the sacrament of penance is explored fully in Nick Gray, "The Clemency of Cobblers: A Reading of 'Glutton's Confession' in *Piers Plowman*," *Leeds Studies in English* n.s. 17 (1986): 61–75. See also Simpson 66.

to Glutton himself "wiþ a galoun ale"; after Glutton has drunk to surfeit, he "pisside a potel in a paternoster while"; only after he has slept through Saturday and Sunday is he "asshamide" and ready to do penance — although contrition is arguably not the chief stimulus for a resolve "to faste, for hungir or þrist" following a two-day hangover.

The confusion of the scene is reminiscent of other representations of the folk on the field — "þe mase" of "alle maner of men" in the Prologue, the throng gathered around Lady Meed, the pilgrims as they "blustreden forþ as beestes" toward Truth. There is, however, an important difference. All these other scenes have an interpreter or guide figure: Holy Church to explain what "bemeniþ . . . þe feld ful of folk" (A I.1 ff.); Conscience to sort out the different kinds of meed (A III.217–76); Piers to show the way and later to separate winners from wasters (A VI.25 ff.). What is missing from the A-Text confession scene is a similarly authoritative voice — one that might probe the sincerity of the penitents, expose and correct their misapprehensions, declare precisely what is and is not a valid confession. When the poet came to revise the scene, apparently feeling the need for such a guide-figure, he found a ready candidate on the spot.

Placed in a crowd of look-alike sorrows, Repentance's first task in the B-Version is self-definition. How can this sorrow be distinguished from others — from the sorrow that is envy and sloth, from the remorse that comes with a hangover, from the regret of bad deals and failed enterprises? The question occupies a central place in the development of penitential theory. One of the challenges facing the early church Fathers was the need to separate Christian *dolor* from the countless pretenders that lurked in and among the word's subtle shades of meaning. *Non omnis dolor paenitentia*, "Not every sorrow is penitence," the pseudo-Augustinian *De vera et falsa paenitentia* warns;[15] and Tertullian castigates those who fail to "regulate the limit of their

---

[15]For example, the treatise says, we might feel sorrow because of exile from our native country (i.e., heaven) or because we are held back from it by our corruptible flesh. "But such sorrow comes more from desire than from self-punishment. Whence it differs from penitence. For penitence is a certain voluntary 'revenge' of the person who sorrows, punishing in himself what he grieves that he has committed" (*PL* 40: 1120; cf. Lombard's *Sentences* IV.15, *PL* 192: 872–77).

repentance," regretting (like Envy) the good with the bad![16] By the high Middle Ages a very elaborate profile of "true repentance" had been established. Raymund of Pennaforte, for example, can tell us all about the three "actions" of repentance, the three "species," the six "causes," the various effects, impediments, and other attributes.[17] When Repentance assumes control of the confessions in the B- and C-Texts, we see a proliferation of such topoi, not only in his speeches but in those of the Sins as well. The tears flow more freely; "shame" appears for the first time (B v.90, 125, 366); finally love of God becomes a prime motive for repentance (C vi.101 ff.).

Along with the "encyclopedic" approach to contrition, there was also the more or less standard definition: *Contritio est dolor pro peccatis assumptus, cum proposito confitendi, & satisfaciendi*[18] ("Contrition is an assumed [that is, voluntary] sorrow for sins, together with the purpose of confessing them and of making satisfaction for them"); or as Chaucer's Parson defines it, apparently translating from Pennaforte, "Contricioun is the verray sorwe that a man receyveth in his herte for his synnes, with sad purpos to do penance, and neveremoore to do synne" (125–30). Although the poet does not quote the definition as a whole (as he does many other penitential maxims[19]), its constituent parts played a role in his revision of the confession scene. First, *dolor pro peccatis*. "Sorwe for synne," Repentance tells Envy, "is sauacion of soules" (B v.127). Sloth acknowledges that "Ne riȝt sory for

---

[16]"But how unreasonably they [the men of this world] demean themselves in the act of penitence it will suffice to make plain by this one fact, that they apply it even to their good deeds. They repent them of their faith, love, simplicity, patience, compassion. According as an act hath met with ingratitude, they curse themselves because they have done a good deed, and they fix in their heart that sort of repentance chiefly, which is employed upon the best acts, taking care to remember never again to perform any good service: on repentance for evil deeds, on the contrary, they lay but a light stress. In fact, they more readily sin through this same repentance, than act rightly by its means," *Of Repentance*, in *Tertullian: Apologetic and Practical Treatises*, trans. C. Dodgson, *A Library of Fathers of the Holy Catholic Church* (Oxford: Parker, 1842), 1: 349–50.

[17]*Summa de Poenitentia et Matrimonio*, Lib. 3 (De poenitentiis, & remissionibus) (Rome, 1603; repr. Farnborough, Hants.: Gregg, 1967), 437–502.

[18]Pennaforte, *Summa* 3.8 (443). Aquinas devotes an article to the definition (*Summa Theologica*, Part 3, Suppl., qu. 1, art. 1).

[19]Many of these are treated by Nick Gray, "Langland's Quotations from the Penitential Tradition," *Modern Philology* 84 (1986–87): 53–60; for a full study of the Latin quotations, see my *Piers Plowman: A Guide to the Quotations* (Binghamton, NY: Medieval & Renaissance Texts & Studies, 1992).

my synnes yet . . . was I neuere" (B V.399); and at the end of his
confession Repentance instructs him in the exact phrasing to use, " 'I
am sory for my synne,' seye to þiselue" (B V.445). The moment is
echoed in Piers's instructions to the penitents on what they should
say to the gatekeeper at the castle of Truth: "Telleþ hym þis tokene:
. . . I parfourned þe penance þe preest me enioyned / And am sory
for my synnes" (B V.597–98).[20] Next, *assumptus*. The fact that contrition is an *assumed* sorrow—an "act of choice" (Aquinas)[21]—is
reflected in the B-Text's greater emphasis on the will. Although the
connection between repentance and the will is made explicit from
the start in all three versions ("Thanne ran Repentaunce . . . and
made wille to wepe water wiþ hise eiȝen"), only in B and C is it
mentioned again; for example, the narrator says that Repentance
"bad me wilne to wepe my wikkednesse to amende" (B V.187); and
Repentance warns that only those "þat with goode wille confessen
hem" shall avoid hell (C VI.336–38). The corollary—if contrition is
an act of will, so is sin—also receives greater prominence. For
example, Envy confesses to an "yuel wil" (B V.122), Sloth to a
"wikked wil" (B V.428); Lechery acknowledges his desire to have
women "to my wille" (C VI.190), and Wrath to have even "weder at
my wille" (C VI.113). Remarkably, it is in the revised confessions
that the word *will* appears for the first time as a part of the Sins'
moral vocabulary.[22] As for the rest of the definition—contrition is an
assumed sorrow for sins *together with the purpose of confessing and making
satisfaction for them*—it can be said that this unified conception of the
sacrament of penance is the most distinctive feature of the revised
scene. Contrition does not exist simply in conjunction with confession and satisfaction; in a virtual sense it *includes* them. The "pur-

---

[20]For additional examples of the phrase, see B X.76 (C XI.56) and B XVII.31 (C
XIX.19.30).

[21]" . . . since the act of contrition is both an act of virtue, and a part of the
sacrament of Penance, its nature as an act of virtue is explained in this definition by
mentioning its genus, viz. *sorrow*, its object by the words *for sins*, and the act of
choice which is necessary for an act of virtue, by the word *assumed*," *Summa Theologica*, Part 3, Supplement, qu. 1, art. 1 (trans. 18:100–1).

[22]The revised versions stress the importance of the will over the act in other ways
as well. For example, Sloth admits that in his prayers, "That I telle wiþ my tonge is
two myle fro myn herte" (B V.401); and Repentance promises salvation to Coveitise,
"By so hit be in thyn herte as y here thy tonge" (C VI.332). This distinction becomes
a major theme in the poem (see below, part III).

pose" of confessing and making satisfaction is a part of contrition —
so much so that where the performance of the external acts proves to
be impossible, contrition may stand in their place. This line of
argument, which the poet later develops in his dilation upon the
maxim *sola contricio delet peccatum* (B XI.81a),[23] expresses itself in the
structure of the present episode. The figure of Repentance is not
merely given more weight as a corrective to the A-Text's underdevel-
oped representation of the sacrament; rather Repentance expands to
contain both the confessions of the Sins and the specific works of
satisfaction they vow to undertake — "to faste," to "drinke but wiþ þe
doke," to "wende to walsyngham."

Within the larger, more unified conception of penance in B and
C, the requirement of restitution also assumes greater importance.
The idea hardly figures in the A-Text. The word itself never occurs
in the confession scene (or anywhere else for that matter), and the
few allusions are too brief (Sloth's "ȝet wile I ȝelde aȝen") or too
cryptic ("Robert þe robbour on *reddite* lokide") to leave a strong
impression. Upon further reflection or perhaps under the influence
of "antifraternal" writings on the subject,[24] the poet made restitution
a major theme of his poem. Coveitise's vow to "wende to walsyngham," apparently an adequate form of satisfaction by the standards
of the A-Text, is no longer enough to bring him "out of dette."
Repentance now tells him that he must also make restitution. At first
Coueitise is confused; he has no idea what the word means —

---

[23]See also the discussion of *sola contritio* in B XII.177, B XIV.16-17, and B
XIV.85-97. The maxim is extremely common in penitential and canon law sources
(see Gray, "Langland's Quotations"). It appears as well in the Parson's Tale, "I seye
that somtyme contricioun delivereth a man fro synne" (305); and the *Speculum
Sacerdotale* provides a gloss on "somtyme": "penaunce of herte may turne to saluacion
of a man withoute confessioun of mouþe; that is to wite, in tyme of nede and in
poynt of deþ, ȝif ther may noȝt be hadde no preste redy . . ." (ed. Edward H.
Weatherly, EETS OS 200 [London: Oxford University Press, 1936], 63). The
question is discussed at length by Aquinas, *Summa Theologica*, Part 3, Suppl., qu. 5,
arts. 1-3 (trans. 129-33). Pennaforte reviews the opinions on the matter: "Qualiter
autem hoc sit intelligendum, vtrum scilicet sola contritio sine confessione tollat
peccata, an contritio cum confessione, variae sunt opiniones" (3.11), 446. For
discussions by *Piers* scholars, see Greta Hort, *Piers Plowman and Contemporary Religious Thought* (New York: Macmillan, 1938), 150-55; Robert Adams, "Langland's
Theology," 101-2; Wendy Scase, *Piers Plowman and the New Anticlericalism* (Cambridge: Cambridge University Press, 1989), 38-39.

[24]Restitution as an important topic in polemical writings against the friars is
discussed at length by Scase, 23-31.

"I wende riflynge were restitucion" (B v.235). But when he learns
that he must restore everything he has gained by fraud, that otherwise he cannot be absolved (*Non dimittitur peccatum donec restituatur
ablatum*), "Thanne weex þe sherewe in wanhope & wolde han hanged
hymself" (B v.279). To counter such despair, Repentance not only
reminds Coueitise of God's infinite mercy but also proposes a remedy to what is evidently, at least in part, a cause of his wanhope:

> And if þow wite neuere to whom ne where to restitue
> Ber it to þe Bisshop, and bid hym of his grace
> Bisette it hymself as best be for þi soule.
>
> (B v.289–91)

Repentance's lecture is not the poet's only instrument for advancing
the theme of restitution. Sloth's simple vow to "ȝelde aȝen" becomes
an entirely new character in C, a Welshman named "ȝeuan-ȝelde-
aȝeyn-yf-y-so-moche-haue-Al-þat-y-wikkedly-wan-sithen-y-witte-
hadde" (C vi.310–11), presumably a bit of irony based on the supposition that a Welshman's nature is to welsh rather than to pay what
he owes. Much later Will learns from the Good Samaritan that
repentance must be joined with restitution, for (again) "*Numquam
dimittitur peccatum &c*"; God's mercy is great, "Ac er his rightwisnesse
to ruþe torne som restitucion bihoueþ" (B xvii.319). Finally all the
action of the poem comes to rest on the issue of *redde quod debes*:
Contrition lies sick, because thanks to the friars sinners no longer
take seriously the command to "pay what you owe."[25]

Contrition and restitution — the two ideas run through the poem's
argument like interwoven threads. In the confession scene, their
intimate connection is implied allegorically by the author's choice of
Repentance as the mouthpiece for restitution, and more directly by
the way in which this figure first introduces the subject —
"Repentedestow euere . . . or restitucion madest?" (B v.230) — as if
the two questions were the same. Certainly a person unwilling to
return "the thing taken" could not say that he was truly sorry to have
taken it. Because the poem's allegorical figures tend to define them-

---

[25]The imperative of *redde quod debes* extends beyond the formal sacrament of penance but, as R. W. Frank, Jr., says, "probably included restitution" — *Piers Plowman
and the Scheme of Salvation* (New Haven: Yale University Press, 1957), 106 n. 2. Cf.
note 40 below.

selves by their speeches — Conscience is given to making fine distinctions (on "mede" for example) and Patience to preaching "fiat voluntas" and "ne soliciti sitis" — we may say that Repentance's remarks on restitution are in a sense "autobiographical."

Nevertheless, many penitential treatises (as well as *Piers Plowman* scholars) treat restitution as a part of satisfaction. For example, to make satisfaction is, according to *Jacob's Well*, "to fulfylle þi penaunce enioyned of þe preest . . . & to restore þat þou hast falsely gett."[26] Myra Stokes states explicitly that restitution and penance together make up *satisfactio operis*.[27] Where does the correct answer lie? Does restitution belong with contrition or with satisfaction? In the view of some critics, restitution in *Piers Plowman* is a kind of floating idea that attaches itself now to one, now to the other. Siegfried Wenzel sees the poet's use of the word as equivocal: in the confession scene, *restitucion* means "restoring ill-won goods to their legal owner," but in the Good Samaritan's speech (B XVII.319-20), it "designates *satisfactio operis*, the third part of the sacrament of penance."[28] Morton Bloomfield puts such slippage (if indeed it is such) into historical perspective: "Although restitution is, strictly speaking, evidence of contrition, it also presupposes satisfaction; and treatments of this part of penance, especially in the high Middle Ages, sometimes involve the problem of restitution."[29] Given the diversity of opinion on where restitution belongs in the sacrament of penance (or where the poet thinks it belongs), we might do well to pause for a moment over the problem. More than the integrity of Repentance is at stake.

As the visible evidence of contrition, restitution comes before

---

[26]Ed. A. Brandeis, EETS OS 115 (London: Kegan Paul, 1900), 189.

[27]*Justice and Mercy in Piers Plowman: A Reading of the B-Text Visio* (London and Canberra: Croom Helm, 1984). For example, "The debt of sin was atoned or paid for, according to medieval theory, by restitution (the return of wrongfully appropriated money or goods) or penance (the undergoing of due punishment for transgressions). This constituted 'satisfaction'" (15). Elsewhere restitution is lumped with satisfaction as "repayment of the spiritual debt" contracted by sin (23). Simpson also classifies restitution under satisfaction (64). Despite her clear distinction in one place between restitution and satisfaction, Hort obscures it in another; for example, "Avarice niggardly intends to make a pilgrimage into Norfolk, a nice, inexpensive way of making restitution and giving satisfaction" (145).

[28]*The Sin of Sloth*, 145-46.

[29]*Piers Plowman as a Fourteenth-century Apocalypse* (New Brunswick, N. J.: Rutgers University Press, 1962), 131.

satisfaction, *quasi praeambulum*, in the view of most authorities.[30] Although both are instances of commutative justice (and hence closely related), they differ in the following respect. Restitution concerns one's debt to *another person*; it is an act of reparation for some injury committed against that person (theft, fraud, slander).[31] Satisfaction concerns one's debt *to God*; it is an act of penance, "the payment of the temporal punishment due on account of the offence committed against God by sin" (Aquinas).[32] The payment of one debt does not cancel the other. To be sure, this rule is somewhat obscured by the penitential practice of adding an unpaid debt of restitution to that of satisfaction. Spiritual bookkeeping of this sort is endemic in early medieval handbooks of penance. For example, the penitential of Silos (ninth century) prescribes, "If anyone commits theft, he shall restore to his master what was stolen and shall then do penance according to the theft. But if he does not restore, he shall do double penance."[33] Such thinking may lie behind the vow of Robert the Robber: unable to make restitution, he will do penance "al his lif tyme" (B v.475). Nevertheless, the reverse logic does not hold, as Innocent V makes clear in his commentary on Lombard's *Sentences* IV.2.iii (*An restitutio sit pars satisfactionis*):

> It would seem that restitution is a part of satisfaction. Because to him who is not able to make restitution, it is customary to enjoin a greater penance: therefore it would seem that restitution is a part of penance itself. . . . But on the contrary, satisfaction is imposed according to the

---

[30]See Peter Lombard, *Sententiarum Libri Quatuor* (*PL* 192: 877) and the commentaries on this passage in Lyndwood, *Provinciale*, V, tit. 16, chap. vii (Oxford: Hall, 1679), 332; Innocent V, *In IV Librum Sententiarum Commentaria* (Toulouse 1651; repr. Ridgewood, N. J.: Gregg, 1964), 4: 165; see also Johannis de Burgo, *Pupilla Oculi* (cited by Frank, 106 n. 2).

[31]"Restitution," *The Catholic Encyclopedia* (New York: The Encyclopedia Press, 1913), 12: 788–89.

[32]*Summa Theologica*, Part 3, Suppl., qu. 12, art. 3, quoted in "Penance," *The Catholic Encyclopedia*, 11: 628.

[33]John T. McNeill and Helena M. Gamer, *Medieval Handbooks of Penance: A Translation of the Principal Libri Poenitentiales* (1938; repr. New York: Columbia University Press, 1990), 287; similarly, Regino's *Ecclesiastical Discipline* (tenth century) states that if you have committed theft, "thou shouldst do penance for one year and repay the value. If thou dost not repay it, thou shalt do penance for two years" (317).

judgment of the priest, while restitution certainly is not within his judgment.[34]

There were good reasons for keeping restitution and satisfaction separate. One of the complaints lodged against friars in the fourteenth century was that they did, in fact, treat restitution as "within their judgment" and presumed to release penitents from the obligation or, worse, to "convert to their own gain the compensation for wrong-doing which by earthly and heavenly law ought to be restored to the injured parties."[35] This charge apparently lies behind the deal offered Contrition by friar *Penetrans domos*: that in exchange for a "pryuee paiement," "I shal praye for yow / And for hem þat ye *ben holden to* al my lif tyme" (B xx.364–65; emphasis added).[36]

If restitution is not satisfaction, what are we to make of the fact that medieval writers habitually refer to it as such?[37] The question is especially pointed in reference to *Piers Plowman* because the force of its satire against the friars depends partly on keeping the two ideas separate. Yet the Good Samaritan says, concerning God's mercy, "Ac er his rightwisnesse to ruþe torne som restitucion bihoueþ; / His

---

[34]"Videtur quod restitutio sit pars satisfactionis. 1. Quia illi qui non valet restituere, consuevit iniungi maior poenitentia: ergo videtur quod restitutio sit pars ipsius poenitentiae. . . . Contra. 1. Satisfactio imponitur secundum arbitrium sacerdotis, restitutio vero non est in eius arbitrio: ergo &c." (4: 165).

[35]Bill delivered to the Convocation of Canterbury in May 1356, translated in W. A. Pantin, *The English Church in the Fourteenth Century* (Notre Dame: University of Notre Dame Press, 1962), 159–60 (cited in Frank 107 n. 2).

[36]E. Talbot Donaldson translates the lines: "I shall pray for you / And for all that you're beholden to all my lifetime" (*Piers Plowman: An Alliterative Verse Translation* [New York: Norton, 1990], 241). J. F. Goodridge interprets the obligation as a familial one: "And I shall pray for you . . . and for all your loved ones, all my life" (*Piers the Ploughman*, rev. ed. [Harmondsworth: Penguin, 1966], 255).

[37]To cite only a few examples, *satisfactio* is used in the following instances where *restitutio* is meant: "Let them not be admitted to absolution unless they make satisfaction," Edmund Rich, Archbishop of Canterbury, *Constitutions* (1236), quoted in Oswald J. Reichel, *A Complete Manual of Canon Law*, Vol. 1: The Sacraments (London: Hodges, 1896), 168 note; "And when such usurers want to do penance, they must not receive Communion until they have made complete satisfaction," *Fasciculus morum: A Fourteenth-Century Preacher's Handbook*, ed. and trans. Siegfried Wenzel (University Park: Penn State University Press, 1989), 353; "Ubicumque aut quocumque modo aliquem damnificasti, satisfacias ei per te, vel per interpositam personam si damnum times vel scandalum," Robert of Flamborough, *Liber Poenitentialis*, ed. J. J. Francis Firth (Toronto: Pontifical Institute of Mediaeval Studies, 1971), 300.

sorwe is satisfaccion for swich þat may noȝt paie" (B XVII.319–20).
As it happens, the problem of such usage is addressed explicitly in
medieval sources. For example, William Lyndwood (*Provinciale*),
commenting on Peter Lombard's discussion of satisfaction in the
Sentences (IV.15), notes that the word can have both a specific and a
general meaning.[38] In its narrow, more technical sense, "satisfaction"
does not include restitution. In its general sense, "satisfaction" includes both restitution and satisfaction of works (penance), and thus
can stand for either—just as, for example, "tree" can signify an oak
and a tree of life (arborvitae). Normally there is no confusion. We do
not infer that because an oak and a tree of life are both "trees," they
must therefore be identical to each other. Yet the discussion of such
terms as *satisfaccion* and *redde quod debes* in *Piers Plowman* comes peril-
ously close to this kind of reasoning.[39] Let us return to Wenzel's
inference from the Good Samaritan's speech that " 'restitution' designates *satisfactio operis*." The analysis goes wrong in two ways. First, it
reverses the relation between the terms in the text (where satisfaccion is used as a synonym for restitucion, not vice versa) and, sec-

---

[38]Lyndwood's comment, which follows closely the wording of Innocent's commentary on the *Sentences* (4: 165), is as follows:

> Sed quaero, nunquid Restitutio, de qua sequitur, sit pars satisfactionis? Dic quod pars
> satisfactionis potest dici dupliciter. Uno modo, communiter omne illud quod ad debitam
> satisfactionem exigitur, & sic Restitutio est pars Satisfactionis. Alio modo dicitur proprie
> id in quo consistit Satisfactio, & sic non est pars, quia dicit cessationem tantum ab injuria,
> sed est fundamentum & quasi praeambulum. Fit enim inaequalitas justitiae ad Proximum
> tripliciter: aliquando in rebus tantum, ejus res retinendo; aliquando in actionibus &
> passionibus, injuriando; aliquando in utroque simul, ut ei per vim res auferendo. Et
> secundum hoc tripliciter fit emenda: nam in primo casu fit restitutio, sicut quando solvitur
> debitum; in secundo sufficit satisfactio; in tertio requiritur utrumque. (*Provinciale*, 332)

[39]The relation between restitution and *redde quod debes* is especially complicated.
Frank states that "restitution, or rather that larger doctrine of *redde quod debes* which
probably included restitution, may have been more or less identified in the poet's
mind with satisfaction" (106 n. 2). Morton Bloomfield, citing Will's description of
his progress ("Thoruȝ Contricion and Confession til I cam to vnitee" [B XX.213]),
comments: "Here Unity must in some sense correspond to satisfaction and *redde
quod debes*. In spite of Aquinas and Scotus, Langland must regard restitution as part
(at least) of satisfaction in the Sacrament of Penance" (*Piers Plowman as a Fourteenth-
century Apocalypse*, 223 n. 68). The heart of the issue remains the definition of *redde
quod debes*, which is clearly broader than *operis satisfactio*; as Frank says elsewhere, it
may include not only restitution and satisfaction but even "man's debt of love to
God and to his neighbor" (108). Inclusion of all these things in the concept of *redde
quod debes* warrants the conclusion that they are in some way associated but not that
they are to be "identified" with one another. Further study of these complex relations is needed.

ond, it assumes that satisfaccion here is meant in the narrow sense of "*satisfactio operis*, the third part of the sacrament of penance" — which is, in fact, the issue to be decided.[40] Since the focus of this part of the Good Samaritan's speech (B xvii.305-20) is restitution, not satisfaction of works, there is no reason to take the Samaritan's use of *satisfaccion* in the technical sense. The lines simply state that restitution is necessary to turn God's justice into mercy, but for the person who is unable to pay what he owes, his "sorwe" may satisfy or make up the difference.[41] This is precisely the situation in which Robert the Robber finds himself — and he is riddled with anxiety (as we shall see) that his "sorwe" may not be enough.

II

The troubling episode of Robert the Robber brings the whole matter of restitution down to a concrete and personal level:

> Roberd þe Robbere on *Reddite* loked,
> And for þer was noȝt wherwiþ he wepte swiþe soore.
> Ac yet þe synfulle sherewe seide to hymselue:
> "Crist, þat on Caluarie vpon þe cros deidest,
> Tho Dysmas my broþer bisouȝte þee of grace
> And haddest mercy on þat man for Memento sake,
> So rewe on þis Robbere þat Reddere ne haue

---

[40]Wenzel's analysis, in full, is as follows:

In this passage "restitution" designates *satisfactio operis*, the third part of the sacrament of penance. However, in the confession of Covetousness (V, 232ff., 276ff.), "restitution" is used with the meaning of restoring ill-won goods to their legal owner (or the Church). In Langland's use of this term, therefore, we observe what is very much a peculiarity of his poetry in general: that the lines between the concrete and the abstract, or between the individual and the universal, or between the temporal and the spiritual dimensions of a concept, are fluid, and that Langland apparently employed this fluidity as a device of poetic discourse. Just as "mede" in the poem means a good many things from a bribe to the use of temporal goods, so does "restitution" imply both the returning of stolen or borrowed objects and making satisfaction for man's debt before God. (*The Sin of Sloth*, 145-46)

Although I disagree with Wenzel's reading of the passage, I want to emphasize how much I am indebted throughout this essay to his learning, as other references to his work partly indicate.

[41]It should be noted here that the Samaritan's logic presents discursively what was earlier conveyed allegorically through Repentance, a figure that combines the twin themes of sorrow and restitution.

> Ne neuere wene to wynne wiþ craft þat I owe;
> But for þi muchel mercy mitigacion I biseche:
> Dampne me noȝt at domesday for þat I dide so ille."
> What bifel of þis feloun I kan noȝt faire shewe.
> Wel I woot he wepte faste water wiþ hise eiȝen,
> And knoweliched his coupe to crist yet eftsoones,
> That *penitencia* his pik he sholde polshe newe
> And lepe wiþ hym ouer lond al his lif tyme,
> For he hadde leyen by *Latro*, luciferis Aunte.
>
> (B v.461–76)

Although this incident hardly changes from one version to the next (it has dropped two lines from A and will lose yet another in C), its changing place in the narrative invites different readings. Because Robert is the last of the penitents in A and B, some critics take him to be the embodiment of all the sins.[42] Others treat him as part of the particular sin that immediately precedes him — Sloth in A and B, Coveitise in C.[43] But let us try out a new perspective. How does the expansion of Repentance, his words now enveloping those of Robert the Robber, bear on our understanding of this pathetic figure?

Repentance's lecture to Coveitise on the necessity of restitution has prepared us for the episode of Robert the Robber. The episode is much clearer in B, not because it has been significantly changed (it hasn't), but because it now stands in exemplary relation to Repentance's speech. Readers of B are in a far better position than readers of A to understand what Robert's looking upon *reddite* means and why the fact "þer was noȝt wherwiþ" causes him such grief. (In C Repentance's words on restitution do more than anticipate the episode of Robert the Robber; they swallow it whole. Robert is moved from the rear of the procession of Sins to the center of Repentance's lecture to Coveitise, where he joins another newcomer, Evan the

---

[42]For example, Elizabeth Kirk and Siegfried Wenzel; see note 49.

[43]T. P. Dunning writes concerning the A-Text that "the confession of Robert the Robber is somewhat unexpectedly associated with Sloth instead of with covetousness" — *Piers Plowman: An Interpretation of The A Text*," 2nd edition, revised and edited by T. P. Dolan (Oxford: Clarendon Press, 1980), 56. Bloomfield states flatly: "In C, Robert the Robber is portrayed as a type of avarice" (218). John Bowers sees Robert the Robber as both the embodiment of all the sins and of sloth in particular, "the vice toward which all the other vices move" (87–88).

Welshman. They are foils, the Welshman who can "ȝelde aȝeyn" and the robber who cannot.)

Repentance's speech activates a number of latent meanings in the robber image, an image that had become conventional in penitential literature. His response to Coveitise's confusion of restitution and "riflynge" — "That was no restitucion . . . but a robberis þefte" (B v.233) — identifies the opposition at the heart of the image. For the failure to make restitution is, in itself, an act of robbery. As *The Catholic Encyclopedia* explains:

> This obligation [to make restitution] is identical with that imposed by the Seventh Commandment, "Thou shalt not steal." For the obligation not to deprive another of what belongs to him is identical with that of not keeping from another what belongs to him. As theft is a grave sin of its own nature, so is the refusal to make restitution for injustice that has been committed. ("Restitution," 12:788)

The image of Robert the Robber succinctly captures the theoretical basis of restitution. His way of life and his inability to pay what he owes are partly convertible, each standing for the other. Anyone who is unable or unwilling to make restitution is, by definition, a robber.

Repentance's prayer, following immediately upon Robert's own, brings additional light to other facets of the robber image. One cannot help noticing the contrast between Robert's petition, "Dampne me noȝt at domesday for þat I dide so ille," and Repentance's, "And haue ruþe on þise Ribaudes þat repenten hem soore / That euere þei wraþed þee in þis world in word, þouȝt or dedes" (B v.504-5). The motives are different. Robert's petition is based on fear of punishment; Repentance's on regret for having offended God (like that of Haukyn the Active Man, who "wepte water wiþ hise eighen and weyled þe tyme / That euere he dide dede þat deere god displesed" [B XIV.327-28]). The contrasting petitions reflect the theological distinction between *attrition* (imperfect repentance arising out of fear) and *contrition* (perfect repentance arising out of love of God).[44] Robert's attrition belongs, again, to the very image in which

---

[44]See "Penance," *The Catholic Encyclopedia*, 11: 624-25. The relation of the distinction to *Piers Plowman* is discussed briefly by Adams, "Langland's Theology," 101.

he finds himself trapped. The "robber" is the standard example used to illustrate imperfect contrition. We read in the pseudo-Augustinian *Liber de vera et falsa poenitentia*, a seminal work in the penitential tradition:[45]

> Since not all penitence is good, let us speak in some manner about the things that distinguish true penitence from false, sterile from fruitful. For there are those who repent of having sinned only because they are in immediate pain. Thieves see their sins clearly when they are being punished. But let there be no punishment; the thief reverts to his crimes. Such penitence, proceeding neither from faith nor from charity or unity, remains ineffectual and without mercy. It neither cleanses the conscience nor washes away the sins. In it lies no hope of pardon, no expectation of indulgence. To this kind of penitence belong those who confess unwillingly, not for love of the good, but in order that they might avoid damnation or worldly harm.[46]

To the extent that Robert fits the penitential type of imperfect contrition, he has cause to worry about his eventual fate.

But the figurative meanings of "robber" are not all negative. Indeed, Robert's entire hope is fastened on a different, more positive image of his kind, the thief on the cross. He prays that just as Christ had mercy on Dismas, "so rewe on þis Robbere þat *Reddere* ne haue." His prayer belongs to the so-called "libera" type, attributed to St. Cyprian, in which the petitioner draws a parallel between his situation and that of a biblical character delivered through the mercy of God; for example, "Just as Thou didst deliver Daniel from the den of lions (or Susannah from the elders, or David from his enemies), so

---

[45]The treatise is widely quoted (for example, by Thomas Aquinas, Robert of Flamborough, Vincent of Beauvais) and forms a significant part of Gratian's *Decretum* and Peter Lombard's *Sentences*.

[46]"Sed quoniam poenitentia non omnis est bona, dicamus aliqua quae separant veram a falsa, sterilem a fructifera. Sunt enim quos peccasse poenitet propter praesentia supplicia. Displicent enim latroni peccata quando operantur poenam. Deficit vindicta; revertitur ad crimina. Ista poenitentia non ex fide procedens, nec [a] caritate vel unitate, sterilis manet et sine misericordia. Haec non purgat conscientiam, nec lavat crimina. In hac nulla est spes veniae, nulla expectatio indulgentiae. Huic concordant qui confitentur inviti, non amore boni, sed ut fugiant damnum vel incommodum saeculi" (Cap. IX.23; *PL* 40: 1121).

deliver me from. . . ." [47] It would be easy to regard Robert as a contemporary version of the thief on the cross, an antitype, but the crucial question is whether the parallelism extends any further than their common way of life.

In fact, Robert's appeal to the biblical precedent of the thief is a double-edged sword. On the one hand, the story offers the possibility that even a thief may hope for salvation; on the other, it implies a condition that Robert may not be able to meet. The account of the thief is the *locus classicus* in discussions about the place of contrition in the sacrament of penance.[48] That a sinner can be absolved by contrition alone is proved, Aquinas argues, by Christ's words to the thief,

---

[47]The type is discussed by Marie Pierre Koch, *An Analysis of the Long Prayers in Old French Literature with Special Reference to the "Biblical-Creed-Narrative" Prayers* (Washington, D. C.: Catholic University of America Press, 1940), 168. The "libera" formula is a common feature in several kinds of liturgical prayer as well; for example, the *Ordo commendationis animae quando infirmus est in extremis*:

> Receive, O Lord, thy servant into the place of salvation which he may hope of thy mercy.
> Deliver, O Lord, the soul of thy servant from the pains of hell, etc.
> Deliver, O Lord, his soul as thou didst deliver Enoch and Elijah from the common death of the world.
> Deliver, O Lord, his soul as thou didst deliver Noah from the deluge.
> Deliver, O Lord, his soul as thou didst deliver Isaac from sacrifice and from the hand of his father Abraham.

Translated excerpt from Walter Lowrie, *Art in the Early Church* (New York: Harper, 1947), 41.

[48]A few examples must suffice. In the *Revelations* (Book 6, chap. 115) of St. Bridget (1303–1373), Christ replies to her prayer for a penitent sinner who had no means of confession:

> He laments because he has none to hear his confession; tell him that the will is sufficient. For what benefitted the thief on the cross? Was it not his good will? [Homo ille qui te consuluit plorat quod non habet auditorem confessionis suae. Dic ei quod sufficit voluntas. Nam quid profuit latroni in cruce? Nonne voluntas bona?] (*Revelationes S. Brigittae* [Antwerp, 1611], 527)

Thomas Brinton (1320–89), Bishop of Rochester, cites the thief in support of the doctrine that contrition alone blots out sin:

> Econtra vero sola contricio delet omnem maculam quo ad Deum et habilitat ad Dei regnum. Exemplum de bono latrone, qui vere contritus cum partem petisset a Christo, dicens *Memento mei, Domine, dum veneris in regnum tuum*, Christus sic respondit, *Hodie mecum eris in paradiso*. (*The Sermons of Thomas Brinton, Bishop of Rochester [1373-1389]*, ed. Mary Aquinas Devlin, Camden Society, 3rd series, 85–86 [London: Royal Historical Society, 1954], 1:81)

Thomas Aquinas had already made the same connection in his argument for *sola contritio*:

"This day shalt thou be with me in paradise" (Luke 23:41). Like his "broþer" Dismas, Robert is a thief; like him he cannot make restitution; but whether his own "sorwe" qualifies as contrition is in doubt. Given the rich and contradictory implications of the robber image, perhaps the narrator's conclusion is the only one possible: "What bifel of þis feloun I kan noȝt faire shewe."

Although Robert the Robber may be seen as "a confessing individual who is collective in representing all the sins,"[49] he is clearly inadequate for the role. His main concern — "Dampne me noȝt" — is too limited to encompass the sorrow of perfect contrition, and his literal inability to make restitution sets him apart from most of the other penitents. He is a solitary figure. In the A-Text his timid prayer ends but does not really *conclude* the confession scene; in B and C the task is transferred to the truly "collective" supplication of Repentance, offered on behalf of all the Sins.

The prayer of Repentance (B v.480–505)[50] is a set-piece, a magnificent example of the *ars orandi*. Its weight and formality call for a liturgical setting, which the poet creates in a stroke by the addition of Ps. 84:7. "The fact that this prayer ends with Hope blowing his horn of 'Deus tu conversus vivificabis nos,'" Burrow points out, "suggests that Langland is here thinking of public liturgical, rather than private sacramental, penance; for this verse from the Psalms occurs after the Confiteor and the absolution-prayer Misereatur in the Mass."[51] Thus the prayer of Repentance stands in place of the Mis-

---

The affections of the heart are more acceptable to God than external acts. Now man is absolved from both punishment and guilt by means of external actions; and therefore he is also by means of the heart's affections, such as contrition is. Further, we have an example of this in the thief, to whom it was said (Luke xxiii.43): *This day shalt thou be with Me in paradise*, on account of his one act of repentance. (*Summa Theologica*, Part 3, Suppl., qu. 5, art. 2; trans. 18:131)

[49]Kirk, *The Dream Thought of Piers Plowman*, 62–63; cf. Wenzel, *The Sin of Sloth*, "Robert may very well be a comprehensive figure representing, and repenting for, several or even all the seven deadly sins" (144).

[50]In Kane and Donaldson's punctuation, the prayer begins in the preceding line with "do mercy to vs alle." The punctuation of Skeat, Bennett, Schmidt, and other editors — who see the prayer as opening with the phrase "God, þat of þy goodnesse" — is followed here, and is supported moreover by the argument that the prayer is modeled after the form of a collect.

[51]"The Action of Langland's Second Vision," 251 (Blanch 213). It might also be noted that Repentance's "public" prayer follows upon the "secrets" (private prayers) of the Sins (viz. Robert's prayer which he "seide to hymselue"), in correspondence with the order of the liturgy.

ereatur, the priest's answer to the confession of the people: "Almighty God have mercy upon you, and forgive you all your sins, deliver you from all evil, preserve and strengthen you in all goodness, and bring you to everlasting life."[52]

The structure of Repentance's prayer is a crucial part of its significance in the poem. Where the liturgical setting might lead us to expect a form closer to the Misereatur, the poet gives us something quite different — a classical collect. Pius Parsch provides a good analysis based on the following example from the feast of the Epiphany:

> O God, who by the guidance of a star didst on this day reveal Thine only-begotten Son to the Gentiles; grant in Thy goodness that we who have known Thee by faith may be brought to the vision of Thy glory: through the same Jesus Christ, Our Lord.[53]

Parsch comments: "The above prayer, like the majority of the Collects constructed on classical lines, falls naturally into three parts. First, we have the invocation: 'O God'. . . . The second part consists usually of a relative clause and includes the motive of the petition. . . . The third part is the actual petition, and we notice how this flows naturally and harmoniously from the main idea of the feast" (127). Not only does Repentance's prayer reflect the basic syntax of the collect ("God, þat of þi goodnesse gonne þe world make . . . be merciable to vs"), it also shows a careful regard for the relation between parts. The *narratio* of the extended relative clause — a virtual history of salvation from the Fall through the Resurrection — provides a basis for the petition. The connection is that of an *a fortiori* argument: "And by so muche it semeþ þe sikerer we mowe / Bidde and biseche" (B v.501-2). Although no feast day is specified, Repentance's petition for mercy certainly "flows naturally and harmo-

---

[52]From the Use of York, *The Lay Folks Mass Book*, ed. Thomas F. Simmons, EETS OS 71 (London: Trübner, 1879), 93. In his edition, *Piers Plowman: The Prologue and Passus I-VII of the B Text*, J. A. W. Bennett comments that the beginning of Repentance's prayer "may be regarded as a reflection or equivalent of *Misereatur vestri omnipotens Deus, etc.*, said before the celebrant goes up to the altar" (Oxford: Clarendon, 1972), 182.

[53]*The Liturgy of the Mass*, 3rd ed. (St. Louis: Herder, 1957), 127-28.

niously" from the Lenten and Eastertide associations of the passage.[54]

As a collect, Repentance's prayer is perfectly suited to its place in the narrative. A collect is a community prayer. As Parsch says, "The priest recites it for the people and in their name" (128). So does Repentance:

> Thanne hadde Repentaunce ruþe and redde hem alle to knele.
> "I shal biseche for alle synfulle oure Saueour of grace
> To amenden vs of oure mysdedes: do mercy to vs alle. . . ."
>
> (B V.477–79)

The medieval understanding of the function of a collect, generally accepted by modern liturgists as well, is based on the word itself. A collect, Walafrid Strabo explains, is "the 'collecting' of the petitions of the several members of the congregation into a single prayer"[55] — exactly the function of Repentance's prayer.

Few collects (or none) meant for liturgical use, however, reach the length of Repentance's prayer. For comparable examples, we must go to literary sources — to French epic and romance. In content Repentance's prayer conforms to a generic type known as the "biblical-creed-narrative" prayer. Marie Pierre Koch defines it as "a narration of biblical events with the person praying affirming his belief in them and adding a petition."[56] Numerous examples survive in Old French, embedded (like Repentance's prayer) in larger poetic works.[57] Repentance's prayer not only contains the necessary elements — a narration of biblical events (from the creation through the Resurrection), an affirmation of belief ("And for the beste as I bileue"), a petition ("be merciable to vs . . .") — but it does so within a

---

[54]For which see Bennett, 182–86.

[55]*The Oxford Dictionary of the Christian Church*, ed. F. L. Cross (London: Oxford University Press, 1958), 310.

[56]*An Analysis of the Long Prayers in Old French Literature*, 11.

[57]Koch's survey finds 117 long prayers (all reproduced) in 45 different poems; the prayers are classified under ten types, the most common being the "biblical-creed-narrative-petition" (the prototype of which she traces to the *Song of Roland*). To her list of 117 prayers should be added another example from the *Roman de Silence*. See Sarah Roche-Mahdi, ed. and trans., *Silence* (East Lansing, MI: Colleagues Press,

framework that is itself a credal statement: the major elements of the prayer, as Robertson and Huppé point out, correspond to the articles of the Apostles' Creed.[58]

No less important is the narrative function of the type. In French sources the "biblical-creed-narrative" prayer normally occurs in moments of high excitement, as just before a battle. In *Piers Plowman* it marks what is surely one of the most dramatic moments of the poem:

> A þousand of men þo þrungen togideres,
> Cride vpward to Crist and to his clene moder
> To haue grace to go to truþe . . . .
>
> (B v.510–12)

Like the carefully placed set-pieces of Chaucer — for example, the *Canticus Troili* in. *Troilus and Criseyde* (1:400–20) or the roundel at the end of *The Parliament of Fowls* — the prayer of Repentance can be appreciated as an independent composition, a compressed vision of the poem, inserted at a critical point in the action. The prayer not only brings the confession scene to a rhetorically splendid close; it also launches the pilgrimage that, in one form or another, will oc-

---

1992), 22–24 (lines 427–72). Long before Koch's work (1940), Johannes Altona had made a similar study of "biblische" prayers in the *chansons de geste*: "Eine eigentümliche Form des Gebetes . . . ist die biblische. . . . Indem nun der Betende auf diese Täten der Gottheit hinweist, bittet er sie gewissermassen indirekt, auch ihm seine Bitte zu gewahren. 'Wie dieses alles wahr ist, und wir es glauben, errette Du (welcher so vielen geholfen) auch meinen Leib vor Tod und Bedrängniss!' Dies ist zugleich der Schluss des Gebetes. Mit geringen Modificationen hat dieser in fast allen Gedichten denselben Wortlaut" (*Gebete und Anrufungen in den altfranzösischen Chansons de Geste* [Marburg, 1883], 12–13).

[58]"The prayer of Repentance is essentially a statement of faith followed by a plea for amendment and mercy, combining most of the elements of the Apostolic Creed" (*Piers Plowman and Scriptural Tradition* [Princeton: Princeton University Press, 1951), 74. A full analysis of the prayer cannot be undertaken here. I should like to note, however, that literary compositions based on creeds of the church are extremely common. One of the most elaborate is Joinville's *Credo*, ed. Lionel J. Friedman, *Text and Iconography for Joinville's 'Credo'* (Cambridge, Mass.: Medieval Academy of America, 1958). Friedman compares Joinville's development of the *Credo* to that of a medieval preacher's expansion of a biblical text. Medieval sermons themselves are sometimes based, in part, on the creed; for example, Woodburn O. Ross, ed., *Middle English Sermons*, EETS OS 209 (1940), 26–27. Like Repentance's prayer, this particular sermon uses the creed as the preface to a petition for mercy.

cupy the poet to the end. "In this short passage," Elizabeth Kirk says of the prayer, "we have in embryo the whole future development of the B text."[59]

III

The expanded role of Repentance has consequences far beyond the confession scene. As noted already, the emphasis now falls "not on the objective ritual of penance but on the psychological reality of repentance" (Adams), and this new emphasis places the scene in a different relation to other parts of the poem.

Certainly an earlier scene that invites comparison is the confession of Lady Meed (B III.35–63). Contrition is no part of it: Lady Meed "shrof hire of hire sherewednesse, *shamelees* I trowe."[60] The whole process is described as a commercial transaction. Meed's confessor, "coped as a frere," promises absolution "for a seem of whete" and salvation itself in exchange for financing "a wyndow in werchynge." As Greta Hort points out:

> From the two different specimens of confessions given in passus iii and v of *Piers Plowman* we may gather Langland's idea of a "bad" and a "good" confession. Meed's confession is obviously intended to be a picture of everything a confession should not be, just as the confessions of the Seven Deadly Sins are descriptions of "model confessions." The two instances of confessions which Langland gives supplement each other and should be read together. (142)

The extent to which these words are more applicable to the B-Text than to the A is one measure of the significance of the poet's revisions. The original confessions can hardly be called "model confessions." To say that the sinners are "shamelees" like Meed would be a gross distortion, but (as noted already) the emphasis in the A-Text is clearly on the exterior elements of the sacrament — oral confession

---

[59] *The Dream Thought of Piers Plowman*, 69.

[60] For a full discussion of the word *shamelees* in this context, see T. P. Dolan's essay in this collection, pp. 81–88.

and works of satisfaction — rather than on the "interior penance" of contrition of the heart.

The growth of Repentance not only heightens the contrast between the two confession scenes; it also signals the emergence of that contrast, in a variety of forms, as a fundamental theme of the poem. Almost immediately we see it again. As the penitents "blustreden forþ" in search of Truth (B v.514), they encounter a professional pilgrim, decked out in full gear and (above all) in "signes" — "Signes of Synay and shelles of Galice, / And many crouch on his cloke and keyes of Rome" — in order that people "sholde knowe / And se bi hise signes whom he souȝt hadde" (B v.521–24). Despite his wide travels (not only in Sinai, Galicia, and Rome, but also "At Bethlem, at Babiloyne . . . In Armonye, in Alisaundre, in manye oþere places"), he cannot direct the folk to Truth. It is, after all, not a question of geography. In pointed contrast, Piers the Plowman knows the way "kyndely"; "Conscience and kynde wit kenned me to his place." He offers the folk an interior map of the will, in which the significant landmarks are "places" like the brook of "beþ-buxom-of-speche," the ford of "youre-fadres-honoureþ," the croft of "Coueite-noȝt-mennes-catel-ne-hire-wyues" — all leading to (or more accurately, perhaps, *constituting*) the moral destination of Truth: "And if grace graunte þee to go in in þis wise / Thow shalt see in þiselue truþe sitte in þyn herte . . ." (B v.605–6).

No sooner do the folk arrive at Truth, however, than the antithesis is played out again, this time in Piers's tearing of the pardon (strictly speaking, an indulgence, a common reward for the completion of a pilgrimage[61]). Angered by the priest's fixation on the letter of the document, by his inability to see more deeply, Piers destroys the *signe*. As Burrow summarizes the meaning of the incident: "Langland's fear, as so often, is that the external form or institution — even though it is acceptable in itself — may come to usurp the place of the inner spiritual reality."[62] Indeed, this fear, revisited over and over, is the note on which the poem ends. Lady Meed's confession to the friar is reenacted: in exchange for a "pryuee paiement," friar *Penetrans domos* reduces or even waives the obligations of penance and restitution, and so debases the sacrament "Til

[61] See my essay, "The Design of the Poem," *A Companion to Piers Plowman*, 42–43.
[62] "The Action of Langland's Second Vision," 260 (Blanch 220).

Contricion hadde clene foryeten to crye and to wepe" (B xx.369). Contrition is no longer contrite—it is *nomen sine re*.[63] The *signe* has triumphed over the substance; and so again the pilgrimage "to seken Piers þe Plowman" (B xx.382), who is the embodiment of perfect truth, must be renewed. Yet even this is not the poet's final statement. His fear of the tyranny of form not only lies behind the repeated narrative shedding of the outer forms of penance, pilgrimage, and pardon; it also drives his own restless need to constantly remake his poem. The displacement of one version after another is the poet's final and most profound expression of his dissatisfaction with *signes*, of his own yearning to reach "the inner spiritual reality."

The emergence of Repentance as a guide figure in passus V of the B-Text is not an isolated event; it is a part of the poet's total reconceptualization of his work—a process which by the very nature of its dependence on signs could never be completed.

---

[63]The idea of the empty signifier returns us to the very beginning of the poem: "Dum rex a regere dicatur nomen habere / Nomen habet sine re nisi studet iura tenere" (B Prol.141–42). Langland's picture of a Contrition that is no longer contrite may also be compared to the saying in *De vera et falsa poenitentia*, "Ubi enim dolor finitur, deficit et poenitentia" (*PL* 40:1124).

Struggling with Will:
Jangling, Sloth, and Thinking in *Piers Plowman* B

LINDA J. CLIFTON

PIERS PLOWMAN SIGNIFICANTLY extends the conventions of medieval dream visions as it repeats, over and over, its protagonist's wakings and sleepings and dreamings. This pattern of recurrent dreaming produces interesting resonances with the idea of "waking sleep," which appears in a number of fourteenth-century English manuals for contemplative practice, some of them translations of earlier Latin texts. These manuals, describing the process and fruits of contemplation, teach the seeker how to discipline the self for the experience of union with God. Since a number of these works appear in the Vernon manuscript, together with a copy of the A-Text of *Piers Plowman*, we may fruitfully examine what a fourteenth-century reader of such a volume might have understood by the recurrent wakings and dreamings that punctuate *Piers*.

To locate that understanding, we will also need to examine the meaning of "jangling" as it appears in these contemplative texts and to determine what particular sin this "jangling" marks by its presence. Since such jangling recurs throughout the Dreamer's struggle in *Piers Plowman* B, defining its moral referents will be crucial to interpreting the nature of that stuggle. Before turning to the poem, therefore, we will look at what these manuals say "jangling" does to contemplative practice and what sin it betrays. Then, by looking at how the Dreamer struggles with his jangling, just as the contemplatives do, we will be prepared to explore more completely how these references to jangling clarify the roles of Thought and Will in *Piers Plowman* B.

The search of the contemplative for the experience of union with God has been called by Joseph Wittig a "commonplace program of spiritual ascent."[1] Wittig asserts by this label the notion that, by the fourteenth century, contemplative practice was not a secret knowledge or teaching. In fact, numerous texts from the fourteenth century describe in detail exactly how to conduct such practice. Wittig finds this "commonplace program" described in the writings on contemplation of the Victorines and St. Bernard, and he and A. V. C. Schmidt in particular have drawn connections between *Piers Plowman* B and the contemplative writers. Schmidt links the inner dreams with Rolle's Holy Name devotion in the *Form of Living* and with his *Ego dormio* and St. Bernard's *Sermons on the Song of Songs*.[2] Wittig demonstrates that the author of *Piers Plowman* knew at least two "syncretistic compilations" of these traditions, for the beginning of passus XI quotes from the incipit of one of these compilations. Further, Wittig links certain contents of passus IX-XII with this "tradition of spiritual ascent through self-knowledge" (212-13).

A large number of texts describing contemplative practices survives from this period. These include reports of their mystical experiences by Richard Rolle, Julian of Norwich, Margery Kempe, and the author of *The Cloud of Unknowing*; instructional manuals such as *A Ladder of Foure Ronges* and the writings of Walter Hilton, St. Bernard and St. Bonaventure; and treatises explaining the psychology of contemplation such as *Benjamin Minor*. The explicit purpose stated in many of these texts is to instruct the reader in techniques for reaching spiritual perfection, and subsequently salvation, through contemplative union. The texts frequently gloss the verse *Ego dormio et cor meum vigilat* from the "Song of Solomon," and often use the image of the waking sleep as a figure for characterizing meditation and contemplation. For instance, *The Cloud of Unknowing* advises that, as a contemplative practice, one "sit ful stylle, as it were in a slepyng sleiȝt."[3] The same author, in *The Book of Privy Counselling*,

---

[1] Joseph S. Wittig, " 'Piers Plowman' B, Passus IX.-XIII.: Elements in the Design of the Inward Journey," *Traditio* 28 (1972): 212.

[2] A. V. C. Schmidt, "The Inner Dreams in *Piers Plowman*," *Medium Ævum* 50 (1986): 32.

[3] Phyllis Hodgson, ed., *The Cloud of Unknowing and The Book of Privy Counselling*, EETS, OS 218 (London: Oxford University Press, 1944), 83.

says that the state of sleep to the world is not only most desirable, but most safe from the fiend:

For, as Salamon seiþ in þis processe, 'ȝif þou slepe' in þis blynde beholdyng from al þe noise & þe steryng of þe fel fende, þe fals woreld & þe freel flessche, 'þou schalt not drede any peril' ne any deceyte of þe feende. . . . for 'þou schalt gracyously rest' in þis louely onheed of God & þi soule; '& þi sleep schal be ful softe.' (147–48)

One group of these texts in particular has a direct association with *Piers Plowman*, since, as I've said, they appear with *Piers Plowman* A in the Vernon Manuscript, a large compendium of religious and contemplative tracts. The Vernon manuscript was compiled in the early 1380s from earlier texts. Its language localizes the manuscript in the southwest Midlands — from South Staffordshire, south Shropshire, or north Worcestershire,[4] an area of England near the "Malverne hilles" — named as the site of the Dreamer's experience in *Piers Plowman*. The manuscript contains, among others, Hilton's *Scale of Perfection* and *Of Mixed Life*, *The Mirror of St. Edmund*, part of the *Ancren Riwle*, Rolle's *Prick of Conscience*, his *Ego dormio* and *The Form of Perfect Living*, Hilton's translation of Bonaventure's *Stimulus Amoris*, "A talkyng of þe loue of god," *The Abbey of the Holy Ghost* and *The Charter of the Abbey of the Holy Ghost*.

Linguistic and structural affinities exist between *Piers Plowman* and other contents of the Vernon manuscript. For example, Horstman claims, concerning "A talkyng of þe loue of God," which is written as prose in alliterative long lines, "Several of its peculiar words are found again in Piers Ploughman (as daunselen)."[5] Structural similarities link Vernon to later versions of *Piers*. For instance, in the unfolding personification allegory of the progress of Conscience toward perfection in *The Abbey of the Holy Ghost* and *The Charter of the Abbey of the Holy Ghost*, one finds a number of elements which appear in *Piers Plowman* B, one of the most fully developed of

---

[4] A. I. Doyle, *The Vernon Manuscript: A Facsimile of Bodleian Library, Oxford Ms Engl. Poetry a.1* (Cambridge: D. S. Brewer, 1987), 11. For recent discussion of texts in this manuscript see the essays in Derek Pearsall, ed., *Studies in the Vernon Manuscript* (Cambridge: D. S. Brewer, 1990).

[5] C. Horstman, ed., *Yorkshire Writers: Richard Rolle of Hampole, An English Father of the Church, and His Followers*, 2 vols. (New York: Macmillan, 1895–96), II.345.

these being the debate of the four daughters of God, Mercy, Truth, Peace and Love.[6] Although this debate is found in a number of medieval texts, only the *Abbey* texts and *Piers* show the debate as occurring after the fact of God's decision to send Christ to mankind. In the other versions, the debate occurs as part of God's deliberations.

The *Charter of the Abbey of the Holy Ghost*, like several of its companions in the Vernon manuscript, including Hilton's treatise on the mixed life, is addressed not to religious but to laity:

> A dere brethir and systirs, I see þat many walde be in religyone bot þay may noghte, owthir for pouerte or for drede of thaire kyne or for band of maryage, and forthi I make here a buke of þe religeon of þe herte, þat es, of þe abbaye of the holy goste, that all tho þat ne may noghte be bodyly in religyone, þat þay may be gostely. (Horstman I.321)

Thus in at least one important manuscript, an early version of *Piers Plowman* is found associated with treatises describing contemplative practice. Further, material from one of these, *The Charter of the Abbey of the Holy Ghost*, turns up included in *Piers Plowman* B at the same point in the progress of the subject toward salvation, that is, after the initiation of Christ's passion. In both, the writer evinces concern with lay people seeking salvation.

Finally, these manuscripts present direct parallels in word usage between these contemplative texts and *Piers*. In the Prologue of *Piers Plowman*, the Narrator, describing the folk in the field, says,

> Ac japeres and jangeleres, Judas children,
> Feynen hem fantasies, and fooles hem maketh —
> And han wit at wille to werken if they wolde.
> That Poul precheth of hem I will nat preve it here:
> *Qui loquitur turpiloquium* is Luciferes hyne.
>
> (Prol.35–39)[7]

---

[6] In the Vernon manuscript, the *Charter* and the *Abbey*, separate texts in Thornton and Laud 210, are joined into one text (Horstman I.321). See also Hope Traver's study of the versions of this debate allegory in *The Four Daughters of God*, Bryn Mawr College Monographs VI. (Philadelphia: Bryn Mawr College, 1907).

[7] A. V. C. Schmidt, ed., *The Vision of Piers Plowman: A Complete Edition of the B-Text* (London: Dent, 1978). All my references to the poem are to this edition.

Hilton, in the Vernon manuscript of his *Qui Habitat*, condemns jangling in language nearly identical to that employed in *Piers*. Commenting on the phrase *"Non accedet ad te malum: & flagellum non appropinquabit in tabernaculo tuo,"* Hilton says,

> But, þou, louere of god, whiles oþur men rennen out and fihten and striuen, sweren and be-gylen, *Iapen and Ianglen*, pleyen & syngen, holde þe stille in þi tabernacle, & þou schalt ben in pes, sikerliche huled with þe schadewe of vr lord from þe knotte of þis scharpe scourge.[8]

The alliterative phrases referring to jangling, such as "Iapen and Ianglen" recur in *Piers* and in other contemplative texts. Examining to what particular deadly sin they are attached, and what that might mean for a reader's perception of the Dreamer's struggle in *Piers*, provides the focal point of the remainder of this article. A reader making this examination finds that the words "jangling" and "japing" point in the contemplative texts to dangers the seeker must avoid, and point in *Piers Plowman* to one of the chief dangers faced by the poem's protagonist in his long and wandering pilgrimage, the danger of substituting his own arguments, his own busy assertion of meaning, for the patient listening which can lead to understanding and finally to grace. The distraction of jangling causes Will to ignore information to which he should attend, until finally he can move beyond insisting upon his own arguments, and his deeper instruction begins.

I do not seek to trace *Piers Plowman* directly to the Vernon manuscript, nor to connect it explicitly to any specific source text, but merely to show that, in the aggregate, contemplative texts circulating at the time *Piers Plowman* B was written, and localized to that region of England in which the poem has its setting, contain among them a body of directives for action which might have been readily available to readers of *Piers* and which might illuminate a reader's perception of this work. The Vernon manuscript provides a contemporary witness placing the A-Text of *Piers*, while its versions B and C were still in formulation, in the context of contemplative writing in English, and the contents of Vernon display particularly interesting

---

[8] Bjorn Wallner, *An Exposition of Qui Habitat and Bonum Est in English*, Lund Studies in English 23 (Lund: Gleerup, 1954), 36. Italics mine.

points of comparison with *Piers Plowman* B. I will not confine my
comparison of *Piers Plowman* B to this single source in Vernon, but
will use the Vernon manuscript's material as one set of several repre-
sentatives of Wittig's "commonplace program of spiritual ascent"
developed over the course of several centuries.

In many Middle English contemplative texts, jangling appears as a
specific danger to the contemplative life, and is so identified in text
after text. *A Ladder of Foure Ronges* says that one of the signs that a
soul has turned from "pryvy abydyng of the Holy Gost" and been
"cast to wyckyd thou3tys and to vanite" is the tongue's indulgence in
"ianglyng." This text goes on to assert that what draws man down
from the ladder of ascent to union with God is "vanyte of this
worlde"[9]: "It is not semely that . . . the tunge þat a litel before . . .
hath tillyd hir spouse to hyr bowre . . . by oon & by oon turnyd into
vanite & to fowle speche, to waryyng & to forsweryng & to other
ianglyng"(117; italics mine). In *Benjamin Minor*, one's reason must
have "refreinid þe greet jangelyng of þe ymagynacioun, & haþ put
hir to be vnderloute to God" (*Deonise* 26) if the soul is to progress
toward contemplation. This jangling imagination, says the treatise,

> crieþ so vnkunnyngly in þe eres of oure hertes, þat for ou3t þat reson hir
> lady may do, 3it sche may not stille hir. And þerfore it is þat oft-tymes
> whan we schuld praye, so many diuerse fantasies of yuel þou3tes crien in
> oure hertes þat on nowise we mowen by owre owne my3tes to driue hem
> awey. And þus it is wel prouid þat Bala [Imagination] is a foule jangeler.
> (13)

As we saw above, Walter Hilton's *Qui Habitat* condemns "Iapen
and Ianglen, pleyen & syngen." Hilton identifies such jangling, even
though it seems mere playfulness, with "þe bigininge of all synne.
ffor anon as a mon leoneþ to him-self, þen entreþ in him al vuel
sturinges of veyn dredes & vein likynges of passaunt þinges and
drawen him doun to þe vanite of þe world"; what you should do
instead is "sech vre lord in þi þou3t. . . . So þat þou mai freliche &

---

[9] Phyllis Hodgson, ed., *Deonise Hid Diuinite and Other Treatises on Comtemplative Prayer Related to The Cloud of Unknowing*, EETS, OS 231 (London: Oxford University Press, 1955), 116.

restfuliche þenken on him with swete affeccions of loue meltynge in þi soule" (32–34; emphasis added). Jangling is thus a sign of misdirection and an activity which perpetuates the soul's inclining away from the kind of understanding that permits it to come to union or perfection.

Richard Rolle, too, finds jangling antithetical to meditation and perfection. His version of the Psalter translates Psalm 139's *vir linguosus* as "Man iangelere" who "sall noght be righted in erth. . . . *Jangelere* is he til whaim spekynge is lust, and lufis leghis, and behaldis noght what he says."[10] In the *Form of Perfect Living*, he writes, "A foule litchory it is to hafe lykynge & delit in mannes wordes. . . . If we be aboutward to hyde vs fro *Iangelynge* & louyng of þo worlde, god will schew vs til his loueyng & our Ioy."[11] For Rolle, in almost all uses of this word,[12] jangling is any misspending of the "spire. . .of grace" (*PP* B IX.101). In "The Commandment" he says,

And þat silence be in occupacioun of good thoghtes, hit helpeth gretly to Goddis loue; for *ianglers* and bacbiters, þat appeireth other mennes lif with wicked wordes, and al þat loueth har owne state bifor al oþer, . . . þai haue no more sight of þe loue of God in har soule þan þe eigh of a bak hath of þe son. For vayn speche and il wordes ben signe of a veyn herte and il, þat is withouten grace of God. . . .[13]

He tells his reader, "discipline of silence is goed, that we auyse vs or we speke and þe noght mykill ianglande" (Bramley, Psalm 118:11). Jangling constitutes specific danger: "thaire ianglyngis & tresons. . .will make thaim to be lost" (Psalm 11:3).

The Cloud of Unknowing, which criticizes mystics transported in dramatic manifestations of joy in Christ reminiscent of Rolle's mystic transports, speaks as Rolle does of the dangers of jangling. First,

[10]Henry R. Bramley, ed., *The Psalter, or Psalms of David and Certain canticles, with a translation and exposition in English by Richard Rolle of Hampole* (Oxford: Clarendon Press, 1884), Psalm 139:12. Italics mine.

[11]Horstman 18–9. I follow the text of MS Harley 1022; the emphasis is mine.

[12]His uses of "jangling" as an action following successful contemplation, rather than as an action preventing the contemplative from progress in his journey will be discussed below, pp. 39–40.

[13]Sarah J. Ogilvie-Thomson, ed., *Richard Rolle: Prose and Verse Edited from MS Longleat 29 and Related Manuscripts.* EETS, OS 293 (Oxford: Oxford University Press, 1988), 34.

the *Cloud*-author says his book must be kept from "Fleschely ianglers, opyn preisers & blamers of hem-self or of any oþer, tiþing tellers, rouners & tutilers of tales, & alle maner of pinchers: kept I neuer þat þei sawe þis book." The book is only for one who "in a trewe wille & by an hole entent, purposed him to be a parfite folower of Criste" (*Cloud* 2). Second, the *Cloud*-author condemns the appearance of contemplation without its substance and "nice corious contenaunces in bodily beryng" who look as if they were meditating, who go "waggyng wiþ þeire fete," tossing their arms about, or "euermore smyling & leiȝing at iche oþer worde þat þei speke, as þei weren gigelotes & nice japyng jogelers lackyng kontenaunce." And he sees such unseemly behavior, if they "ben gouernors of þat man þat doþ hem," as "tokenes of pride & coryouste of witte" (*Cloud* 99). In other words, he takes them as signs of the evil results of the voice that jangles. Last, he warns against voices that jangle of Christ. Speaking of the attempt to push oneself to think of God, he warns,

> For paraventure he wil bryng to þi minde ful feire & wonderful pointes of his kyndnes, & sey þat he is ful swete & ful louyng, ful gracious & ful mercyful. & ȝif þou wilt here him, he coueiteiþ no beter; for at þe last he wil þus *jangle* euer more & more til he bring þee lower to þe mynde of his Passion. & þere wol he lat þe see þe wonderful kyndnes of God. (*Cloud* 27; emphasis mine)

But this result is actually a scattering, a sweet meditation, not the desired piercing of the cloud of unknowing. The agent of this jangling which misdirects, he says, is

> a scharp & a clere beholding of þi kindely witte, preentid in þi reson wiþinne in þi soule. . . . good in his kynde. . .a beme of þi licnes of God. Bot þe vse þerof may be boþe good & iuel. Good, when it is openid bi grace for to see þi wrechidness, þe Passion, þe kyndnes, & þe wonderful werkes of God. . . . Bot þen is þe vse iuel, when it is swollen wiþ pride & wiþ coriouste of moche clergie & letterly conning as in clerkes. (*Cloud* 30)

He then connects this kind of jangling devotion, even when it is good, to active life, "troublid & trauailid aboute many þinges; bot contemplative sitteþ in pees wiþ o þing" (*Cloud* 31).

In *Our Daily Work*, a work "of the same kind as Bonaventura's *Speculum disciplinae ad novitios*. . .and similar works of Hugo de St.

Victore, St. Bernhard &c. . . .but. . .not written for monastic life" (Horstman I.137n), jangling is clearly a useless spilling out of something precious. *Our Daily Work* says each man needs three things: honest work without wasting time, work done with a "fredome of spirite" (137), and honesty and fairness in doing what one does for the love of God and by God's direction. The goal is a great reward by God's grace: "til mikel his mede þurgh goddis grace helpand" (137). The manuscript then draws a connection between wrong use of time, "bisynes," "Ianglyng," and the misspending of speech in the following passage:

> Wonder it ware þat man þat gifs him to bisynes of þe werld mare þen
> nedis: had na lettyng in praier, in rest of hert, in sothefastnes of worde,
> in perfeccione of gode werks, in luf to god & all cristen men. For-þi hali
> men bifore þis tyme þat knew þir lettyngs: þai fled þe werld with all þe
> vanitees as it had bien cursid. . . . Thre maners of occupacions are, as
> sere *Iangling* & mikil, Raykyng aboute, Mikil trauailing aboute werldli
> thinges. Agayn mikil *Iangling*: sais Salomon: *Qui dimittit aquam: caput est
> iurgii.* "Lat þe water oute": is lat þe tonge flete oute in *Ianglinge*. Bot to þe
> knowyng of god ne of him-selfe mai nane come: þat latis his hert flete
> oute with mikil vnnaite speche; for he makis waie to þe fende in him-
> selfe. (140; emphasis mine)

Immediately following this passage, we find the silent rest that is desirable contrasted with the wrongful flowing out of wasted speech:

> Agayn þas þat eauer rakis aboute to fede þaire wittis with vanitees and
> lustis: is þe leryng of þe angel how he lerde þe hali Abbote Arsenius &
> said: "Arseni flee þe werld & his ȝernyngs, hald þe in reste, bridil þi
> tonge": þat it flete noght oute in *Ianglynge* ne idel speche. (140; emphasis
> mine)

So, not only is jangling fatal to the soul, but the desired state is to "hald þe in reste" and turn one's back on the business and busyness of the world. This is as true for the lay person, who is the audience for *Our Daily Work*, as for the religious, according to this text.

This kind of busyness is specifically identified as a form of sloth or *acedia*, according to Cassian. In his description of the sloth that besets the solitary monk in his desert cell, Cassian characterizes *acedia* thus:

It instils in its victims abhorrence of the place, disgust of the cell, and contempt for the brethren. The monk becomes disinclined to any work within the cell. He deems his life spiritually useless and imagines that he could make better progress elsewhere. If he does not leave the place, he might even forego his salvation. The slackness of his body, hunger, and the heat make him unquiet and confused in mind. He begins to think it better to go out and perform some deed of mercy: visiting the sick or bringing comfort to a brother. Then the monk either sinks into slumber or leaves his cell and looks for consolation in other people's company. If flight becomes a habit, the monk will soon give up his profession altogether. (*Inst.*, X, 2-6)[14]

Here, busy actions which take one away from one's contemplative practices are identified as signs of sloth just as are the more obvious laziness or slumber. Wenzel demonstrates that later centuries emphasized wandering and laziness as the major hallmarks of sloth. But the Vernon text of *The Mirror of St. Edmund*, in its instruction about the knowledge of the seven deadly sins which those who would live the life of perfection must have, includes distracting busyness in its description of sloth: "Off Accidie waxen: heuinesse, Malice, Whonhope, Necligence aboute godes comaundemens, *bisi þouht aboute þinges defendet*" (Horstman I.246; emphasis added). Busyness, not sleep, is the enemy of perfection here. Busyness is, paradoxically, the form of sloth most dangerous to contemplatives, making them restless when their devotion should be to remain in solitary focus on spiritual things (Wenzel 31). Sloth is the "ambiguous" vice,[15] both lazy and busy, despairing and overzealous, marked by frantic activity and marked by sleep. This sleep of sloth, says Hilton, is the "flesschli reste"[16] that occurs when will and desire for God grow cold and that leads "sumtyme to ydelnesse" (36), not the "reeste in deuocion" (32) associated with "goosteli swettenesse in deuocioun and contemplacion" (31-32) which the contemplative should seek. As Bowers demonstrates, busyness and overzealousness are the as-

---

[14]Siegfried Wenzel, *The Sin of Sloth: Acedia in Medieval Thought and Literature* (Chapel Hill: University of North Carolina Press, 1967), 19.

[15]John M. Bowers, *The Crisis of Will in Piers Plowman* (Washington, D. C.: Catholic University of America Press, 1986), 61.

[16]Walter Hilton, *Walter Hilton's Mixed Life: Edited from Lambeth Palace MS 472*, ed. Sarah J. Ogilvie-Thomson (Salzburg: Institut fur Anglistik und Amerikanistik, 1986), 36.

pects of *acedia* most dangerous to contemplatives; the Thornton manuscript version of *The Mirror of St. Edmund* says that not only does *acedia* make "manes herte hevy and slawe in gude dede," it also "makes mann to yrke in prayere or halynes, and puttes man in wykkednes of wanhope, for it slokyns þe lykyngeȝ of gastely lufe" (Horstman I.224–25).

The Cloud of Unknowing characterizes this search as the work of a "trewe wille" (63) and

> not elles bot a trewe knowyng & a felyng of þi-self as þou arte, a wrecche & a filþe, fer wers þen nouȝt: þe whiche knowyng & felyng is meeknes. & þis meeknes deserueþ to haue God himself miȝtely descendyng to venge þee of þine enemyes. (67)

John Bowers emphasizes how this move is an action of the will: "The will had to turn toward the good and act upon it" (2). Though the seeker must recognize and activate his own will in this process, by so doing he can only make himself ready for grace, not guarantee its coming, as *A Ladder of Foure Ronges* advises:

> thouȝe the fre wille of man may not make grace in man, netheles he may doo that in hym is — caste oute the olde dowe, which is the olde corruptible synne þat withdrawith man from grace, and so make hym redy þat he may receyve this grace. (*Deonise* 103)

In all these passages, the contemplative writers identify jangling as a distraction from contemplative practice and thus from the wordless union with God toward which these practices aim. Jangling is a form of sloth, active rather than passive, but deadly to union nevertheless. Even jangling, however, despite this strong association with deadly sin, presents occasions that may have gracious fruits. According to *Benjamin Minor*, for instance, while Bala the imagination is a "foule jangeler," as a man learns to restrain his imagination he learns what he needs to advance along the contemplative path:

> þus it is semely in a mans soule for to be, þat fro þe tyme þat reson haue refreined þe greet jangelyng of þe ymagynacioun, & haþ put hir to be vnderloute to God, & makiþ hir to bere sum frute in helpyng of hir knowyng, þat riȝt so þe affeccioun refreyne þe lust & þe þrist of sen-

sualyte, and make hir to be vnderloute to God, & so to bere sum frute in helpyng of hir felyng. (*Deonise* 26)

These fruits, it turns out in *Benjamin Minor*, are abstinence and patience, after which "discrecioun & contemplacioun risen in þe resoun" (39). So jangling presents the seeker with a challenge, and by overcoming that challenge the seeker progresses toward union with God.

In at least two references, Richard Rolle puts jangling in a different context than the *Benjamin Minor*, seeing it as a positive outcome of progress along the contemplative path, rather than as a barrier on the journey. In "The Commandment" he says, "If þe lyste speke, forbere it at þe begynnyng, for Goddes lufe; for when þi hert feles delyte in Criste, þe wil not liste to speke, ne jangell, bot of Criste."[17] In his prose lyric "Gastly Gladnesse" he sings, "Lufe makes me to melle, and joy gars me jangell" (Allen 52). For Richard of St. Victor, then, jangling presents occasion for the seeker to work to attain the fruits of contemplation, while for Rolle jangling is both distraction from the search and a sweet babbled outpouring of the successful seeker's love of Christ, the "spire," or sprout, of Grace.

Like the contemplative texts we've just examined, *Piers Plowman* B consistently condemns jangling. Jangling is mentioned in *Piers* as one activity listed among various actions of men, most of them the apparently benign occupations of ordinary secular men, the "settynge and sowynge" and "[w]erchynge and wandrynge as the world asketh" (Prol.19–21), what Wyclif calls "bysynesse of worldly occupacion."[18] But some forms of busyness are condemned as soon as mentioned. In the first of these condemnatory lists of busyness appear "japeres and jangeleres, Judas children" who "[f]eynen hem fantasies, and fooles hem maketh — / And han wit at wille to werken if they wolde" (Prol.35–37). Jangling and japing are thus condemned the very first time the poem mentions them. In fact, each time janglers and japers are mentioned in the poem, they are con-

---

[17]Hope E. Allen, *English Writings of Richard Rolle: Hermit of Hampole* (Oxford: Clarendon Press, 1931), 75.

[18]Kenneth Sisam, ed., *Fourteenth Century Verse and Prose* (Oxford: Oxford University Press, 1923), 127.

demned. Later in the Prologue, the Dreamer describes the angel's descending to speak in Latin because "lewed men ne koude / Jangle ne jugge that justifie hem sholde, / But suffren and serven — forthi seide the aungel" (129-31). This statement might appear to praise jangling, along with praising the action of passing judgment, as actions which learned men can and should perform, when they dispute and discriminate among arguments to vindicate themselves, as Schmidt's note puts it (Prol.130-31n). In context, however, the value of disputation and judging is cast into doubt by the poem's subsequent events, when the angel's words are challenged by "a goliardeis, a gloton of wordes" (Prol.139), and the angel's words sink, lost beneath the babble of the Rat Parliament.

Jangling and judging are further condemned in passus II, where "Glotonye he gaf hem ek and grete othes togidere, / And al day to drynken at diverse tavernes, / And there to jangle and jape and jugge hir evencristen" (II.93-95). This gluttonous action leads directly to "Sleuthe and sleep. . .And thanne wanhope" (99-100). In passus IV, "Waryn Wisdom wynked upon Mede / And seide, 'Madame, I am youre man, what so my mouth jangle" (IV.154-55); here jangling is clearly identified with false or misused speech since Waryn Wisdom's pledge of loyalty is made to the false Lady Mede. The king soon condemns such false disputation, angrily telling the lawyers defending Mede, "I wole have leaute in lawe, and lete be al youre jangling" (IV.180). Not only does jangling defend the false and therefore undermine "leaute," but it corrupts marriage and the community. In passus IX, the marks of an "uncomly" marriage are "jelousie joyeless and janglynge on bedde" (IX.166) which bring forth the fruit of "[manye] foule wordes" (168) rather than children. Jangling corrupts the religious community too, preventing its proper issue. The confession of Wrathe in passus V reveals: "I was the prioresse potager and other povere ladies, / And maad hem joutes of janglyng. . . . Of wikkede wordes I Wrathe hire wortes made, / Til 'thow lixt!' and 'thow lixt!' lopen out at ones / And either hitte oother" (V.155-62). This jangling is clearly connected with disruption of religious practice, since Wrathe is pictured as a friar who, by introducing mendacity to the preaching friars and jangling gossip to the convent, causes them to argue about "spiritualte" (V.147) rather than follow the true intent of their vows.

Jangling becomes the occupation of those diverted from simple necessity, as the well-fed workman, despising the poor food he appreciated when Hunger was his master, now "[a]yeins Catons counseil comseth. . .to jangle: / *Paupertatis onus pacienter ferre memento*" (VI.314-15a). He thus forgets to bear patiently the burden of poverty as he should do, and the sign of his forgetting is his jangling. Wit, of whom the Dreamer says he "dorste meve no matere to maken hym to jangle" (VIII.121), preaches against jangling, as does his wife Dame Study. Wit criticizes Christians by pointing out that "a Jew wolde noght se a Jew go janglyng for defaute. . .and he amende it myghte" (IX.82-83), stating that if Jews "that we jugge Judas felawes" (IX.85) prevent jangling, surely Christians in their more enlightened state should do the same.

Wit moves on to analyze right use of speech. He praises using speech rightly: "He dooth best that withdraweth hym by daye and by nyghte / To spille any speche or any space of tyme: / *Qui offendit in uno, in omnibus est reus*" (IX.97-98a). He calls speech the "spire. . .of grace" (IX.101), which makes jangling a spilling of speech, a waste of grace, even if that jangling is a complaint against poverty rather than the wasted speech of false lawyers, wrathful gossipers, Jews who refuse to recognize Christ, or Judas, Christ's betrayer. Even to spend the "spire. . .of grace" in speaking of good things may be unnecessary and therefore blameworthy. As Richard Rolle says, "if a man say soth withouten nede he is a iangelere" (Psalm 139:2). Dame Study speaks more directly, heartily condemning "japeris and jogelours and jangleris of gestes" (X.31) and launching herself into an impassioned condemnation of all such "vile harlotrye" and "[l]echerie, losengerye and losels tales" (X.45-49). When she says this jangling and japery will prevent each of these harlots from receiving "to his yeresyyve the value of a grote" (X.47), her word choice reminds us of the friars' telling the Dreamer in passus VIII. that his "yeresyyve" was free will and wit (VIII.53-54). When Dame Study includes in these harlotries the behavior of those who prefer to "carpen of Crist" (X.51), she anticipates Will's further struggles, such as those we will see in the banquet in passus XIII. "God is muche in the gorge of thise grete maistres," Dame Study says, "Ac amonges meene men his mercy and hise werkes" (X.66-67). Thus, as Wit and Study suggest, jangling is a serious obstacle to progress toward grace. Later, in passus XVI, Jews are portrayed as denying grace by jangling when they object to Christ's being called "leche of lif and lord of high hevene" (XVI.118). Here their jangling and judging are definite signs of their fault: "Jewes jangled therayein that juggede lawes" (XVI.119). In this same way, jangling is a sign of his fault when Judas "jangled thereayein" (XVI.144) in denying falsely that he will betray Jesus. Both Judas and the Jews, therefore, misuse speech by denying Christ, and this misuse is called "janglyng."

A chief enemy of the Dreamer's search, against which he is repeatedly warned, is therefore jangling, that aspect of sloth which manifests itself as busyness, the distraction from the quiet focus of the will which allows it to approach the will of God. Busyness has been condemned from the very onset of the poem. The entire series of the Dreamer's visions begins by characterizing busyness as ignoring a better heaven than this world:

> Sestow this peple —
> How bisie they ben aboute the maze?
> The mooste partie of this peple that passeth on this erthe,
> Have thei worship in this world, thei wilne no bettre;
> Of oother hevene than here holde thei no tale.
>
> (I.5–9)

These are just like Rolle's condemned busy folk in *The Form of Living*:

> Gangerels and janglers and kepers of comers and goers arly and late, nyght and day, or any þat takeled is with any syn wilfully and wittyngely, or þat hath any delite in any erthly thynges, þei ben as ferre þerfro as is fro heuyn to erth.[19]

The Dreamer is busy, not like these busy folk, but busy with question and argument, as even his early questions of Lady Church reveal. Desirous of understanding, which is commendable, but not understanding himself nor the right means for seeking understanding, the Dreamer goes wandering and questioning "ful ofte of folk that I mette / If any wight wiste wher Dowel was at inne" (VIII.3–4). Thus he seeks, as according to St. Edmund he should, by asking those who appear to be wise. St. Edmund says a seeker has questions to ask:

---

[19] Ogilvie-Thomson, *Rolle* 17.

þou hast ma[t]ere of spekyng to Clerkes ben þey neuere so wyse, and to
lewede, ben þei neuere so boystes. Whon þou spekest to wyse, meue
summe of þeose materes, and aske. And whon þow spekest to symple,
teche hem bleþeliche and sweteliche. For whi? þou hast inouȝ wherof to
speken, and hou þou schalt þin owne lyf leden & oþure amenden. (Horstman I.254)

In other words, it is proper for the Dreamer to seek Dowel by
questioning others. However, as the cautions against jangling reveal, he should not engage in disputing their words. Thus, for a
reader of contemplative texts, the repeated references throughout
the poem to jangling warn against the Dreamer's particular problem, manifested in his continual arguing, his busyness not of the
involvement in the world but of succumbing to that sloth which is
manifested as distracting activity. The Dreamer's challenge, if he is
to advance, is to fight off sloth's attacks upon his will, and the aspects
of sloth which concern him are precisely those that beset the desert
fathers and later contemplatives. It is this sin of which Will has been
guilty in his intellectual busyness, and this sin is most often identified in *Piers Plowman* by references to jangling.

Accordingly, when in passus VIII he meets two friars, men of
apparent wisdom, he is too quick to argue and to judge, immediately reacting to the friars' claim that Dowel dwells with them with
his own "*Contra!*" and by posing an argument "as a clerc" (VIII.20).
The effect of this argumentation is so to catch him up in his dispute
with their claim that he fails to hear their message. They tell him
that Dowel is "charite the champion" (VIII.45–46) and that God "yaf
thee to yeresyyve to yeme wel thiselve – / And that is wit and free
will, to every wight a porcion . . .; / Ac man hath moost therof, and
moost is to blame / But if he werche wel therwith, as Dowel hym
techeth" (VIII.53–57). He simply responds that he has "no kynde
knowyng . . . to conceyve alle thi wordes" (VIII.58), though he does
muster enough humility to promise he will "go lerne bettre" (VIII.59).

The Dreamer has thus mistaken the outward signs of the way of
the friars, and their proprietary claim that Dowel dwells with them,
for the inner truth they have been willing to share. His wit and free
will are his gift from God, just as they tell him. But he prefers the
assertion of his own powers of disputation to a humble attending to
the truth he should heed despite its being offered by friars. More-

over, because as yet he does not know his own will and wit, he cannot understand the application of their message to his own situation. He thus questions as St. Edmund bids, but because he has yet to understand his own nature and to learn enough humility to cease his jangling arguments, he cannot comprehend what he hears.

He therefore disputes with the friars and then wanders "widewher, walkyng myn one, / By a wilde wildernesse" until the "[b]lisse of the briddes" makes him stop and the "[m]urthe of hire mouthes made me ther to slepe," bringing him "the merveillouseste metels . . . That ever dremed [dr]ight in [doute], as I wene" (VIII. 63-70). In this dream, invoked by his concentration upon the repetitious song of the birds, he begins to learn himself and to receive the "yeresyyve" of which the friars told him, an introduction to his wit and free will.

The first agent of this knowledge is Thought. *Piers* makes Thought the figure who first identifies Will as Will: "Thanne Thoght in that tyme seide thise wordes: / Wher Dowel and Dobet and Dobest ben in londe / Here is Wil wolde wite if Wit koude teche . . ." (VIII.125-27). Thus "Thought" is the figure who begins the process by which the Dreamer comes to know himself.

The identity of Thought is not immediately obvious. A. C. Spearing argues in *Medieval Dream Poetry* that " 'thought' . . . is the term used by Chaucer in *The House of Fame* to mean 'memory', the faculty that has inscribed in his brain the events of his dream"; and in *Piers*, this figure called Thought "is presumably one of the faculties involved in the creation of [the] poem so far."[20] Since Thought is identified as one who has followed Will "this seven yeer" (VIII.76), it is possible to assign him the role usually taken by memory. If we do agree with Spearing's identification of Thought and memory, and then attempt to relate this identification to materials found in contemplative texts, we must look at the passage in which Thought introduces the Dreamer as "Wil" to Wit. Here, if we follow Spearing, the action of the poem which juxtaposes Thought, Wit, and Will symbolically presents us with Bonaventure's three agents of contemplation: memory (Thought), intelligence (Wit), and will (the

---

[20](Cambridge: Cambridge University Press, 1976), 148.

aspect of the Dreamer now identified as Wil). For Bonaventure, memory, intelligence and will are the trinity through which the mind rises to the "contemplation of the Blessed Trinity."[21] However, such an interpretation does not explain why Will and Thought dispute three days together, nor how this disputation differs in quality from the earlier jangling disputation with the friars, as it certainly differs in result.

Examining references to use of the words "thought" and "thinking" in contemplative texts reveals more than one function for thought. Thought is a vital functionary in the search for God in the Vernon text of *The Mirror of St. Edmund*, where we find:

> Two þinges wiþ-outen mo makeþ mon holi, þat is to witen Knowynge and Loue. Knowynge of soþnesse, and Loue of godnesse. But to kno-wyng of God þat is soþnesse, ne maiзt þou not comen but þorw kno-wynge of þi-self. . . . To þe knowyng of þy-self maiзt þou comen wiþ ofte þenkynge; to þe knowyng of God: wiþ clene contemplacion. To þe kno-wynge of þi-self þou maiзt comen in þis Manere: Þenk inwardliche and ofte what þou art, what þou were, and what þou schalt ben. Furst as to þi bodi, after as to þi soule. (Horstman I.241–42)

Thought, in these texts, is much more than memory. According to an anonymous fourteenth-century fragment of the *Benjamin Major*, it is one of the modes of the "thre wyrkings of cristen mans saule" (Horstman I.82). This fragment in Cambridge Ms. Dd V.64 says that "A Grete clerk þat men cals Ricard of Saynt Victor" identifies these modes of work as:

> Thoght, Thynkyng, And contemplacioun. And þat a man may witerly knaw ilkane by þaim-self, He tells qwat differens es by-twyx þam thre. He says þat thoght es wyth-owten trauayl & wyth-owten froyte, And thynkyng es wyth trauayle & wyth froyte. Þou sal wyt þat thynkyng and meditacioun er bath ane. (Horstman I.82)

If we examine the fuller text of the *Benjamin Major*, we find the following distinction drawn:

---

[21]St. Bonaventure, *The Mind's Road to God*, trans. George Boas, (Indianapolis: Bobbs-Merrill, 1953), 26.

Contemplation is a free and clear vision of the mind fixed upon the manifestation of wisdom in suspended wonder. . . . Meditation however, is an industrious attention of the mind concentrated diligently upon the investigation of some object. . . . But thinking [translating the Cambridge manuscript's "Thoght"] is the careless glance of the soul prone to restless wandering.[22]

In the Vernon manuscript of *The Mirror of St. Edmund* no distinction is made between thought and "þenkynge," but all forms of introspection seem to coalesce in this one term, as they do in the Vernon manuscript's version of Walter Hilton's *Epistle on Mixed Life*, which seeks to make no such distinctions but says, "Þer are moni maner of þenkynges, wȝuch are best to þe I can not say" (Horstman I.284). Similarly, the Vernon manuscript version of *The Mirror of St. Edmund* distinguishes between thought and "bisi þouht." The author blames the latter, which is thought "aboute þinges defendet," calling it deadly because it impedes the work of seeking "þe seuene ȝiftes of þe holigost" (Horstman I.246-47). "Bisi þouht" thus functions within the mind much as "jangling" does in the world, as a distraction from that object which the will should seek. Thus a distinction is made between thought that is productive in the search for God, and that which, like jangling, proves primarily a distraction. Richard of St. Victor goes on in the chapter referenced above to discuss the utility of even such "vain and frivolous considerations, throwing off the bridle of discretion to interfere or rush headlong into everything" by saying:

> Yet it often happens that in the wanderings of our thinking, the soul meets with something which it passionately desires to know and presses on strongly towards it. But if the mind satisfying its desire applies itself with zeal to this kind of investigation it already exceeds the bounds of thinking by thinking, and thought passes over into meditation. (*Selected Writings* 138-39)

Even as a distraction, it seems, such thought, like jangling, can lead to God, as we saw earlier in the example from the *Benjamin Minor* of

---

[22]Richard of Saint Victor, *Selected Writings on Contemplation*, trans. Claire Kirchberger (London: Faber & Faber, 1957), 138.

Bala the jangler whose noise precedes the restraint which bears the fruit of advancement in the spiritual journey.

Will's encounters with the friars and with Thought seem to follow just this pattern. He begins his argument with the friars by asserting clear opposition to their words—"*Contra!*"—and listens only to answer back in jangling argumentation. He responds to the friar's parable that he cannot "concyve alle thi wordes" (VIII.58) and says he will "lyve and like" for himself (58). Immediately thereafter, he sleeps and in his dream meets Thought who calls him by name. In contrast to his negative response to the friars, his first words to Thought are "What art thow?" (73), and his next is to trust Thought to tell him of Dowel:

> "Art thow Thought?" quod I, "thoo thow koudest me wisse
> Where that Dowel dwelleth and do me to knowe."
>
> (77–78)

Once Thought has answered, Will thanks him "that he me [so] taughte" (109), though he seeks to know still more: "How Dowel, Dobet and Dobest doon among the peple" (112). He and Thought then go about "thre daies. . . / Disputyng upon Dowel day after oother" (115–16). Will's humble attitude toward Thought makes this activity, in context, an exploration of meaning like the *Benjamin Major*'s "thynkyng" which is "wyth trauayle," a working out of the meaning of Thought's words, not a disputation asserted to pose one idea against another as Will's encounter with the friars had been.

Thought, even "wyth trauayle," can only reveal limited information, however. Thought's explanation of Dowel, Dobet and Dobest defines only modes of behavior in the world. For him, Dowel is the laborer for whom virtue means avoidance of gluttony and avarice. Dobet's virtues are humility, help of those in need, and avoidance of arrogance. Dobest bears a bishop's crosier and practices virtue by putting down wickedness. In fact, Thought admits he reaches his limit, for he cannot give the Dreamer the "kynde knowynge" he "coveite[th] to lerne" (VIII.111–12). Because Thought realizes he cannot answer this request, he says he will direct Will to Wit because "Wit konne wisse thee" (113) and soon, "er we war were, with Wit gonne we mete" (117). Wit is grave, soft in speech, and wears clothes that are not prideful, neither in rich show nor in demonstration of poverty (119–20). He is "lik to noon oother" (118), a figure who cannot be made by any means to "jangle" (121), unlike Thought, who has been arguing with Will for three days together (115–16). When Thought introduces him to Will—"Here is Wil wolde wite if Wit koude teche" (127)—Wit immediately begins his long descripton of the Castle of Kynde, his allegory of the location of Dowel, Dobet and Dobest. Thought is thus portrayed as one willing to "jangle" while Wit is not, and thus more limited than Wit in what he can contribute to Will's "kynde knowynge." At the end of Wit's instruction, Will is introduced to Study when she intervenes with a diatribe against sharing such knowledge, and against jangling.

The Dreamer's encounter with Thought in passus VIII thus bears some similarity to the nature of Thought in the *Benjamin Major*. This time with Thought bears definite fruit for the Dreamer, however, in the form of an advance in knowledge of himself. The first fruit of this vision appears almost despite the Dreamer's sojourn with Thought when Wit appears "er we war were" (VIII.117). Thus, even though Thought and the Dreamer are engaged in an argument which distracts them both ("er *we* war were"), together they travel the road by which they encounter Wit. Thought, who earlier told the Dreamer his "kynde name" (72) advances him in the knowledge of self he must have if he is to progress toward perfection. In action, then, this episode functions just as Richard of St. Victor describes the fruitful proceeding of "Thynkyng" from the vagaries of Thought. Thought, though he engages in a disputation with Will, functions as the figure who finally names the Dreamer to himself. His lengthy "[d]isputying" with Thought "upon Dowel" (116), unlike the argument with the friars, functions not as the distraction of jangling but as an encounter that furthers his search by introducing him to Wit. The action of the poem thus demonstrates clearly that the Dreamer's process of self-discovery, the very process St. Edmund and Bonaventure have been describing and advocating, while impeded by jangling, is not halted altogether. The process works just as the Vernon manuscript of *The Mirror of St. Edmund* suggests when it says, "To þe knowyng of þy-self maiȝt þou comen wiþ ofte þenkynge" (Horstman I.241).

I would argue, then, that Thought be read not as the Dreamer's faculty of memory, as Spearing would claim, but as the personification within his dream of the activity, described by St. Edmund and

Bonaventure, which, despite its limitations, leads him toward self-knowledge. The sum effect of this episode is thus to move the Dreamer by means of the limited meditative action called "thought" toward the self-knowledge required in the contemplative process and thus to take a crucial step in the soul's attempt to progress toward perfection. One implication of this move in the poem is to reveal jangling as an impediment that the soul can overcome by wit.

This movement toward self-knowledge will prove an increasingly difficult travail, full of disputation, false starts, numerous questionings, visions which offer more puzzles than answers, and answers the Dreamer misapprehends. His constant refrain—"I have no kynde knowyng"—marks his continued difficulty, and the very existence of such difficulty marks his process as a parallel to that described in the contemplative texts as the travail of contemplation. These interior struggles of Will, these intellectual wanderings within his visions reminiscent of his physical wanderings in this waking life, taken in the context of these repeated references to jangling, serve (as John Bowers argues) as indicators of Will's struggles with the sin of sloth.

I believe Bowers is right in bringing attention to the relationship between the progress of Will in the poem and the notion that "If sloth was a sin, then it must involve a perverse movement of the will and therefore stem from a volitional defect. But *acedia* was unique among the seven deadly sins because it could result from no movement of the will at all" (63). Initially the Dreamer displayed a passive, or at least unfocused, will, wandering about and falling into vision rather than passionately desiring God. As the Dreamer intensifies in focusing his will upon truth and accepting as his own "kynde knowyng" the truth he's being shown, the form of sloth called "bisiness" and exemplified by jangling becomes his chief impediment to progress. His actual progress in the poem demonstrates his learning to focus his will and, with the help of grace, to defeat those sins of which he has indeed been guilty.

For a reader of the contemplative texts, important, if not primary, among those sins is "busyness." Busyness has delayed the Dreamer's understanding the lessons of Holy Church. Busyness has distracted his attention away from hearing that wit and free will are his "yere-syyve" from God, and moved him instead to dispute with the friars who gave him that news. Only his meeting, in dream, with Thought and then with Wit and Study, allows him to progress. His sin of "busyness," or jangling, is not the act of arguing *per se* but the nature and occasion of that disputation. Jangling, as in the external dispute with the friars, is a negative and distracting assertion of what our times call ego; the internal, self-conscious disputation with Thought, on the other hand, proves to be a positive and productive exploration central to the Dreamer's search.

Even this productive sort of argumentation must be controlled with patience, however. In the banquet scene, rejection of jangling becomes crucial to the Dreamer's progress when he refrains from his desire to "jangle to this jurdan" (XIII.83) . In that scene, Will has learned enough during the last five passus to voice his early objections to the doctor "to myself so Pacience it herde" (63), but the more disturbed the doctor makes him, the more he desires to "jangle to this jurdan." But Patience "preynte on me to be stille" (85). In other words, his lessons since he met Wit have aroused the Dreamer's patience by demonstrating to him how his will's lack of this quality has prevented his learning what he seeks. Now the Dreamer's own patience helps his will hold his tongue. This stay proves only momentary, however, as the doctor's actions "in that ye eten the puddyng . . . and we no morsel hadde" (106–07) rouse Will's anger at this hypocrisy. Will declares to the doctor that he himself is "in point to dowel" (110). This time, both Conscience and Patience quell Will's talk: "Thanne Conscience ful curteisly a contenaunce he made, / And preynte upon Pacience to preie me to be stille" (111–12). Will understands little of what Patience and Conscience say in their subsequent discussion of Dowel with Clergy, but he does understand he must try to be silent. His submitting to Conscience and Patience to curb his jangling leads directly in the action of the poem to a vision of the life of one ordinary Christian, Haukyn. This provides a move forward in the process of his own quest since, as Carruthers points out, in Haukyn "Will should be able to see much of himself,"[23] and knowledge of the self is crucial to the quest for "kynde knowynge."

Discretion and patience are precisely the two qualities evoked in the banquet scene, a scene that immediately follows Will's meeting

---

[23]Mary Carruthers, *The Search for St. Truth: A Study of Meaning in Piers Plowman* (Evanston: Northwestern University Press, 1973), 115.

with Ymaginatif. Thus in the poem, as in the *Benjamin Minor*, the fruits for the Dreamer of his long struggle with his will about his propensity to jangle are the appearance of Patience and Conscience, as "discrecioun & contemplacioun" begin their struggle to rise in his understanding. As in so many of the contemplative texts, the process is a series of advances and backslidings, as Will's attempts at obeying Patience demonstrate. Or so a reader of those texts might view the action of the poem.

Reading *Piers Plowman* B's references to "jangling and japing" in the expanded context of the contemplative writers' uses of those terms focuses attention on the interior nature of the recurrent struggle the poem figures forth. In this context, the enemy to spiritual progress is not the friars' teachings, though some of these teachers be proud or false, but that within Will himself which causes him to approach their words with "*Contra!*" In this context, it is not the jangling of the world but the jangling of our selves that prevents our wills from proceeding on their journeys to the truth. Within ourselves, too, according to this context, are found those faculties which can advance us on the journey, should we, like Will, seek to make it.

Diuerse Copies Haue it Diuerselye:
An Unorthodox Survey of *Piers Plowman*
Textual Scholarship from Crowley to Skeat

ERIC DAHL

M OST *PIERS PLOWMAN* SCHOLARS in the early and middle decades of the present century accepted two questions about
the poem as fundamental: 1) Can modern editorial procedures establish reliable texts for three versions of a work when each version is
attested by diverse manuscripts? and 2) Were the various versions of
the poem created by one author or by more than one? In more
recent decades, scholars have generally avoided stirring the waters
of textual uncertainty or the unity of authorship. While it is not
uncommon for *Piers* scholars to deplore the conflict and acrimony
that flared earlier in the century among textual scholars, many fail to
recognize that much of the recent flood of enterprising scholarship
concerned with *Piers Plowman* does not flow from a better understanding of fundamental textual issues, but rather proceeds from an
unwarranted confidence that the uncertainties of text and authorship
somehow can be brushed aside with vague claims that new critical
approaches make them irrelevant, or by doxologizing some subset of
editorial simplifications. The outcome has been the shaping of an
orthodoxy which assumes that all versions of the poem were created
by the same man, that it is appropriate to harmonize the three
versions textually in order to bolster the assumption, and that the
textual critical heritage should be retrieved only to the extent that it
contributes to the current critical consensus and textual status quo.

No scholar in her or his right mind should invest serious effort
now in the study of *Piers Plowman* without analyzing the main discussions of those underlying textual realities which might disqualify

much of what is being written about *Piers Plowman* today. Such an analysis is no light undertaking, especially if one independently seeks the wisdom and experience of those who have published on both sides of the debate about authorship in this century. The present essay is intended as a concise preliminary to such a weighty project, a survey of the scholarship which focused on textual issues relating to *Piers Plowman* prior to the authorship controversy. It summarizes editorial and other textual critical activity from the appearance of Robert Crowley's *editio princeps* in 1550 to W. W. Skeat's 1886 parallel text edition of the A-, B-, and C-Versions of the poem. This survey is offered as an alternative to the account provided recently by George Kane, whose editorial work is fundamental to the single authorship orthodoxy.[1]

The first editor of *Piers Plowman* was Robert Crowley (1518?-1588), a scholar trained at Oxford who was acutely interested in the doctrines of the Reformation. He probably learned the art of printing while three of his controversialist essays were being prepared and brought to press in London during 1548. Within a year he had established his own small press at Ely Rents, Holborn. During 1550 he issued all three of his editions of "The Vision of Pierce Plowman." He was ordained a deacon by Bishop Ridley in 1551 and apparently gave up his printing at that time. He was among the exiles at Frankfort in 1554, and at the death of Mary returned to England for an active career in support of the new Protestant doctrines.[2]

In producing his first edition of *Piers Plowman*, Crowley was able to "gather togyther suche aunciente copies as I could come by" and to select what Thomas Wright and Walter Skeat both considered to be "an excellent manuscript" that is otherwise unknown to us today.[3] Crowley did not explain why he chose this particular text or offer any general discussion of diversity in his manuscript sources. He was, however, aware of textual variation, and in his introduction he

---

[1] George Kane, "The Text," in John A. Alford, ed., *A Companion to Piers Plowman* (Berkeley and Los Angeles: University of California Press, 1988), 175-77.

[2] "Crowley, Crole, or Croleus, Robert," *The Compact Edition of the Dictionary of National Biography*, 1975.

[3] *The Vision of William Concerning Piers the Plowman in Three Parallel Texts*, ed. Rev. Walter W. Skeat, 2 vols. (1886; London: Oxford University Press, 1924), 2: lxxiii, lxxvii. Citations from this volume will hereafter be noted in brief form, using the editor's name.

offers the first recorded suggestion that some texts of *Piers* have variations that go beyond scribal error and involve composition by someone other than the original author. Interested in variants of one of the poem's prognostications, Crowley offers his reader two lines from each version for comparison. First he quotes from the manuscript that he selected for his own edition (a B-Text — compare Skeat 1886, B vi.327–8). The passage explains that death and dearth will come after several signs have been revealed:

> And when you se the sunne amisse, & two monkes heades
> And a mayde haue the maistrye, and multiplie by eyght.
> (Skeat 2:lxxiv)

Crowley explains that this version "is spoke by the knowledge of astronomie as may wel be gathered bi that he saith, Saturne sente him to tell" (in the previous line). He then suggests that another version from a different manuscript uses a contrasting technique and "geueth it the face of a prophecye." This second example comes from what is now recognized as a C-Text (compare Skeat's C ix.351-52):

> Three shyppes and a shefe, wyth an eight folowynge
> Shall brynge bale and battell, on both halfe the mone.
> (Skeat 2:lxxv)

Though the distinction between "astronomie" and "prophecye," as two methods of predicting the future may be obscure to us today, Crowley believed this textual difference represented divergent outlooks that derived from two distinct intellects. He concluded that the second version "is lyke to be a thinge added of some other man than the fyrste autour. For diuerse copies haue it diuerslye" (Skeat 2:lxxiv). In other words, as Crowley prepared the first printed edition of *Piers Plowman*, he came to believe that manuscript variation resulted from more than simple scribal error. He believed that a significant change of text found in another manuscript was produced by a writer other than the author of the editor's chosen source.

In his preface, Crowley identified "Roberte langelande, a Shropshere man borne in Cleybirie" (Skeat 2:lxxiii) as the author of the text being published. Crowley probably learned this opinion from John Bale (Skeat 2:xxviii). Like the many names proposed for an author of *Piers Plowman* by modern scholars and in one famous manuscript ascription, this one likely derives ultimately from lines in the poem itself. Bale's "Robert" probably originates from a misreading of the verb "yrobbed" as "I Robert," a variant that is found in two extant manuscripts.[4] The more commonly proposed "William Langland" is given backwards in a signature line added by the B reviser, later repeated as an ascription in a C-Text, and not found in any association with the A-Text.[5] The name "William" would also, of course, be a typical guess, given that the narrator/dreamer in the poem is named Will. In any case, the name William Langland adopted widely in our time and used in reference to all versions of the poem is little more than a prop used by proponents of single authorship and an expository convenience for those who have opted for the single-authorship assumption in their critical writing.[6]

The point to emphasize here is that after 1550 the presence of an edited text of the poem, which had been attributed by Crowley to a named author, had much more influence on future scholarship than Crowley's more tentative and obscure comments about textual variation in the wider collection of manuscripts. From 1550 to the present, most scholars have preferred a reduction of manuscript diversity and the simpler implications of single authorship to the more problematical alternatives. Though Crowley reported direct observations of manuscript diversity and suggested multiple authors were responsible, the manuscripts were less accessible than his printed edition of a single version. For most readers, one version of the poem implied one author, identified through the subsequent

---

[4]Skeat 2:xxviii. See also George Kane's *Piers Plowman: The Evidence for Authorship* (London: Athlone Press, 1965), 42–43.

[5]The line "I haue lyued in londe, quod I my name is longe wille," appears at B xv.148 in Skeat's edition. The C-Text ascription is found in Trinity College Dublin MS. 212 (D.4.1.) and reads, "Memorandum, quod Stacy de Rokayle, pater Willielmi de Langlond, qui Stacius fuit generosus, et morabatur in Schiptone under Whicwode, tenens domini le Spenser in comitatu Oxon., qui praedictus Willielmus fecit librum qui vocatur Perys Ploughman."

[6]Kane, *Evidence* 21–35 and 46–51, argues tortuously that the Dublin ascription did not derive from the line in the B-Text and that its reference to "librum qui vocatur Perys Ploughman" refers to the A-, B-, and C-Texts of the poem. These conclusions are central to his claim that a single author named William Langland wrote all three versions of *Piers Plowman*.

years not only as Robert Langland but as John Malvern, William Langland, and Piers Plowman himself.[7]

Crowley's second edition adopted new readings from what was probably another B manuscript (also now lost) and in addition included some lines to the Prologue normally found in A-Text manuscripts.[8] He was silent about this use of these other manuscripts in forming his revised text of the poem. He mentioned only that he had "added certayne notes and cotations in the mergyne, geuynge light to the Reader" (Skeat 2:lxxv) as well as offering a new summary of the poem's contents. This same announcement accompanied his third edition in the same year, which apparently drew on yet another manuscript.

It has been suggested that medieval scribes who altered their exemplars to suit their expectations or those of their patrons, or combined several texts to form more complete versions of a work, are the "medieval editors" of those works.[9] We might as easily suggest that editors like Crowley who revised or recombined varying texts of medieval poems in more recent times are actually "modern scribes." Like some of his medieval predecessors, Crowley suffered from an "inability, in numerous instances, to read the text correctly" and altered his text "arbitrarily."[10] In other words, Crowley did not, apparently, ask many questions about editorial procedure in handling multiple manuscripts, and his editions are unsatisfactory for having many misreadings of the original texts and for conflating them. This should come as no surprise. *Piers Plowman* was the only medieval work in the vernacular that Crowley ever printed, and he lacked a consistent method for dealing with his diverse sources. His scholarly descendants in our own century would eventually become deeply concerned about this problem, addressing it with commentaries, collations, or both, and finally evolving elaborate rationales

---

[7]Skeat rejects Stow's ascription of the poem to "John Malvern" and also discusses the curious confusion of "Piers" with the poem's author (2:xxviii-ix and xxiv-xxv).

[8]*Piers Plowman: The B Version. Will's Visions of Piers Plowman, Do-Well, Do-Better, and Do-Best*, ed. George Kane and E. Talbot Donaldson (London: The Athlone Press, 1975), 7; Skeat 2:lxxvi.

[9]Anne Hudson, "Middle English," *Editing Medieval Texts*, ed. A. G. Rigg (New York: Garland, 1977), 34.

[10]Skeat 2: lxxvii; and Kane and Donaldson 7.

to systematize and validate their editorial decisions in establishing modern critical editions.

The next edition of *Piers Plowman*, by Owen Rogers in 1561, is, according to Skeat, "a careless reprint of Crowley's *third* issue, and is almost worthless" (Skeat 2:lxxvi). One point of interest is a false claim by the editor which amounts to the first enunciation in *Piers Plowman* scholarship of an editorial desideratum that has, in many forms, bedeviled print-oriented scribes-errant down to the present. Rogers claimed that his new edition was "imprynted after the authours olde copy" (Skeat 2:lxxvi). While no such authorial copies have survived, editors in our own time have found more sophisticated rationales to claim authority for their reconstructions of the poem. One problem with such claims is that they seek to validate a hypothetical certainty which can distract attention from the persistent analysis of the textual diversity that has actually survived. In general, scholarly uncertainty about substantial variation in texts is positive, both because it is a logical necessity and because it is conducive to productive study of an open manuscript culture in which the diversity of texts is one basis for understanding a poem's reception and its historical meaning.

While Crowley's methods for deriving the editorial particulars of his text can be understood as similar to those of his medieval scribal predecessors, the effect of his work upon subsequent literary scholarship can only be understood in terms of a quite different technological context. In spite of his arbitrary treatment of sources, his difficulty in interpreting these, and perhaps partly because of his silence about both problems, Crowley produced, in the terminology of our own era, a "definitive edition." Except for the "careless reprint" of Rogers and the misgivings of one or two particularly perceptive scholars, the Crowley editions went unchallenged until the nineteenth century. Without denying that the printing press brought the tremendous advantage of making books widely available, and that analytical editorial scholarship would not have evolved without it, we should be aware that it could and still can create and institutionalize, almost overnight, a textual *status quo* inherently flawed and misleading.

In an era which did not sustain analytical discussion of editorial procedure, it was editorial practice, however faulty, that could determine the direction of scholarly inquiry. Literary luminaries such as

John Seldon (1622), Anthony à Wood (1674), George Hickes (1705), Elizabeth Cooper (1737), Thomas Warton (1754), Thomas Percy (1765), and many others accepted Crowley's edition as *the* text of *Piers Plowman*.[11] A few minor objections surfaced. Based on a misreading by Bale rather than on any attention to manuscript evidence, Warton offered the erroneous emendation of "hotte was the sun" for "sette was the sun" at the beginning of the prologue. Thomas Percy accepted this emendation but suggested an alternate spelling.[12] No scholar, as far as we know, considered it necessary to check the manuscripts on this point. The definitive edition had displaced the extremely varied medieval manuscript sources for the poem. Scholarly assumptions about the poem were almost inevitably as flawed as Crowley's text, and the wide range of uncertainties inherent in a literary work of this nature were given only the narrowest basis for consideration, or simply not recognized at all.

The lack of attention to *Piers Plowman* manuscripts during the early period correlates with the more general history of editing medieval texts at this time. Anne Hudson has referred to this era as "the most barren" for the scholarly investigation of Middle English manuscripts (35). She did identify a striking exception, the editorial work of Thomas Hearne (1678–1735), an underkeeper of the Bodleian Library, whose edition of Robert of Gloucester's *Chronicle* (1724) was

> the first true scholarly edition of a Middle English text. . . . Hearne's achievement is difficult to overestimate: here we have an extremely accurate text, an introduction showing critical acquaintance with five manuscripts and an attempt to understand the origins of the text, and a full and intelligent glossary compiled by Hearne himself. Hearne followed this edition with one of Mannyng's translation of Peter of Langtoft's *Chronicle* in 1725. But the next fifty years saw few if any successors. (35)

---

[11]This may be seen by surveying the relevant entries in Vincent DiMarco, *Piers Plowman: A Reference Guide* (Boston: G.K. Hall, 1982). This excellent book has made the full range of *Piers* scholarship much more accessible, though some scholars seem reluctant to cite it as a basis for their summaries.

[12]DiMarco 26–28 gives an account of the conjectures of Warton and Percy. Kane, "The Text" 176, discusses the same exchange more briefly.

Hearne also commented on the diverse texts of *Piers Plowman*, suggesting that its varying manuscripts might have arisen in ways similar to the diverse manuscripts of Robert of Gloucester's *Chronicle*. Hearne's ideas about the multiple authorship of this *Chronicle* thus provide the necessary context for understanding his views about *Piers Plowman*, a notion originally suggested by Vincent DiMarco.[13]

Hearne wrote that his interest in Robert of Gloucester's *Chronicle* arose from familiarity with one manuscript in the Bodleian, which he decided not to edit because he had heard there were better ones. Years later he obtained one of the preferable manuscripts:

> I laid aside my Design of publishing this Author, and did not resume it 'till above a Year agoe, when the Loan of a MS. . . . was procured for me out of the Harleyan Library . . . accompanied with another MS. of Robert of Gloucester, the Loan of which was obtained for me out of the Heralds Office. . . . As soon as I saw the Harleyan MS. I presently concluded, that it was a very good one and authentick, and therefore I immediately transcribed it, and resolved to make it my Text.[14]

Hearne explained that the manuscript from the Herald's Office is quite different, and that in his edition he "inserted my Observations from it . . . at the bottom of the page, always subjoyning *Ar* [i.e., the manuscript of the College of Arms] to them" (liii). Hearne's edition of the *Chronicle* thus offers a careful transcription of a single manuscript (Harley), selected as the best possible text, with collations from another source (from the Herald's Office), printed at the bottom of every page. He also consulted a good and longer manuscript in the Cotton Library but did not use it for emendation or to extend his edition. Instead he discussed it as an interesting example of an orginal text being reworked later by its author:

> Nothwithstanding the Harleyan MS. breaks off so early, yet since it ends about the middle of a Page, and with a full Line, 'tis justly look'd upon by Criticks as a perfect Book. So that, in all liklyhood, the Author carried on the Work at first no farther, but after some time resumed it again, and brought it down to his own time. . . . The Harleyan MS.

---

[13]DiMarco 22, and see note 16 below.

[14]Robert of Gloucester, *Robert of Gloucester's Chronicle*, ed. Thomas Hearne (Oxford: Printed at the Theatre, 1724), lii.

agrees, (abating some Variations in the Language) so far as it goes, with the Cottonian one, and yet, without doubt, they were transcrib'd from different Copies, one from the Work as it was first finish'd by the Author, the other from a MS that was compleated after the Author set about it again after some Intermission. (lxvi)

While the Harley and Cotton texts are, according to Hearne, the work of a single author, the manuscript from the Herald's Office suggested a different conclusion: that it resulted from additional development of the material by a second author.

> But then as to that of the Heralds Office, I found not only the Language of Robert of Gloucester to be altered throughout in it, but the Work quite changed in several respects, by having some Passages transposed, others omitted, and divers inserted that were never written by Robert of Gloucester, who was of different Principles from this Author. (lii-liii)

Hearne not only knew about multiple manuscripts but, unlike Crowley, explored the question: how are they related? His edition of the *Chronicle* presents the specific differences in his sources which back his conclusion that MS H (Harley) and MS C (Cotton) are by the same author while MS Ar (Herald's Office) represents a significantly different version of the work which is in fact a text composed by a second author. Hearne also explains why the expansions in the Herald's Office manuscript suggest a different author. They involve the use of excerpts in prose from other historical writers, the addition of "Rhythmical Accounts" of the kings of England in meter unlike that of the original, the inclusion of "strangely Romantick" pseudo-historical episodes, as well as reproducing a royal pedigree of Henry VI. While identifying these extensions as the work of a new writer, Hearne acknowledges that this later version is skillfully done, by someone who often exercises what we now recognize as authorial prerogatives. His description could equally apply to the B reviser[15] of *Piers Plowman*: "The Author, undoubtedly, took a great deal of pains in new modelling Robert of Gloucester and in adapting every Thing to his own Scheme."

---

[15]The term "B reviser" can be understood as a neutral term, referring to either the same person who wrote the A-Text or a second author who transformed it into the B-Text.

Hearne's careful attention to the complexities of a multiply attested work resulted in the formulation of sophisticated ideas about
medieval authorship, including the recognition that one author
could alter his own work and that a second author could assimilate
and extend the first author's work intelligently — all within the same
multiple manuscript context. Such hypotheses could not occur to
readers unfamiliar with the multiple variants of a work, whether
they were reading a single manuscript of Robert of Gloucester's
Chronicle prior to Hearne's edition, or reading *Piers Plowman* in a
printed edition by Crowley which conflated a variety of manuscripts
without editorial comment.

Hearne never edited *Piers Plowman*, but he did come to recognize
that the existing editions did not adequately represent the complexities of the extant manuscripts. This view is recorded in Hearne's
Remarks and Collections, and one particular passage should be valued
as another of his percipient comments about the nature of multiply
attested works. Summarizing one of his earlier letters that replied to
a query about the variations in an unpublished manuscript of *Piers
Plowman*, Hearne wrote,

> What to say, unless I could see the Ms., I know not. This is certain, that
> the Work hath been much altered at different times. I saw a MS. of it
> lately in wch the difference from the print is so great that the Work seems
> to have undergone the same Changes with Robert of Gloucester.[16]

In another entry of his journal and also in his notes on the
flyleaves of Crowley's edition of the poem, Hearne again mentioned
the comparison between the variety of manuscripts of *Piers Plowman*
and the manuscripts he had studied of Robert of Gloucester's *Chronicle*.[17] Although Hearne had earlier written about a single author of
the poem when he knew only one version, his later encounter with
significant textual variation brought him to conclude that the vari-

---

[16]Thomas Hearne, *Remarks and Collections of Thomas Hearne*, ed. C. E. Doble et al.,
8 vols. (Oxford: Oxford Historical Society, 1907) 8: 395. Kane, "The Text" 176,
quotes the second sentence of this passage but not the third. He also points out that
Hearne here probably refers to the Cotton Caligula A XI text of *Piers* which contains
elements of all three versions. The same manuscript was the source for Hearne's
"Cotton" version of Robert of Gloucester's *Chronicle*. This connection was earlier
made obvious by DiMarco 22.

[17]Hearne 8:411 and DiMarco 22.

ous texts of *Piers Plowman* resulted from a composition process similar to that he had discovered for Robert of Gloucester's *Chronicle*. At least one scholar from our own era has come to a similar conclusion. Like Hearne, who concluded that two authors were responsible for three differing texts of the *Chronicle*, David Fowler has proposed dual authorship for the three versions of *Piers Plowman*. Hearne suggested that a first author of the *Chronicle* produced the original version and a second revised version, then a second author produced the more divergent third version. Fowler's theory for *Piers Plowman* involves similar elements in a different order: he suggests that the original or A-Version was composed by one author, then a second author produced the greatly lengthened, thematically different and metrically inferior B-Version. Finally the similarly long but rearranged C-Version was produced by the same second author.[18] The proposal that two authors composed the three versions of *Piers Plowman* has been attacked repeatedly by the editors of the Athlone Press editions and overlooked by most other contemporary scholars.

The affinity of Fowler's dual authorship theory with the ideas of so astute an early scholar as Thomas Hearne should be noted. Hearne, working largely on his own in the 1720s, looked closely enough at multiply attested works to recognize that in some cases differing configurations of what is nominally the same work can result from substantial efforts by more than one writer. The kind of perspective he brought to this issue was notably lacking among his contemporaries. Fowler, unconvinced that all versions are the work of one author, has continued to insist that the A- and B-Texts be read independently. This view is in opposition to a widespread preference for the blending of the textual sources. As one recent writer has aptly described it, most scholars

> have shown a tendency in the case of obscure passages to move across versions in search of help, a practice encouraged by Skeat's parallel-text edition (1886). The implications of this have not always been appreciated. To use one version as a touchstone for the interpretation of another

---

[18]David Fowler, *Piers Plowman: Literary Relations of the A and B Texts* (Seattle: University of Washington Press, 1961). His theory of dual authorship is developed throughout the book. A general outline of the B reviser's transformations of the A-Text is found at 166–67.

suggests that *Piers Plowman* exists, inter-textually, in all three versions at once.[19]

The theory of dual authorship counters this tendency. Whether espoused by Hearne or by Fowler, it is essentially concerned with keeping diverse medieval sources distinct and valuing each independently, reading the extensions of Robert of Gloucester's *Chronicle* in the College of Arms manuscript as valid apart from the more closely related Harley and Cotton texts, or reading the A-Version of *Piers Plowman* without burdening it with themes and conclusions from an expanded version produced years later.

The first widely available statement about textual variation in the sources for *Piers Plowman* was published by Thomas Tyrwhitt (1730–1786), who was an editor of Chaucer, and who possessed a remarkable knowledge of medieval literary works, many at that time known only in manuscripts.[20] In his 1775 edition of *The Canterbury Tales*, Tyrwhitt discussed the state of English poetry at the time when Chaucer wrote. Of Crowley's editions Tyrwhitt wrote, "I cannot help observing, that these Visions have been printed from so faulty and imperfect a MS. that the Author, whoever he was, would find it difficult to recognize his own work."[21] This often repeated statement is really only interesting in the context of Tyrwhitt's editorial experience. In editing Chaucer, Tyrwhitt had devised a technique for comparing manuscripts that allowed him to record variants conveniently. He wrote his collations from several Chaucer manuscripts onto separate pages of Chaucer's text cut from an earlier edition by Speght. He then pencilled in his emendations and a regularized orthography (Windeatt 123–25). While this process of using a "copy text" is familiar to us today, it seems to have been unique in Tyrwhitt's time. When he turned his attention to *Piers Plowman*, Tyrwhitt found at least two C-Texts of the poem. Comparison of

---

[19]John A. Alford, "The Design of the Poem" in John A. Alford, ed., *A Companion to Piers Plowman* (Berkeley and Los Angeles: University of California Press, 1988), 29–30.

[20]B.A. Windeatt, "Thomas Tyrwhitt," in Paul Ruggiers, ed., *Editing Chaucer: The Great Tradition* (Norman, Oklahoma: Pilgrim Books, 1984), 117–43, esp. 138–39.

[21]Geoffrey Chaucer, *The Canterbury Tales of Chaucer to which are added, An Essay upon his Language and Versification; and Introductory Discourse; and Notes*, ed. Thomas Tyrwhitt, 5 vols. (London: Payne, 1775) 4:74. Tyrwhitt's comment is mentioned by Skeat 2:lxxvii; and by Kane, "The Text" 176.

these with Crowley's edition based mainly on a B-Text, especially if he was thinking about collating them, might have caused some dismay. He was not inclined to recognize the full significance of these manuscript variants; instead he believed that the textual problems with *Piers Plowman* were analogous to those for a multiply attested work that he had already collated, *The Canterbury Tales*. He interpreted the diversity in the sources for *Piers Plowman* to be the result of an accumulation of scribal and editorial corruption of a single authorial original, as he had already found to be the case with Chaucer. Like Hearne, he came to a conclusion about the text of *Piers Plowman* based on his previous editorial experience, but in Tyrwhitt's case, the analogy was wrong. No one today believes that the differences between the B- and C-Versions could have arisen from scribal corruption. Tyrwhitt might have realized the inadequacies of such an explanation if he had also been aware of the even more dramatic differences between the A- and B-Versions.

Joseph Ritson (1752–1803) was the first textual scholar to suspect that the *Piers Plowman* manuscripts could be grouped as they are today. He disagreed with Tyrwhitt about Crowley's editions being wildly inaccurate, surmising correctly that Crowley had given a reasonably sound edition based mainly on one version of the poem (now called B), as found in several extant manuscripts. Ritson distinguished these from another group of manuscripts now recognized as C-Texts, and he concluded that two separate versions resulted when

> the author had revised his original work, and given, as it were, a new edition; and it may be possible for a good judge of ancient poetry, possessed of a sufficient stock of critical acumen, to determine which was first and which was second.[22]

Ritson believed the larger differences between *Piers Plowman* manuscripts could result from conscious and thematically consistent revisions of an authorial original rather than from random scribal corruptions. His conclusion that the same author produced the B- and

---

[22]Joseph Ritson, *Bibliographia Poetica: a Catalogue of Engleish* [sic] *Poets of the Twelfth, Thirteenth, Fourteenth, Fifteenth, and Sixteenth Centurys, with a Short Account of Their Works* (London: Nicol, 1802), 26–31. See DiMarco 35–36.

C-Versions is a matter of consensus today—even among most who propose that two separate authors produced the A- and B-Versions. Ritson also identified a new direction of inquiry that would occupy scholars in the coming decades down to the time of Skeat's work and beyond: if separate versions could be isolated, their chronological sequence could perhaps be discovered.

In addition, Ritson seems to have suspected before anyone else that the extant *Piers Plowman* manuscripts could be grouped into three separate versions. First he distinguished between B manuscripts (which resembled Crowley's edition) and all other manuscripts. Then he recognized that these others (he had consulted several C-Texts and at least four manuscripts of the A-Version) could be separated further into two groups that were quite unlike each other. Unfortunately, this recognition was not published by Ritson, having been recorded only as the following manuscript entry in his own hand. The second sentence must be a reference to the differences between the A- and C-Versions:

> The differences as well between the printed copies on the one hand and most if not all the MSS. on the other, as between the MSS. themselves is very remarkable. Of the latter indeed there appears two sets, of which the one has scarcely 5 lines togr. in common with the other.[23]

In the first half of the nineteenth century, three scholars studied the manuscripts closely. Thomas Whitaker (1759–1821) published an edition of *Piers Plowman* in 1813, based on Phillips MS 8231, a C-Text. Whitaker argued that this faithfully represented the author's original and that Crowley's edition represented a late and bad manuscript of the poet's revised text, thus reversing the order for B and C commonly accepted now (DiMarco 37). It was possible for Whitaker to reach this erroneous conclusion because he was unaware of the A-Text. Thus passages found in the B-Text which derived from the A-Text and were omitted in the C-Text could be mistakenly understood as additions by a B reviser to the original C-Text.

In the following decade Richard Price (1790–1833) employed col-

---

[23]Quoted by E. Talbot Donaldson, *Piers Plowman: The C-Text and Its Poet*, Yale Studies in English, vol. 113 (New Haven: Yale University Press), 4–5n3. See DiMarco 36.

lation to show that Crowley's edition of the B-Text was based on a good manuscript. He used the same procedure with two C-Texts to correct portions of Whitaker's edition. Finally, and most importantly, he announced the discovery of the A-Text:

> Among the Harley MSS. there is a fragment of this poem written upon vellum, (No. 875.) of an equally early date with Vespasian B. xvi. and in a character nearly resembling it. Unhappily this fragment only extends to the 151st line of the 8th passus, nor is it free from lacunae even thus far. Our loss is however in some measure repaired — perhaps wholly so — by the preservation of a transcript on paper, in the same collection (No. 6041), which, though considerably younger, and somewhat modernized in its orthography, exhibits a much more correct and intelligible text. From this manuscript it is evident, that another and a third version was once in circulation; and if the first draught of the poem be still in existence, it is here perhaps that we must look for it. For in this the narrative is considerably shortened; many passages of decidedly episodic cast — such as the tale of the cat and the ratons, and the character of Wrath — are wholly omitted; others, which in the later versions are given with considerable detail of circumstance, are here but slightly sketched. . . .[24]

Price also concluded that the version edited by Whitaker did not precede Crowley's. In other words, he not only discovered and put into print what Ritson had suspected — that three different versions of the poem are represented by the extant manuscripts — but also in the process answered Ritson's question about the sequence of these versions.

In 1834 Thomas Wright (1810–1877) reviewed Whitaker's 1813 edition and rejected Whitaker's view that MS Phillips 8231 represented an earlier version of the poem than Crowley's source. Wright inspected seven manuscripts, finding two to agree with Whitaker's text and five to resemble Crowley's.[25] Wright failed to notice that one of these manuscripts, Trinity College Cambridge R.3.14, diverged significantly from both in its first half, being an A-Text through its

---

[24]Thomas Warton, *The History of English Poetry, from the Close of the Eleventh Century to Commencement of the Eighteenth Century*, 3 vols., ed. Richard Price (1824; London: Thomas Tegg, 1840), 2:63–64. See DiMarco 40.

[25]*The Vision and Creed of Piers Ploughman*, ed. Thomas Wright, 2nd ed., 2 vols. (London: Reeves and Turner, 1887), 1:xxxviii-xxxix.

first eleven passus, with its remainder supplied from a C-Text. Thus Wright failed to recognize that there was a third version of the poem and spent his energy distinguishing between B and C. He managed independently to determine that B preceded C. He concluded that Whitaker's C-Text represented a version of the poem containing revisions and additions "made by some other person, who was per- haps induced by his own political sentiments to modify passages, and was gradually led on to publish a revision of the whole" (Wright 1:xxxiv). Like Hearne, Wright understood that the composition and transformation of a work in a manuscript-oriented culture could involve thorough revision and expansion by a second author. It is unfortunate that he did not test this knowledge on the question of the A-Text's authorship. He was unaware of Price's discovery of the A-Version ten years earlier and of Ritson's unpublished comments.

Wright's 1842 edition of *Piers Plowman* was the first text of the poem to approach the editorial quality achieved over a century ear- lier by Hearne in his editions of the chronicle literature. Wright's introduction, repeating and amplifying arguments made in his 1834 review of Whitaker, displayed a knowledge of many different manu- scripts and offered the fullest rationale up to that time for dividing the manuscripts into two distinct groups (the B and C versions as Skeat later named them), and for determining the order of composi- tion for these two. His extensive notes to the text included numerous passages for comparison from Whitaker's C-Text and many useful historical explanations, some of which were later adopted and ex- panded by Skeat. Although Wright divided the text into narrow half-line columns and modernized the orthography and punctua- tion, he was otherwise conservative in the handling of his text, only rarely introducing variants from other manuscripts and consistently giving reasons for doing so in the notes to his text. Thus he adopts "guiltless" from his second Trinity College Cambridge MS (B.15.17) in place of "synneles" early in the Prologue "to preserve the allitera- tion" (Wright 2:505). But such changes are rare in his edition and supported by variants from the other manuscripts.

By the end of the decade, in the introduction to his edition of Chaucer, Wright complained that deriving a text for a multiply attested work by inserting variants from many manuscripts was "the most absurd plan which it is possible to conceive." Instead, he opted for what became known as the "best text" method. He asserted that an editor

> must give up the printed editions, and fall back upon the manuscripts; and that instead of bundling them all together, we must pick out one best manuscript which at the same time is one of those nearest Chaucer's time.[26]

As Skeat later noted, Wright did not follow this rule perfectly himself, at least not in his edition of Chaucer (Ross 155). But Wright's comments were aimed at Thomas Tyrwhitt, whose wide knowledge of Middle English language and manuscripts resulted in an edition of Chaucer which was emended eclectically, that is, by selecting variant readings from many manuscripts to produce what is hypothetically the author's original. Tyrwhitt was perhaps the most qualified of the early practitioners of this method. In England, editors had offered such hybrid texts in print since Caxton, whose second edition of Chaucer was revised rather than completely redone when he was lent a better manuscript. Crowley's successive editions of *Piers Plowman* conflated multiple sources. In our own century the most elaborate example of eclectic editing and the emphasis on editorial judgment above the manuscript record has been championed by E.T. Donaldson and George Kane in their Athlone Press edition of the B-Text.[27]

Wright advocated the best-text method in his edition of Chaucer, but he was actually a better practitioner of the method in his 1842 edition of *Piers Plowman*. It has been suggested that Wright may have known the Tuebner Series of classical editions, which employed the same method. This continental influence, however, is not necessary to explain Wright's practice. Hearne had already taken this course, offering an unemended best text, with collations, more than a century before. Wright undoubtedly knew of Hearne's editorial work, for in the introduction to his edition of the French text of Peter

---

[26]Thomas W. Ross, "Thomas Wright," in Ruggiers 148.

[27]For an account of their editorial practice see Kane and Donaldson 128–220. Hudson responds tactfully, ". . . one blenches from the thought of this method applied by scholars of less acuity and energy than Kane and Donaldson" (45). Also of interest is E. Talbot Donaldson, "The Psychology of Editors of Middle English Texts" in his own *Speaking of Chaucer* (New York: Norton, 1970), 102–18.

Langtoft's *Chronicle*, he discusses Hearne's edition of the English translation.[28]

The obvious initial problem with this method is in choosing a "best text." Wright's judgment in such matters was not infallible, as may be seen in his selection of the texts for his editions of Chaucer and the Chester plays.[29] But though Wright's choice of a source for *Piers Plowman* (Trinity College Cambridge MS B.15.17) was passed over in favor of Laud Misc. 581 by Skeat when he edited the B-Text of *Piers Plowman*, the Trinity MS is a close second at worst, having more errors but also a more regular orthography. Kane and Donaldson selected this manuscript as the basis for their own eclectic edition.

Skeat, who made careful use of the Trinity MS and Wright's second edition, referred to the latter as "excellent" (Skeat 2:lxvii) while finding about forty misprints but only about ten examples of misreading, most involving the confusion of *n* and *u* (Skeat 2:lxxviii). Compared to Crowley's "inability, in numerous instances, to read the text correctly" (Skeat 2:lxxvii) and compared to Whitaker, who "frequently misunderstood his author" and "often failed in deciphering the not very difficult characters in which the MS. is written" (Skeat 2:lxxxi), the edition of Wright represents a significant editorial landmark. Though Skeat disagreed with Wright's theory of multiple authorship, he wrote of the importance of Wright's edition with characteristic candor: "it would hardly be just not to confess my *very great* obligations to it. Without its help my work would, at least, have been doubled" (Skeat 2:lxxvii, n5).

Walter W. Skeat (1835–1912) published a volume of parallel extracts from twenty-nine manuscripts of *Piers Plowman* in 1866 and pointed out that they represented three distinct versions of the poem.[30] It is Skeat who named the versions the A-Text, B-Text, and C-Text, and he credited Price with the discovery of the A-Text. Skeat's separate Early English Text Society (EETS) editions of the

---

[28]Thomas Wright, ed., *The Chronicle de Pierre de Langtoft* (London: Longmans, 1866–68).

[29]Ross 156; and W.W. Greg, *Bibliographical and Textual Problems of the English Miracle Plays* (London: A. Moring, 1914), 41.

[30]*Parallel Extracts from Twenty-Nine Manuscripts of Piers Plowman, with Comments, and a Proposal for the Society's Three-Text Edition of this Poem*, EETS, OS 17 (London: N. Trübner, 1866).

A-, B-, and C-Texts appeared in 1867, 1869, and 1873. His monumental two volume edition of the three versions printed as parallel texts appeared in 1886.

Like most of the other scholars who produced editions in the EETS series during the last four decades of the nineteenth century, Skeat was recruited by F. J. Furnivall even though he was not an expert in paleography or textual criticism.[31] At Christ's College, Cambridge, Skeat had studied theology and mathematics. In 1860 he took orders and soon afterwards began a career in the Church. This was ended by illness after two years, and Skeat returned to Christ's College to accept a lectureship in mathematics in 1864. The EETS was formed that same year and Skeat was enlisted to help prepare early texts for eventual use in developing the *New English Dictionary*. Skeat was handed a manuscript of *Lancelot of the Laik*, and his edition of it appeared a year later, in 1865. The next year he began his work with *Piers Plowman*, which was to occupy him for the next twenty years.

As an editor of *Piers Plowman*, Skeat was the inheritor of an extensive but varied body of textual and scholarly material. His primary tasks were the tireless gathering of manuscripts and other sources and the organized presentation in print of a vast amount of textual, historical, and other information. He eventually became aware of forty-five manuscripts of the poem and classified these into ten different groupings based on their formal treatment of the poem: 4 types of the A-Text, 2 of the B-Text, 2 of the C-Text, and 2 types of mixed texts combining A and C or B and C.

More than a century after its publication, Skeat's 1886 parallel text edition is still an extremely valuable modern source in the field of *Piers Plowman* scholarship. The first volume prints his three versions in a format that allows specific passages in the three versions to be compared with ease. The second of the two volumes contains, in addition to a description and classification of the multiple manuscripts, nearly three hundred pages of notes in which Skeat interprets the text, gives historical background, suggests parallels from other medieval sources, and offers many other kinds of information. The specificity and range of Skeat's insight constantly remind us that he was either directly involved or familiar with a number of other

[31]A.S.G. Edwards, "Walter Skeat," in Ruggiers 172.

editorial projects at the time he was working with *Piers Plowman*. During the years that Skeat composed his notes to *Piers Plowman*, he was also editing the *Treatise on the Astrolabe*, *The Bruce*, and his *Etymological Dictionary*, while becoming Erlington and Bosworth professor of Anglo-Saxon at Cambridge and founding the English Dialect Society. From this milieu his notes and introduction communicate a wealth of relevent historical and textual information as well as conveying the scholarly sensibility of a key member in an active community of philologists.

Skeat's role is pivotal in the history of early and modern *Piers Plowman* scholarship. He provided an essential map for a previously mysterious textual frontier and also a synthesis of much of the best interpretive scholarship up to his time. He contributed more substantive textual discussion than his predecessors combined, as well as producing separate editions of the three versions, each an editorial construct determined by the particular nature of its sources. For the A-Text he knew ten manuscripts of differing length and chose to base his edition on the Vernon MS as far as it goes into the tenth passus, with an ending supplied from Trinity College Cambridge MS R.3.14. He collated five manuscripts with his main text and in so doing identified several variants that suggested emendations, all of them clearly identified. His B-Text was more closely based on a single manuscript, MS Laud Misc. 581, which Skeat considered to be the author's autograph, perhaps corrected in his own hand. It was one of fourteen B manuscripts known to the editor, who felt they were generally in close agreement. Skeat found his eighteen C-Text manuscripts to be more varied. He identified two main subclasses — one slightly earlier than the other — and he chose a manuscript from the more recent subclass, Phillips 8231. Against this text he collated five manuscripts throughout and another four occasionally. He also identified other subclasses among his C-Text sources, based on their affinities with his two main C-Text groups.

These three editions reveal not only the "brilliantly organized intellect" (Kane, "The Text" 177) of their editor but also a creative sensibility capable of the kind of conjecture which allowed Skeat to systematize and interpret a previously overwhelming body of manuscript evidence. Although the Vernon MS went out of favor as the basis for studying the A-Version, and Laud Misc. 581 is no longer believed to be the B-Text author's autograph, scholars in our own century remain indebted to and continue to imitate Skeat, whose carefully edited texts were also demonstrations of ambitious textual and authorship hypotheses.

Skeat adopted the view that only one author created all the versions of *Piers Plowman*. His opinion is still cited on this question, but usually without going into detail, perhaps because Skeat's ideas about single authorship are so surprisingly naive on some points, and sometimes tellingly honest about his uncertainty. For example, his 1881 notice for the *Encyclopaedia Britannica* suggests that the author's name was not "Langland" but "Langley" (DiMarco 64). This statement adopts the conclusions of Charles Henry Pearson (DiMarco 55), published a decade earlier. The advantage of Pearson's account is that it manages to link the name "Langley" with the names of two different people and two locations in two ascriptions given by John Bale and a C manuscript. However, in 1884 Skeat rejected the name "Langley" (DiMarco 65). In his 1886 edition, he repeats this skeptical view, but offers also Pearson's "plausible theory" which adopts "Langley" as the author's name. Then Skeat adds,

> Yet I confess that I still hesitate as to whether we should do so; for it is very difficult, in such a case, to see how the traditional name of Langland came to be mentioned at all. It involves the unlikely substitution of the comparatively rare name of Langland for a name which was much commoner and more widely spread; and this is a difficulty which I can hardly get over. In a matter so obscure, I now prefer to keep to the traditional name, though I confess that at one time I thought otherwise. (Skeat 2:xxxi)

Nevertheless, when Skeat constructs a biography of the author traditionally named William Langland, he manages to incorporate all the names mentioned in both ascriptions and linked by Pearson, even the references to two different locations of origin. Skeat proposes that the poet's family had moved from the location mentioned in one ascription to the location mentioned in the other (Skeat 2:xxxii).

Skeat's account of the author's life is, incidentally, a tour de force in the construction of literary biography out of every possible fragmentary reference to "the poet" in ascriptions, the texts of the poem, and elsewhere. This generally resembles Skeat's editorial procedure with the manuscripts — he gathers all possibly relevent elements and assimilates these into an all-inclusive chronological pattern. In the field of textual criticism the outcome was a very useful assemblage of the textual data in a thoroughly logical array. In the field of biography, however, Skeat's imagination seems to get the better of him as we follow Will Langland from his schooldays to the confessions of his declining old age, observing incidents along the way that remind us of tales from another mathematician of the era, Charles Dodgson. Skeat's account of Long Will is built upon the autobiographical fallacy — assuming the narrator within a literary text gives a true autobiographical account of the author's actual life:

> In one passage he tells us that he was loath to reverence lords and ladies, or persons dressed in fur or wearing silver pendants; he would never say 'God save you' to serjeants whom he met, for all of which proud behaviour, then very uncommon in a poor man, people looked upon him as a fool, and few approved of his mode of life (B.xv.3–10). It requires no great stretch of imagination to picture to ourselves the tall gaunt figure of Long Will, in his long robes and with his shaven head, striding along Cornhill, saluting no man by the way, minutely observant of the gay dresses to which he paid no outward reverence. (Skeat 2:xxxv-vi)

However charming we may find this account, such a narrative can do nothing to substantiate any theory of authorship; it has as much evidential validity as horsefeathers. Still, this passage has its place in a tradition of concocting single authors for *Piers Plowman* that has survived into our own era.

Earlier we considered a period in which the existence of a printed text for one (and only one) version of the poem caused almost all scholars to assume that *Piers Plowman* was written by a single author. Their interpretive criticism for more than two and a half centuries both derived from and bolstered confidence in this assumption. When multiple versions of the poem were discovered, multiple authorship became tenable, a fact recognized before Skeat only by scholars who had actually come into contact with variant sources — Wright in the 1830's, Hearne a century before, and, to a lesser degree, even Crowley in 1550. Once Skeat clearly distinguished and published three parallel versions of the poem in 1886, the text was no longer presentable as a once coherent literary unity which had been garbled during centuries of scribal transmission. Instead it would now be apparent to anyone who took the evidence seriously that markedly different texts had arisen during an early period of about thirty years and that these different texts represent quite distinct versions, possibly composed by more than one person, despite Skeat's conclusion to the contrary.

A shift in scholarly rhetoric and critical emphasis was indicated. The considerable and heterogeneous textual information, once simply understood in the singular as a "work" or "poem" that had survived in various states of corruption, was now available in its multiplicity, with a standardized nomenclature for its three versions, and a good descriptive list of its many manuscript sources. The new textual reality implicitly invited scholars in our century to shift their attention to issues of attribution or the fundamental nature of the textual record instead of simply taking part in a generalized academic exploration of theological satire in an allegorical mode.

The theory of multiple authorship which soon arose had negative implications for some nearly sacred scholarly traditions. The possibility that the most widely known version (the B-Text) involved extensive revision of one author's work by another was an obvious threat to a mode of criticism which interpreted "the poem" as an individual writer's uniform expression of his literary imagination. If the A-Text was the only version written by the original author, the entire corpus of *Piers Plowman* scholarship was perhaps focussed on the wrong text. Dual authorship for the A- and B-Versions allowed new and very different evaluations of their significance, for example the view that an original work's attack on corrupt institutions and failures of the individual will (A-Text) was subsequently modified and expanded by someone with less radical social and political views and less artistic ability (B-Text). These considerations perhaps help to explain the intense resistance even today to the notion that more than one author created the multiple texts of *Piers Plowman*.

The recognition and publication of the multiple versions of *Piers Plowman* in the nineteenth century did not by any means bring an end to widespread satisfaction with the hypothesis of single authorship. Single authorship had received all but unanimous (though widely uninformed) support during more than two centuries of commentary, and it had the advantage of being the simpler assumption to keep untangled by those writing about the poetry with inadequate understanding of its textual vagaries — a factor still relevant today.

The identification of separate versions of the poem did cause an elaboration of the single authorship hypothesis. In one view (implied by Ritson, developed by Price, and accepted by Skeat) the multiple versions resulted from a single poet's revisions throughout a long life which involved personal conflict and change that could explain shifts in theme and emphasis among the versions. This explanation recurs throughout our century's discourse on authorship. In our own era it has become a very pliant psychological construct indeed. Almost any degree of variation between one version and another can be explained by citing extreme shifts in a single author's political outlook, or his bouts of confusion, or, if necessary, more dramatic disruptions of his mental faculties.[32]

As stated at the outset, part of the value of this survey of the early scholarship should come from the perspective it can give to those studying the related scholarly activity of the twentieth century. During the centuries we have reviewed, textual scholars discovered and catalogued a range of manuscripts. While this effort went a long way toward characterizing uncertainties about the nature of the manuscript sources, it also provided the basis for a new debate about authorship. The theory that more than one author was responsible for the multiple versions of the poem, as advocated in our century by scholars from Manly[33] to Fowler, is not peculiar to this era; it was considered possible or likely by such earlier textual scholars as Hearne and Wright, the best editors of Middle English texts in their respective eras. Given the status of extant evidence, the modern debate about authorship could not be won on the basis of fact alone. Instead, a general consensus in favor of single authorship has been achieved through the rhetoric of editorial authority[34] and the inclination of academic scholars to accept the least arduous of uncertain paths, especially if that option is ready-made, presented confidently

---

[32]See, for example, Elizabeth Kirk, *The Dream Thought of Piers Plowman* (New Haven and London: Yale University Press, 1972) and Priscilla Martin, *The Field and the Tower*, (London and Basingstoke: Macmillan Press, 1979).

[33]John Mathews Manly, "The Lost Leaf of 'Piers Plowman,'" *Modern Philology* 3 (1905-06): 359-66.

[34]In the second chapter of Kane's *Evidence* a straw-man account of the multiple authorship argument is constructed and easily knocked down. The third chapter then argues for single authorship by very carefully interpreting what is actually an absence of reliable evidence. This sort of unbalanced argument by assertion is announced early in the book. Discussing the ongoing authorship debate and the

in magisterial editions, and if access to the underlying manuscript evidence is difficult.

It should also be understood that the intensity of the authorship debate early in our own century provided the impetus for further textual scholarship and influenced the shaping of all the printed texts of *Piers Plowman* available today. For this and other reasons the texts commonly in use are seriously flawed—a subject too large to be outlined here. A direction of textual scholarsip for the coming century, however, can be inferred from the work of the best of the textual scholars we have discussed. Hearne understood the need to compare all major variants and thus published his texts with collations from multiple manuscripts—the best mechanism in the eighteenth century for recording the kind of analysis in which he excelled. Skeat understood that the textual issues could only be assessed legitimately through a comprehensive grasp of the multiplicity of manuscripts, and therefore he produced a careful listing of every manuscript of the poem that he knew to exist and a parallel text edition to facilitate comparison of the three main versions. What we now need is not a reduction of all variations according to some theory of authorship and for the supposed advantages of working from a received text, but access instead for all scholars to the complete set of extant *Piers Plowman* manuscripts in a carefully prepared and convenient format—an electronic parallel text edition encompassing all the manuscripts, made manageable by the technically competent Hearnes and Skeats of our own era. The goals of such an effort are likely to be different from those determined for textual criticism by the tradition of the printed book:

> The difficulty, at the point of editing, with deciding among these readings—attempting to find the "best" one of the bunch—is that by printing the "best" reading, one does not resolve the diversity of variants into a single text accompanied by an apparatus of rejected readings, one

---

opposition to his views, Kane declares, "This continued opposition is intolerable: there should, in principle, be a reasonable, a correct way of interpreting the whole body of evidence, one that will provide an unambiguous answer, final at least in the present state of knowledge. If correctly assessed this evidence should point to a single truth, and that it has not done so implies, for me at least, that the assessment has been faulty" (1). This is nearly a call for *a priori* interpretation of otherwise inconclusive evidence, and it is remarkable that such assertions have been so influential.

only alters the materials of study from the extant medieval versions of the text to a modern one based on an editor's best judgment. The selective record of variants of the manuscripts presented by Skeat, Knott and Fowler, and the fuller collation provided by Kane, while helpful in displaying how significant textual decisions have been based on available variants, does not show how in any given manuscript these variants work together to convey the meaning of the text. The manuscripts of the A-text exhibit a diversity of readings and this diversity leads to the recognition of a range of potential meanings. . . . A single printed text cannot adequately present this diversity of readings. Yet one must know the readings in their diversity — and not just as given by a critical text — in order to understand the medieval text as preserved by its historical forms.[35]

Modern printed texts of *Piers Plowman*, such as the eclectic editions produced by Kane and Donaldson, offer a reduction of the textual data, a leveling of variation, to produce a uniform compilation of guesses in support of an editorial theory. The theory of single authorship for all the versions of *Piers Plowman* is the bedrock of the editorial practice of Kane and Donaldson. Though not stated overtly, this theory affects their determinations of typical scribal practice, which is the principle invoked to justify their idiosyncratic emendations. The resulting emended texts of the poem in turn determine which interpretations of the work can be sustained. It should come as no surprise that the current textual status quo so created has no need for the less streamlined theory of multiple authorship, since the texts of the different versions have been harmonized to exclude it.[36] While the editions by Kane and Donaldson have great interest as the fullest demonstration of a highly subjective approach to reducing manuscript variation, they should not be understood as having ended the discussion of the extant manuscript sources.

[35]Gerald Barnett, "The Representation of Medieval English Texts," diss., University of Washington, 1988, 214–15.

[36]David Fowler, "A New Edition of the B text of *Piers Plowman*," *Yearbook of English Studies* 7 (1977): 23–42. This very significant review of the Kane-Donaldson B-Text is partly concerned with the harmonization of the A- and B-Versions by the editors of the Athlone edition. The meter of the A-Version is easily discerned, whether one is reading David Fowler's edition or George Kane's. But in editing the B-Version, Kane and Donaldson adopted variants and even provided many readings of their own invention in order to make their B-Version far more regular metrically than

Textual uncertainty has traditionally been a source of vitality in the study of *Piers Plowman*, and the diversity of our sources for the poem is a topic now most in need of unencumbered scholarly attention. Some progress has been made in the discussion of discrete manuscripts and what they tell us about both the processes of composition and the reception of works in an open manuscript culture. We have only begun to consider the separate meaning and coherence of separate manuscripts, whatever their relation to an authorial original. At a higher level of generalization, we need to study the separate versions of the poem independently: reading the B-Version in texts which have not been systematically harmonized with the A-Text by modern editors, for example, and analyzing the A-Version without anachronistically importing themes and conclusions from the much altered and much later B-Version. It is necessary to set aside the imperious notions that uncertainty about authorship is "intolerable" (Kane, *Evidence* 1) or that scribal variation merely "damages the work" and has no intrinsic value for scholarship (Kane, "The Text" 194). Uncertainty about the text and its authorship is to be welcomed and valued for what it is — the honest recognition of a complex reality in need of informed exploration. This effort requires an outlook free of the proprietary assumptions of those who have established the standard editions or who have made such pro-

---

what is found in any extant B manuscript, and therefore much more similar to the A-Version's alliterative artistry than indicated by the B manuscripts. They justified this by arguing that all of the B manuscripts descended from a corrupt archetype in which the meter had been garbled throughout. But Fowler identified a flaw in their theory by arguing as follows: The B-Text is composed of two different kinds of material — poetry adopted from the A-Version (2200 lines) and new material added to this orginal poetry by whoever produced the B-Version (an additional 1100 lines). When Kane and Donaldson "repaired" the meter of the entire B-Text to make it uniform throughout, they were required to emmend only 35 (or 1.5%) of the lines originally deriving from the A-Text, while at the same time they found it necessary to repair 125 (or 11.4%) of the lines original to the B revision. Undoubtedly a convoluted explanation could be devised to explain why the scribe who supposedly produced the "corrupt archetype" of the B-Text made ten times as many scribal errors in copying new B-Text lines as he did in copying the original A-Text lines. A more straightforward explanation of the existing manuscript evidence would be that two different people with differing metrical principles created the A-Text and the lines extending it in the B-Text. In this view, Kane and Donaldson have inadvertently, in their metrical revisions, demonstrated that the metrical practice of the A-Text poet differs from that of the B reviser.

lific contributions to the maintenance of a simplistic and unnecessarily restrictive authorship orthodoxy and textual status quo.

Perhaps in a book honoring a scholar who has remained committed to teaching *Piers Plowman* throughout a very productive editorial and critical career, it will be permissable to offer straightforward advice to future scholars in the field. We may be told that the scholarly consensus today is built on a firm textual analysis. Some scholars would have us believe their work arises from a comprehensive understanding of the textual sources and a resolution of the textual uncertainties. In fact, the textual issues were not resolved, but scholars have moved on, referencing nonsolutions found in a narrow set of critical editions as their warrant — creating an unwarranted confidence about a limited set of textual options. It is not sound scholarship to brush aside the difficulties in order to proceed with a less complicated problem, even if this is done with the support of the majority of one's colleagues. And only the simple minded will insist that the underlying uncertainties about text and authorship are the result of an argumentative minority needlessly complicating the issues. The causes for this uncertainty are not psychological but historical; they can only be addressed by familiarizing oneself with the diversity of the texts and their textual history.

Shame on Meed

T. P. DOLAN

A FTER LADY MEDE'S courteous reception at Westminster she is approached by a friar who offers to absolve her sins, and the narrator describes what happens:

> Thanne Mede for here mysdedes to that man kneled,
> And shroue hire of hire shrewednesses shamelees, I trowe. . . .
> (B III.43–44)[1]

The most significant word in this couplet is "shamelees," which the poet reinforces with the tag "I trowe." The word "shamelees" has a technical meaning, because the absence of shame when confessing to a friar was a major criticism of the friars' administration of the sacrament of Penance. The pointed use of the word here offers further evidence of the poet's familiarity with all the technicalities of the arguments mounted against the friars.

Innocent IV (Pope, 1243–1254) issued a controversial anti-mendicant Bull known as *Etsi Animarum* in 1254. In this Bull he makes the point that shame is a very important part of the sacrament of Penance because there is a psychological difficulty in having to confess one's sins to a priest whom one sees regularly. The parish clergy know their parishioners intimately and it is embarrassing for penitents to reveal their sins to someone they might meet every day.

---

[1] All quotations from *Piers Plowman* are taken from the B-Text in *The Vision of William Concerning Piers Plowman*, ed. Walter W. Skeat. 2 vols. (Oxford: Clarendon Press, 1886).

It should be noted that at that time there was no such thing as a confession-box, with a grille between priest and sinner, which ensures a degree of apartness and anonymity between confessor and penitent. Before it came into general use in the Church, about 1614, the custom was for a sinner to kneel beside the priest at the beginning of the confession and then at the end for the absolution.[2] While confessing his or her sins the penitent sat or stood beside the priest: it was an intimate rite, which often gave rise to scandal. A friar was, by the nature of his calling as a mendicant, a wandering cleric and may never have seen a penitent again after his or her confession. Hence, to confess to a friar was a relatively impersonal, anonymous act, and the shame and embarrassment (*erubescentia*) were absent. This is what Innocent IV has to say on this point:

> verum etiam erubescentia, quae est magna pars poenitentiae, tollitur, dum quis non proprio sacerdoti quem habet continuum et praesentem, sed alieno et aliquando transeunti, ad quem difficilis et aliquando impossibilis est recursus, sua crimina confitetur.[3]

> [But shame, which is a great part of penance, is removed if someone confesses his crimes, not to his own regular priest whom he has on a permanent and regular basis as confessor, but to another visiting confessor to whom it is sometimes difficult, if not impossible, to go back to again.]

Shame was always regarded as an important component in the rite of Confession. In the Pseudo-Augustine tract *De Vera et Falsa Poenitentia*, which Chaucer cites as by Augustine in *The Parson's Tale* (X.985–87), the point is made that:

> Erubescentia enim ipsa partem habet remissionis: ex misericordia enim hoc praecepit Dominus, ut neminem poeniteret in occulto. In hoc enim

---

[2] See Henry Charles Lea, *A History of Auricular Confession and Indulgences in the Latin Church*, 3 vols. (Philadelphia: Lea Brothers, 1896), 1: 394–95; J. O'Connell, *Church Building and Furnishing: The Church's Way: A Study in Liturgical Law* (London: Burns and Oates, 1955), 72; *New Catholic Encyclopedia*, 15 vols. (New York: McGraw Hill, 1967), 4: 136–37, s.v. *Confessional.*

[3] Quotation taken from *Bullarium Franciscanum*, Epitome et Supplementum, ed. C. Eubel (Quaracchi: Franciscan Order, 1908), 260a.

quod per se ipsum dicit sacerdoti et erubescentiam vincit timore Dei offensi, fit venia criminis.[4]

[The feeling of shame has a part to play in the remission of sins; and this is a mercy of the Lord's, so that no-one would claim to be a penitent in secret, by the very fact that he himself goes along and confesses to the priest, and the fear of the God he has offended conquers his sense of shame and thus brings about pardon for his sins.]

The necessity to feel shame was obviously a commonplace requirement for the sacrament of Penance. Indeed, it is one of the sixteen conditions for a good confession, as contained in this mnemonic verse which has been attributed to St. Thomas Aquinas (in his Commentary on Book IV of the *Sentences*), but which is also found earlier:

> Sit simplex, humilis, confessio, pura, fidelis,
> Atque frequens, nuda, discreta, libens, verecunda,
> Integra, secreta, lachrimabilis, accelerata,
> Fortis et accusans, et sit parere parata.

> [Let confession be simple, humble, pure, faithful
> And frequent, unadorned, discreet, willing, ashamed,
> Whole, secret, tearful, thorough,
> Strong and reproachful, and showing readiness to obey.][5]

In dealing with Quaestio *de verecundia* in the *Summa Theologiae* St. Thomas defines what he means by the term "verecundia":

> verecundia est timor ingloriationis

> [To be sensitive to shame is to entertain a healthy fear of being inglorious.] (*S. T.*, 2a, 2ae 144.4)[6]

---

[4]*PL* 40: 1122. Citations of Chaucer are taken from *The Riverside Chaucer*, gen. ed. Larry D. Benson (Boston: Houghton Mifflin, 1987).

[5]See Thomas N. Tentler, *Sin and Confession on the Eve of the Reformation* (Princeton: Princeton University Press, 1977), 106–07. For further explanation of these verses, see *Dictionnaire de Théologie Catholique*, 3: 957–58, s.v. *Confession, Questions Morales et Pratiques*; and 12: 984, s.v. *Pénitence*.

[6]St. Thomas Aquinas, *Summa Theologiae*, Blackfriars Edition, 60 vols. (London: Eyre and Spottiswoode, 1964–66), 66–67.

Crucial to this feeling of shame, as he explains a little earlier, is the
factor of familiarity with the person to whom penitents confess their
sins; this feeling is missing with itinerant priests:

> Et inde etiam est quod quantum ad aliquid magis verecundamur a
> personis conjunctis, cum quibus semper sumus conversaturi, quasi ex
> hoc nobis perpetuum proveniat detrimentum; quod autem provenit a
> peregrinis et transeuntibus, quasi cito pertransit.

> [In this respect we fear disgrace in the eyes of those who are closer to us,
> for we have to live with them constantly and they can cause us continual
> worry, more so than passers-by and strangers who have but a glancing
> effect on us.] (*S. T.*, 2a 2ae 144.3; Blackfriars 43: 64)

Aquinas normally uses the word *verecundia*, rather than *erubescentia*, to
cover the sense of shame. Other commentators, however, make a
distinction between *verecundia* and *erubescentia*, with the former relating "to the reaction to the disgrace incurred in a completed act" and
the latter "to one still contemplated." This seems an unnecessary
distinction because the general view was that it was important to feel
shame and to blush during the act of penance because such reactions
were absent when the sins were perpetrated.[7]

Presumably, then, Lady Mede had not seen that particular friar
previously, and so her confession was "shamelees." The author returns to this theme in passus XX, where he more precisely identifies
the difference between confessing to a curate and confessing to a
friar:

> And euele is this yholde in parisches of Engelonde,
> For persones and parishprestes that shulde the peple shryue,
> Ben curatoures called to knowe and to hele,
> Alle that ben her parisshiens penaunce to enioigne,
> And shulden be ashamed in her shrifte; ac shame maketh hem wende,
> And fleen to the freres as fals folke to Westmynstre. . . .

> (B XX.277-82)

---

[7]See *New Catholic Encyclopedia*, 13: 163–64, s.v. *Shame, Sense of*. See also John T.
McNeill and Helena M. Gamer, *Medieval Handbooks of Penance: A Translation of the
Principal Libri Poenitentiales and Selections from Related Documents* (1938; rpt. New York:
Columbia University Press, 1965), 316, 324–25. Before the Fourth Lateran Coun-
cil shame was less precisely classified: see Allen J. Frantzen, *The Literature of Penance
in Anglo-Saxon England* (New Brunswick: Rutgers University Press, 1983), 177–79.

The parish clergy are called "curates" because they should know and cure their parishioners. The fact that they are local should make their parisioners "ashamed" when they go to confession to them, but to avoid this embarrassment penitents seek out friars who do not know them. Like Lady Mede they go to Westminster and shelter behind the anonymity of a wandering friar-confessor, who would in any case tend to give light penances—a factor which Chaucer identifies in his description of the Friar in *The General Prologue*:

> Ful swetely herde he confessioun,
> And plesaunt was his absolucioun:
> He was an esy man to yeve penaunce,
> Ther as he wiste to have a good pitaunce.
>
> (221-24)

In *Piers Plowman* there is nothing "swete" about Repentance's attitude to the penitents in the passage on the Seven Deadly Sins. He is at pains to make them feel sorry for their sins. In dealing with Glotoun, for instance, he is perfectly clear in stressing that this sense of sorrow involves a sense of shame:

> As thow with wordes and werkes hast wrou3te yuel in thi lyue,
> Shryue the and be shamed ther-of and shewe it with thi mouth.
>
> (B v.372-73)

If Glotoun had confessed to a friar, as Lady Mede did, this sense of shame would have been lacking.

The importance of the element of shame in the sacrament of Penance, as prescribed in Innocent IV's *Etsi Animarum*, had been revived and given prominence in the anti-mendicant controversy in the fourteenth century in the writings and sermons of Richard FitzRalph (Archbishop of Armagh, 1346-1360).[8] During the last ten years of his life he issued a series of addresses and sermons criticising

---

[8]For a full account of FitzRalph's life and work see Katherine Walsh, *A Fourteenth-Century Scholar and Primate: Richard FitzRalph in Oxford, Avignon and Armagh* (Oxford: Clarendon Press, 1981). In several recent studies of *Piers Plowman* FitzRalph's writings have been successfully employed to elucidate the poet's thought: see, for

the friars. In these he continually adverted to the passage concerning *erubescentia* in *Etsi Animarum*. The publicity which he gave to this problem ensured that it became a significant piece of anti-mendicant propaganda, which the poet astutely reflects in his poem.

Aubrey Gwynn argued that the lines concerning the four orders of friars in the Prologue—and in particular the couplet:

> But holychirche and hij holde better togideres,
> The moste myschief on molde is mountyng wel faste.
>
>   (B Prol.66–67)

—probably referred to the continuing public dispute between FitzRalph and the mendicant orders.[9] Whether or not this was the case, it seems reasonable to claim that the poet was aware of FitzRalph's role in the conflict, not least because they were both so keenly aware of the dangers allegedly posed by the friars to the effective ministry of the Church.

In FitzRalph's first major anti-mendicant sermon, preached on the text "Unusquisque in quo vocatus est frater, in hoc maneat apud Deum," which he delivered in Latin at a public consistory before Clement VI in Avignon on 5 July 1350, he says that the shame (verecundia), which is a major part of Penance, is removed or lessened if the penitent sees the confessor only once or twice a year (viz., a friar), whereas he would see a curate every day:

> tollitur omnino verecundia aut multum minuitur, que tamen est penitencie pars magna; quoniam nemo ambigit, quin quiscunque maiorem verecundiam haberet confiteri illi qui eum quasi per singulos dies esset visurus, sicuti curatus per singulos dies conspicit oues suas, quam illi qui fortassis semel tantum aut bis in anno eum videret, qualis est frater.[10]

---

example, Kathryn Kerby-Fulton, *Reformist Apocalypticism and "Piers Plowman"*, Cambridge Studies in Medieval Literature 7 (Cambridge: Cambridge University Press, 1990), 145–53, 229–30; Wendy Scase, *"Piers Plowman" and the New Anti-clericalism*, Cambridge Studies in Medieval Literature 4 (Cambridge: Cambridge University Press, 1989), *passim*; and Penn R. Szittya, *The Antifraternal Tradition in Medieval Literature* (Princeton: Princeton University Press, 1986), 280–83.

[9]Aubrey Gwynn, "The Date of the B-Text of *Piers Plowman*," *Review of English Studies* 19 (1943): 1–2.

[10]See *The Beginning of the Strife between Richard FitzRalph and the Mendicants*, with an Edition of his Autobiographical Prayer and his Proposition *Unusquisque*, ed. L. L. Hammerich (Copenhagen: Levin and Munksgaard, 1938), lines 303–09.

[The feeling of shame, even though it has a major part to play in the sacrament of penance, is completely removed or greatly reduced because no-one can doubt that it causes more shame for a person to confess to one who sees him in the normal course of events every day — for instance, the curate, who is the person who looks after his flock every day — than to one who might see him perhaps only once or twice a year, such as the friar.]

FitzRalph voiced the same view in the four sermons which he preached in the vernacular in London during 1356 and 1357. These survive only in Latin versions.[11] During the course of the third of these sermons, preached on the text "Dic ut lapides isti panes fiant" at St. Paul's Cross, London, on 26 February 1357, he discusses "Erubescencia que est maxima pars penitencie" (fol. 123r, line 6). He takes up the same theme again in the last of these sermons, preached on the text "Nemo vos seducat inanibus verbis" at St. Paul's Cross on 12 March 1357:

Innocencius IIII in illo capitulo *Etsi Animarum* alias raciones istud adducit scilicet quod non tantum contemptus et indevocio in populo prodeunt contra proprios sacerdotes, sed erubescencia que est maxima pars penitentie tollitur, cum quis non proprio sacerdoti quem habet continuum et presentem sed alieno et aliquando transeunti, ad quem difficilis et aliquando impossibilis est recursus, sua crimina confitetur. (fol. 132v, lines 28–32)[12]

[Innocent IV in the document headed *Etsi Animarum* adds other reasons to this, namely, from this practice there comes not only contempt and lack of respect among the people against their own priests, but the feeling of shame, which is a major part of penance, is removed, when someone confesses his crimes not to his regular priest, whom he has on a permanent and regular basis as confessor, but to another visiting confessor, to whom it is difficult and sometimes impossible to go back to again.]

---

[11]See T. P. Dolan, "English and Latin Versions of FitzRalph's Sermons," in *Latin and Vernacular: Studies in Late-Medieval Texts and Manuscripts*, York Manuscripts Conference 1987, ed. A. J. Minnis (Cambridge: D.S. Brewer, 1989), 27–37.

[12]Quotations from FitzRalph's London sermons are taken from British Library MS Lansdowne 393 (an early fifteenth-century paper manuscript).

Here, anticipating the Meed episode, FitzRalph addresses his audience on the importance of confessing sins to a curate whom a penitent would see practically every day, and not to an "alien" confessor like a friar.

FitzRalph's most celebrated address, the *Defensio Curatorum*, which was delivered before Innocent VI in Avignon on 8 November 1357, also includes a section on the necessity for feeling shame in confession, which is absent when confessing to a friar. This highly polemical sermon was translated by John Trevisa some time between 1387 (when he completed the translation of the *Polychronicon*) and 1398 (when he completed his translation of the *De Proprietatibus Rerum*).[13] In this address FitzRalph refers to Innocent IV and *Etsi Animarum* several times. Here is the relevant passages as translated by Trevisa:

> Also Innocencius telliþ anoþer cause, for a man is more shamfast to schryue hym to his ordinarie þan to eny frere, for a man is more schamfast to schewe his synnes to hym that he seeþ al day þan to hym that he seeþ but ones a ȝere.[14]

The authorities adduced in this paper show that Lady Mede made an imperfect confession, because she felt no shame when she was shriven by the maverick friar at Westminster. They also provide further evidence for acknowledging the poet's masterly handling of the intricate details involved in the anti-mendicant controversy.

---

[13]See A. S. G. Edwards, "John Trevisa," in *Middle English Prose: A Critical Guide to Major Authors and Genres* (New Brunswick: Rutgers University Press, 1984), 134–35. See also David C. Fowler, "New Light on John Trevisa," *Traditio* 18 (1962): 289–317, and the same author's "More about John Trevisa," *Modern Language Quarterly* 32 (1971): 243–54.

[14]Quotation from *Dialogus inter Militem et Clericum, Richard FitzRalph's Sermon: "Defensio Curatorum," and Methodius: "þe Bygynnyng of þe World and þe ende of Worldes,"* by John Trevisa, ed. Aaron J. Perry, EETS, OS 167 (London: Oxford University Press, 1925 [for 1924]), 53 (lines 10–13). This corresponds to the reading of BL MS Lansdowne 393, fol. 252r, lines 17–20.

"Covcitisc to Konne," "Goddes Pryvetee," and Will's Ambiguous Dream Experience in *Piers Plowman*

RICHARD K. EMMERSON

I N THE CLOSING PAGES of his magisterial overview of the biblical
tradition in medieval English literature, *The Bible in Middle English Literature*, David C. Fowler concludes his case for approaching
"Piers the Plowman as History" by distinguishing the outlooks of the A
and B versions. He associates the two versions with two related yet
distinct biblical perspectives: the former with the prophetic and the
latter with the apocalyptic. More specifically, he comments that in
the B continuation the Dreamer, who represents "the explosive ideology of the A version," is subjected "to a relentless inquisition, until
Will becomes malleable and is ready to adopt a new attitude (B XI-
XV)."[1] One of the most telling episodes in this inquisition is Anima's
condemnation of Will's desire to attain knowledge simply for the
sake of knowledge. This rebuke is important, because it is the last
time that the feigned spiritual superiority of Will is attacked by a

---

[1]David C. Fowler, *The Bible in Middle English Literature* (Seattle: University of
Washington Press, 1984), 295. I have similarly applied the distinctions between the
prophetic and the apocalyptic outlooks to *Piers Plowman*, but to recognize a parallel
shift in point of view from the Visio to the Vita of the B-Text: *"Piers Plowman*, like
Scripture itself, moves from the prophetic ideal of a renewed society within history
attainable by human action to the apocalyptic hope of individual salvation and
ultimate reward beyond history in another, divine, world." See Richard Kenneth
Emmerson, "The Prophetic, the Apocalyptic, and the Study of Medieval Literature," in *Poetic Prophecy in Western Literature*, ed. Jan Wojcik and Raymond-Jean
Frontain (Rutherford, NJ: Fairleigh Dickinson University Press, 1984), 54.

personified authority of the unimpeachable stature of Anima.[2] This attack, furthermore, serves as a prologue to the lengthy sermon that introduces Anima's exposition of Charity, which is crucial to *Piers Plowman*.

Several critics have noted that passus XV is, in Elizabeth Kirk's words, "transitional — 'finit dowel et incipit dobet' — since it keeps the basic format of the Dowel scenes while synthesizing the argument of Dowel in terms of the action to come."[3] It is not necessary to accept the authenticity of the manuscript rubrics to recognize that in fact the dialogue between Anima and Will represents a turning point in his quest, a shift from the largely passive intellectualizing that characterizes his middle visions to the active historical and apocalyptic visions that conclude *Piers Plowman*.[4] Generally scholars have concentrated on Anima's rather elaborate exposition of Charity and Will's second dream-within-a-dream in passus XVI rather than Anima's preliminary rebuke. Nevertheless, without denying the centrality of Anima's explanation of Charity and Will's swooning vision of Piers and the enigmatic Tree of Charity to the poem's thematic and theological concerns, this essay suggests that closer critical attention to Anima's rebuke of Will and its resonances throughout the poem will provide clues for the understanding of the Dreamer's ambiguous dream experience.

Only briefly into Will's fifth dream that begins B XV, Anima catalogues his several faculties by citing his numerous denomina-

---

[2]A. V. C. Schmidt, "Langland and Scholastic Philosophy," *Medium Ævum* 38 (1969): 152, notes that like *Liberum Arbitrium* in C, *Anima* in B is the single personified speaking character who is identified only by a Latin rather than a vernacular name. Although, as Schmidt suggests, Langland may have sought the greater precision of the Latin, the Latin name also provides greater authority. James F. G. Weldon, "The Structure of Dream Visions in *Piers Plowman*," *Mediaeval Studies* 49 (1987): 272, notes that Anima represents "the highest human faculty."

[3]Elizabeth Kirk, *The Dream Thought of Piers Plowman* (New Haven: Yale University Press, 1972), 159. See also Sister Mary Clemente Davlin, O. P., *"Kynde Knowyng* as a Major Theme in *Piers Plowman* B," *Review of English Studies* n.s. 22 (1971): 1–19. A. V. C. Schmidt, *The Vision of Piers Plowman: A Complete Edition of the B-Text*, rev. ed. (London: Dent, 1984), 343, comments that despite Anima's rebuke, "Will is clearly much better able now to learn, after his sojourn with Patience." Unless otherwise noted, all references to the poem will be to Schmidt's edition.

[4]On the manuscript rubrics, see Robert Adams, "The Reliability of the Rubrics in the B-Text of *Piers Plowman*," *Medium Ævum* 54 (1985): 208–31; for an argument that the markings are authorial, see Lawrence M. Clopper, "Langland's Markings for the Structure of *Piers Plowman*," *Modern Philology* 85 (1987–88): 245–55.

tions.[5] Will, as usual "al bourdynge," slyly but critically compares Anima to a bishop, " 'For bisshopes yblessed, thei bereth manye names' " (xv.40, 41). Apparently accepting the jest, Anima extends it by punning on the Dreamer's name and signaling that he understands the Dreamer perfectly:

> "That is sooth," seide he, "now I se thi wille!
> Thow woldest knowe and konne the cause of alle hire names,
> And of myne, if thow myghtest, me thynketh by thi speche!"
>
> (xv.44–46)

This seemingly innocent response prompts Will into acknowledging his "coveitise to konne":

> "Ye, sire," I seide, "by so no man were greved,
> Alle the sciences under sonne and alle the sotile craftes
> I wolde I knewe and kouthe kyndely in myn herte!"
>
> (xv.47–49)

The Dreamer thus elicits from Anima one of the harshest denunciations in the poem:

> "Thanne artow inparfit," quod he, "and oon of Prides knyghtes!
> For swich a lust and likyng Lucifer fel from hevene:
> *Ponam pedem meum in aquilone et similis ero Altissimo.*"
>
> (xv.50–51a)

By identifying Will as one of Pride's knights, Anima conscripts Will into the very army that, as becomes painfully evident in the concluding passus of the poem, ultimately launches Antichrist's full-fledged apocalyptic attack on Unity:

> Antecrist hadde thus soone hundredes at his baner,
> And Pride bar it bare boldely aboute,
> With a lord that lyveth after likyng of body,

---

[5]Two key changes should be noted in the C-Text treatment of this episode: it does not take place at the beginning of a new dream; and the speaker is Liberum Arbitrium rather than Anima. See C xvi.157–229, ed. Derek Pearsall, *Piers Plowman by William Langland: an Edition of the C-text*, York Medieval Texts, 2nd ser. (Berkeley: University of California Press, 1978).

That cam ayein Conscience, that kepere was and gyour
Over kynde Cristene and Cardynale Vertues.

(xx.69-73)[6]

At the same time, Anima associates Will's "lust and likyng" with
Lucifer's original sin, the source of all evil. Thus Will's insatiable
desire to know "alle" is placed firmly within and yet at the boundaries
of salvation history. Just as the poem's Prologue provides a cosmic
moral perspective on Will's contemporary world, setting the "fair
feeld ful of folk" between "a tour on a toft" and a dungeon in "[a] deep
dale bynethe" (Prol.14-17), so Anima's condemnation provides a
cosmic moral perspective on Will's place in history. Will's quest for
unlimited knowledge is associated with the activities of those deni-
zens of the "derke and dredfulle" dungeon that take place between
the fall of Lucifer and the attack of Antichrist.

Anima's condemnation, moreover, continues. The moral and historical perspective *sub specie aeternitatis* is supplemented with an explanation based on natural reason and a warning drawn from the wisest
man who ever lived—a man whose wisdom, as Will earlier noted
(x.375-86), did not save him:

"It were ayeins kynde," quod he, "and alle kynnes reson
That any creature sholde konne al, except Crist oone.
Ayein swiche Salomon speketh, and despiseth hir wittes,
And seith, *Sicut qui mel comedit multum non est ei bonum,*
Sic qui scrutator est maiestatis opprimitur a gloria."

(xv.52-55a)

Anima then glosses Solomon's warning (Prov. 25:27) against those
attempting to scrutinize the majesty of God in order to teach the
Dreamer that the more he understands "good matere," the more he is
obliged to do good:

To Englisshe men this is to mene, that mowen speke and here,
The man that muche hony eteth his mawe it engleymeth,
And the moore that a man of good matere hereth,

---

[6]On the portrayal of Antichrist in *Piers Plowman*, see Richard Kenneth Emmerson, *Antichrist in the Middle Ages: A Study of Medieval Apocalypticism, Art, and Literature*
(Seattle: University of Washington Press, 1981), 193-203.

But he do therafter it dooth hym double scathe.
"*Beatus est*," seith Seint Bernard, "*qui scripturas legit
Et verba vertit in opera* fulliche to his power."

(xv.56-61)

Anima's citation of Bernard's *Tractatus de Ordine Vitae* is often noted by critics, who count this passage as a crucial lesson in Will's moral education.[7] Despite earlier warnings (e.g., from Ymaginatif [xii.56a]), Will has yet to recognize that Dowel is not so much a concept to be understood as an imperative to be followed.

The force of Anima's rebuke is not spent at this point, however. It is not simply that Will would rather passively intellectualize about Dowel than actively do well. Anima condemns Will's immoderate lust for knowledge in its own right, once again citing it as the root of all sin:

> Coveitise to konne and to knowe science
> Putte out of Paradis Adam and Eve:
> *Sciencie appetitus hominem inmortalitatis gloriam spoliavit.*
>
> (xv.62–63a)

The citation from Bernard's *Sermo IV in Ascensione Domini* recalls Ymaginatif's earlier explanation of the Fall in passus xi.[8] There Ymaginatif, scolding Will for being unable to hold his peace, associated the Dreamer's incessant questioning with Adam's erring appetite:

> Adam, whiles he spak noght, hadde paradis at wille;
> Ac whan he mamelede aboute mete and entremeted to knowe
> The wisedom and the wit of God, he was put fram blisse.
>
> (xi.415–17)

Clearly, Anima condemns Will's "coveitise to konne" not simply because it leads to inaction, but because it is a dangerous action analogous to the primal sin. It is a form of *curiositas*, a sin con-

---

[7]John A. Alford, "Some Unidentified Quotations in *Piers Plowman*," *Modern Philology* 72 (1974-75), identifies the Bernardine citation and notes that "[t]he idea, common throughout Bernard's writings, is probably based on Matthew 7:24" (396). See also Guy Bourquin, *Piers Plowman: etudes sur la genese litteraire des trois versions*, 2 vols. (Paris: Librairie Honore Champion, 1978), 1:422–27.

[8]Alford, "Unidentified Quotations" 396–97.

demned by moralists throughout the Middle Ages.[9] In fact, one of
the key texts often cited in the traditional polemic against *curiositas* is
Proverbs 25:27, which Anima quoted near the beginning of his
rebuke (xv.55-55a). He now returns to Solomon's proverbial image
of the honey to underscore once again the vicious origins of such
intellectual curiosity:

> And right as hony is yvel to defie and engleymeth the mawe,
> Right so that thorugh reson wolde the roote knowe
> Of God and of hise grete myghtes—hise graces it letteth.
> For in the likynge lith a pride and licames coveitise
> Ayein Cristes counseil and alle clerkes techynge—
> That is *Non plus sapere quam oportet sapere.*

(xv.64-69)

The admonition of Will concludes with this quotation from Romans 12:3, another text often cited in condemnation of *curiositas*
where, as in Anima's rebuke, it is paired with Proverbs 25:27. For
example, Hugh of St. Cher cites the Pauline verse in his explanation
of Proverbs 25 and the proverbial warning in his commentary on
Romans 12.[10] Both are linked by the common concerns that certain
knowledge is prohibited because, as Hugh notes, it is sought "ex
libidine" and because it leads to pride, which is exactly Anima's
point: "in the likynge lith a pride and licames coveitise" (xv.67). This
intellectual pride is the very charge that Dame Study earlier leveled
against the great mendicant masters of divinity when she too cited
Romans 12:3 along with Augustine, one of the great spokesmen
condemning *curiositas*:

---

[9]Christian K. Zacher, *Curiosity and Pilgrimage: The Literature of Discovery in
Fourteenth-Century England* (Baltimore: Johns Hopkins University Press, 1976),
21-33. Although Zacher notes that the concept of *curiositas* informs *Piers Plowman*
(5), he does not deal with the poem in this study.

[10]Hugh of St. Cher, *Opera omnia in universum Vetus et Novum Testamentum* (London,
1645). Compare on Prov. 25:25, vol. 3, fol. 57r; on Rom. 12:3, vol. 7, fol. 62v.
These two verses, in fact, serve as a skeleton for Anima's rebuke. For Langland's
use of quotations, see John A. Alford, "The Role of the Quotations in *Piers Plowman*," *Speculum* 52 (1977): 80-99. For Langland's use of Hugh of St. Cher, see
Judson Boyce Allen, "Langland's Reading and Writing: *Detractor* and the Pardon
Passus," *Speculum* 59 (1984): 342-62.

Swiche motyves they meve, thise maistres in hir glorie,
And maken men in mysbileve that muse muche on hire wordes.
Ymaginatif herafterward shal answere to youre purpos.
Austyn to swiche argueres, he telleth hem this teme:
Non plus sapere quam oportet.

(x.115–118a)

Directly linking this vainglory to the *curiositas* of the masters, who speak enigmatically of the Trinity (x.53) and ask paradoxical questions "To plese with proude men" (x.72), Study warns Will to avoid such questioning:

Wilneth nevere to wite why that God wolde
Suffre Sathan his seed to bigile;
Ac bileveth lelly in the loore of Holy Chirche,
And preie hym of pardon and penaunce in thi lyve,
And for his muche mercy to amende yow here.
For alle that wilneth to wite the whyes of God almyghty,
I wolde his eighe were in his ers and his fynger after
That ever wilneth to wite why that God wolde
Suffre Sathan his seed to bigile,
Or Judas the Jew Jesu bitraye.
Al was as he wolde — Lord, yworshiped be thow —
And al worth as thow wolt whatso we dispute.

(x.119–30)

Had Will heeded Study's warning in his third dream to shun inquiries into "the whyes of God almyghty," he could have avoided Anima's rebuke at the beginning of his fifth dream. Yet he did not, for Anima recognizes that Will's questioning is aimed ultimately at knowing "the roote . . . Of God and of hise grete myghtes" (xv.65–66).

Paralleling Study's earlier condemnation, Anima follows the quotation of Romans 12:3 with a condemnation of the friars. No doubt, Will is relieved that Anima has diverted his aim toward another target, especially one that Will has previously impugned. But significantly the general target remains the *curiositas* of which Will is

guilty, even if the arrows are shot directly at the masters of divinity.[11]
Again, they are condemned for dealing with the unfathomable:

> Freres and fele othere maistres that to the lewed men prechen,
> Ye moeven materes unmesurable to tellen of the Trinite,
> That oftetymes the lewed peple of hir bileve doute.
>
> (xv.70–72)

Anima's attack, first against the friars and then against corrupt clerics in general, now becomes particularly shrill. It is clear from his
later comments — where he insists that the Saracens and Jews
(xv.499–501) and indeed all Christians (xv.568–70) should be
taught to believe in the Trinity — that Anima is not condemning the
Trinitarian topic in its own right but its esoteric manipulation by the
friars for their personal advantage and in lieu of more practical
teachings that are to the advantage of "the lewed peple" (xv.72).
Their theologizing about the Trinity epitomizes the pride of the
friars and especially their delving into the secret mysteries and great
majesty of God. Like Will's desire to know "the roote . . . Of God
and of hise grete myghtes" (xv.65–66), it is a sign not only of pride
but of a very dangerous and specific kind of *curiositas*, a "likynge" that
leads mortal man into prying into the private matters of God, into
"Goddes pryvetee." A lyric in the fourteenth-century Vernon manuscript, "This World Fares as a Fantasy," is a traditional condemnation of this form of *curiositas*, associating presumptuous foolishness
with a master of divinity:

> Whar-to wilne we forte knowe
>   Þe poyntes of Godes priuete?
> More þen him lustes forte schowe
>   We schulde not knowe in no degre;
> And Idel bost is forte blowe
>   A Mayster of diuinite.
> Þenk we lyue in eorþe her lowe,
>   And God an heiȝ in Mageste;

---

[11]Penn R. Szittya, *The Antifraternal Tradition in Medieval Literature* (Princeton:
Princeton University Press, 1986), 265, includes Will's "inordinate craving for
learning and knowledge of abstruse theological matters" as a way in which the poem
associates Will with the friars. See also Jay Martin, "Wil as Fool and Wanderer in
Piers Plowman," *Texas Studies in Literature and Language* 3 (1961–62): 535–48.

Of Material Mortualite
Medle we & of no more Maistrie.
Þe more we trace þe Trinite,
Þe more we falle in fantasye.[12]

This tradition barring human reason from such unsolicited specu-
lation concerning the divine is probably best known in a comic form,
as Chaucer plays on commonplace moral teachings in his sparkling
fabliau, the *Miller's Tale*. The drunken Miller, in order to "quite" the
Knight's account of Theseus's speculations on the "Firste Moevere"
and providence, discourses ceremoniously on the foolishness of delving into "Goddes pryvetee." The Miller introduces the subject in his
prologue, responding to the irritated Reeve:

An housbonde shal nat been inquisityf
Of Goddes pryvetee, nor of his wyf.[13]

Here, and throughout the Miller's tale, the notion of "pryvetee" links
through a series of clever double-entendres Nicholas's arcane speculations into the heavenly secrets with his "hendy" quest for the more
mundane Alyson. While recognizing how the comedy turns on
Chaucer's brilliant word play, we should also note the force of John's
comment on Nicholas's feigned gaping:

Men sholde nat knowe of Goddes pryvetee.
Ye, blessed be alwey a lewed man
That noght but oonly his bileve kan!
(3454-56)

---

[12]"This World Fares as a Fantasy," lines 85–96; ed. Carleton Brown, *Religious
Lyrics of the Fourteenth Century*, 2nd ed. (Oxford: Clarendon, 1952), 163.

[13]*Miller's Prologue* 3163–64. All references to Chaucer will be to Larry D. Benson,
gen. ed., *The Riverside Chaucer*, 3rd ed. (Boston: Houghton Mifflin, 1987). Paula
Neuss, "*Double Entendre* in *The Miller's Tale*," *Essays in Criticism* 24 (1974): 331,
comments that in the tale the sexual meaning of *pryvetee* "seems to take precedence
over the more obvious 'innocent' meaning, so that from originally being 'men ought
not to know God's private business' the message emerges primarily as 'husbands
ought not to be nosy about their wives' privates.'" Nevertheless, the full force of the
comedy is dependent upon its burlesque of the moral tradition condemning *curiositas*.

John's self-satisfied praise of the "lewed man" recalls Will's self-righteous conclusion that it is better to be unlearned than learned, since so many wise men have failed to attain salvation (x.450-62).[14] And like John, who is made both a cuckold and a fool by conspiring with Nicholas's newly discovered "pryvetee" (3603), Will also fails to practice what he preaches, pursuing the very esoteric knowledge that he condemns in the friars. Will's relationship to the friars thus roughly parallels John's relationship to Nicholas. And if John's comic strictures against being "inquisityf/Of Goddes pryvetee" suggest the commonplace nature of moralizing warnings against *curiositas*, brief attention to Nicholas's absurd "intellectual" activities helps elucidate the condemnation of misappropriated learning in *Piers Plowman*.

For example, Nicholas investigates "Goddes pryvetee" by means of "myn astrologye" (3514), a form of *curiositas* which Augustine and others condemned as at best superstitious and futile and as at worst demonic and seductively diverting the trust of "dyuynourys" away from God.[15] In *Piers Plowman* Dame Study, contrasting Christian love especially with "Astronomye," condemns it and the other "sotile" sciences as "yvel" and as particular hindrances to Dowel:

> Forthi loke thow lovye as longe as thow durest,
> For is no science under sonne so sovereyn for the soule.
>   Ac Astronomye is hard thyng, and yvel for to knowe;
> Geometry and Geomesie is gynful of speche;
> Whoso thynketh werche with tho t[hre] thryveth ful late —
> For sorcerie is the sovereyn book that to the science bilongeth.
>   Yet ar ther fibiches in forceres of fele mennes makynge,
> Experiments of Alkenamye the peple to deceyve;
> If thow thynke to dowel, deel therwith nevere!
> Alle thise sciences I myself sotilede and ordeynede,
> And founded hem formest folk to deceyve.
>
> (x.205-15)

---

[14]On Will's quoting Augustine, see C. David Benson, "An Augustinian Irony in 'Piers Plowman,'" *Notes & Queries* n.s. 23 (1976): 51-54.

[15]See Augustine, *On Christian Doctrine* 2.20.30-24.37, trans. D. W. Robertson, Jr., The Library of Liberal Arts 80 (Indianapolis: Bobbs-Merrill, 1958), 55-61; and *Dives and Pauper* 1.26., ed. Priscilla Heath Barnum, EETS, OS 275, vol. 1, pt. 1 (London: Oxford University Press, 1976), 1:139-40.

Yet, despite his supposed search for Dowel, Will rejects this lesson. In a clear echo of this passage, he later eagerly divulges to Anima his desire to understand "Alle the sciences under sonne and alle the sotile craftes" (xv.48), ignoring Study's expert advice to seek the love compared to which "is no science under sonne so sovereyn for the soule" (x.206).

Nicholas's purpose in gaping "upward into the eir" (3473) is hardly such Christian love. His immediate purpose is divination, specifically to prophesy the future, the imminent approach of Doomsday, the destruction of the world in a rainstorm much worse than Noah's flood (3512-21).[16] By dating this apocalyptic flood to "Monday next, at quarter nyght" (3516), in fact, the "poure scoler" (3190) trespasses against "Goddes pryvetee" explicitly, for as Christ explained to his apostles — just before comparing the time of the end to the days of Noah — only God the Father knows the day and the hour of the end (Matt. 24:36-37).[17] In his condemnation of Will in *Piers Plowman*, Anima insists that no one "except Crist oone" (xv.53) can know all, but in the *Miller's Tale* Nicholas's certain prediction of the day and hour of this key sign of the end claims a knowledge denied even Christ! Nicholas's ultimate purpose, of course, is adultery, suggesting in comic form how the selfish use of clerical learning leads to *amor* rather than *caritas*.

---

[16]Míceál Vaughan has convincingly argued that Nicholas dupes John by predicting a one-day flood that "corresponds to elements in a very popular and widespread late-medieval apocalyptic tradition: the Fifteen Signs before Doomsday." See M. F. Vaughan, "Chaucer's Imaginative One-Day Flood," *Philological Quarterly* 60 (1981): 119. On the tradition of the signs, see William W. Heist, *The Fifteen Signs Before Doomsday* (East Lansing: Michigan State College Press, 1952).

[17]This warning is paralleled in Acts 1:7, which is cited in condemnations of *curiositas* as well. See *Dives and Pauper* 1.26, ed. Barnum, 1.1:140, which, when condemning "astronomye," cites Acts 1:7 and Isaiah 24:16, stating that God reserves his "pryuyte" to himself:

Crist hydde manye thynggys from hese apostolys & seyde to hem:
Non est vestrum nosce tempora et momenta que pater posuit in sua
potestate, Actus Apostolorum i [7]. It longyȝt nought to ȝow,
seyȝt he, to knowyn tymys, momentys and stoundys queche þe fadyr
of heuene hatz reseruyd in his power. And he seyde be þe
prophete: Secretum meum mihi, secretum meum mihi, Ysaie xxiv
[16], I kepe my pryuyte to me, I kepe my pryuyte to me. And
sithyn he reseruyd sueche counseyl and pryuyte from hese frendys
þat weryn so nyghy of counseyl, mechil more he reseruyd his
counseyl from hese enmyis, sueche foolys, synful wrecchys.

To turn to the serious condemnation of the friars, *Piers Plowman* similarly shows how the selfish uses of learning associated with *curiositas* are contrasted to Christian love, for they lead to an intellectual pride that is in direct opposition to charity. Anima complains, for example, that the friars preach on the complexities of Trinitarian doctrine rather than on the basic and simple moral precepts of Christianity, displaying their pretentious erudition "Moore for pompe than for pure charite" (xv.79). As Hugh of St. Cher notes while glossing Anima's key text (Prov. 25:27), "Scientia inflat, charitas autem aedificat."[18] Hugh thus quotes 1 Corinthians 8:1, one of the most popular scriptural texts condemning *curiositas*, which Ymaginatif cited in his earlier warning of Will:

> Wo is hym that hem weldeth but he hem wel despende:
> *Scient[es] et non facient[es] variis flagellis vapulab[un]t.*
> Sapience, seith the Bok, swelleth a mannes soule:
> *Sapiencia inflat &c.*
> And richesse right so, but if the roote be trewe.
>
> (xii.56–58)

"*Sapiencia inflat &c.*," in fact, serves as the subtext controlling Anima's long exposition in passus xv, which moves from an initial condemnation of Will's "[c]oveitise to konne and to knowe science" (62) and a description of the vicious results of misused knowledge to a Pauline explanation of charity and its exemplification in the active lives of the saints. Along with other scriptural texts commonly cited by the many traditional condemnations of *curiositas*, 1 Corinthians 8:1 informs the progress of Anima's sermon.

The tradition of *curiositas*, furthermore, helps explain several other characteristics of Will. Christian K. Zacher — citing Augustine, Bernard of Clairvaux, and Thomas Aquinas as representative spokesmen — describes three traditional features of *curiositas* which, significantly, apply in all their force to the character of Will: "*curiositas* is a morally useless, dangerous diversion for wayfaring Christians. Moreover, it was seen as a vice that feeds on the senses (mainly sight) and affects one's entire intellectual outlook. Finally . . . moralists thought *curiositas* signified a wandering, errant, and

---

[18]Hugh, *Opera omnia*, vol. 3, fol. 57r.

unstable frame of mind and was thus best exemplified in metaphors of motion and in the act of travel."[19] We have already seen how the first (moral) characteristic of *curiositas* applies to Will. *Curiositas* is "morally useless" and a "dangerous diversion" because it morally immobilizes Will; it substitutes passive talk about Dowel for active doing well and leads to an intellectual arrogance that makes Will and the friars compatriots in the army of Pride (xv.50). Will's personification of the third (mental) characteristic of *curiositas* — the "wandering, errant, and unstable frame of mind" — has also been noted by critics, who comment on the Dreamer's ambiguous status as wanderer, "jangeler," and fool. David Lawton has shown, for example, that "Will as open persona" shares much in common with members of the several disreputable professions condemned by contemporary penitential handbooks: "According to the judgments explicit in these books, these members of the 'crafte of foly' are all cousins of Langland's dreamer, who hoards their attributes in himself. They are the natural inhabitants of a world in which 'Wyl es rede/Witte es quede/God es dede,' and in which 'the wey of a fole es ryght in hys syght.' "[20] It is thus significant that one of the most explicit examples of Will's "unstable frame of mind" introduces the dream in which Anima rebukes the Dreamer's *curiositas*:

> Ac after my wakynge it was wonder longe
> Er I koude kyndely knowe what was Dowel.
> And so my wit weex and wanyed til I a fool weere;
> And some lakked my lif — allowed it fewe —
> And leten me for a lorel and looth to reverencen
> Lordes or ladies or any lif ellis —

---

[19]Zacher, *Curiosity and Pilgrimage* 21.

[20]David Lawton, "The Subject of Piers Plowman," *Yearbook of Langland Studies* 1 (1987): 16-17; Lawton quotes from *Speculum Christiani*, ed. Gustaf Holmstedt, EETS, OS 182 (London: Oxford University Press, 1933), 130. Lawton convincingly argues that *"Piers Plowman* is a dialogic, not a monologic, poem" (3) and that "the anxieties and faults of the dreamer and his society are identical" (12). John M. Bowers, *The Crisis of Will in Piers Plowman* (Washington, DC: Catholic University of America Press, 1986), has also recently commented on the "studied ambiguity" of Will's character: "In a work so deeply concerned with judging correctly — deciding between alternatives and choosing the right knowledge, the right beliefs, the right actions for the good life — it is not surprising that Langland should have made any final judgment about the poem's central character so extremely hard" (131). See also his discussion of Will as "fool" (149-54).

As persons in pelure with pendaunts of silver;
To sergeaunts ne to swiche seide noght ones,
"God loke yow, lordes!"—ne loutede faire,
That folk helden me a fool; and in that folie I raved,
Til reson hadde ruthe on me and rokked me aslepe. . . .

(xv.1–11)

We have already noted briefly how the first and third characteristics that Zacher identifies as typifying *curiositas* are evident in Will. The second (sensual) characteristic, which is related to Will's moral immobility and physical and mental wandering, now deserves greater attention. From the beginning of the poem it is clear that Will's primary motivation—which, in fact, leads into his first vision—is a desire "wondres to here":

In a somer seson, whan softe was the sonne,
I shoop me into shroudes as I a sheep were,
In habite as an heremite unholy of werkes,
Wente wide in this world wondres to here.
Ac on a May morwenynge on Malverne hilles
Me bifel a ferly, of Fairye me thoghte.

(Prol.1–6)

As John Bowers comments, "Such roaming after curious sights connotes a mental vagrancy that would have been recognized as *curiositas*, condemned since the days of John Cassian."[21] What is less obvious but in the long run more significant, however, is the extent to which the *curiositas* that "feeds on the senses (mainly sight)" and that attempts to meddle into "Goddes pryvetee" entirely underlies Will's perplexing visionary experience, explaining the dubious sources of the dreams, their confusing manner, and their unusual recurrence. Will's dream experience—his "ferly, of Fairye me thoghte"—is of

---

[21]Bowers, *Crisis of Will* 135. Bowers argues that this wandering is also a sign of Sloth. Kathleen L. Scott's recent study, "The Illustrations of *Piers Plowman* in Bodleian Library MS. Douce 104," *Yearbook of Langland Studies* 4 (1990): 1–86, provides support for connecting the Dreamer with Sloth. Scott notes that the manuscript (fol. 1r) illustrates the Dreamer/Narrator in a posture that was "used in depicting Sloth and its associated vice, wanhope or despair" (17; see fig. 1). See also Siegfried Wenzel, *The Sin of Sloth: Acedia in Medieval Thought and Literature* (Chapel Hill: University of North Carolina Press, 1967).

questionable origin and ambiguous significance, and this ambiguity undermines the truth value and authority traditionally associated with the dreamer's experience.[22]

Critics have often acknowledged that *Piers Plowman* is not a typical dream-vision, although in general they persist in studying it in terms of the dream-vision form.[23] Perhaps misled by Chaucer's references to Macrobius and the *Somnium Scipionis*, they have tended to read most late-medieval poems relating dreams as belonging within the Macrobian tradition, what Kathryn L. Lynch has recently called the tradition of the "classic" or "philosophical" vision.[24] But as Alison M.

---

[22]Bowers, *Crisis of Will*, notes that "Langland's suggestion that Will's vision had fairy causes would not have been taken lightly by his first readers. Although the contents of the vision are not especially sinister, we should not underestimate the initial impact of the reference to fairies for a first audience that did not know what kind of dream would follow" (139).

[23]See, for example, Morton W. Bloomfield, *Piers Plowman as a Fourteenth-century Apocalypse* (New Brunswick: Rutgers University Press, 1961), who argues that "Langland certainly chose the dream form with deliberate intent, because he believed it could convey in proper fashion what he wanted to say" (11). The standard and best study of the dream-vision form remains A. C. Spearing, *Medieval Dream-Poetry* (Cambridge: Cambridge University Press, 1976). Interestingly, even while claiming that the three versions of *Piers Plowman* reflect Langland's recognition that he needed to "create a radically new kind of dream-poem," Spearing argues that "much light is thrown on it if it is seen specifically as a dream-poem" (140, 138). For recent, although not fully satisfactory, generic approaches to the poem, see George D. Economou, "The Vision's Aftermath in *Piers Plowman*: The Poetics of the Middle English Dream-Vision," *Genre* 18 (1985): 313-21; Weldon, who sees *Piers Plowman* as "an interconnected sequence of dream vision poems, similar in some ways to the sonnet sequences of the Renaissance" ("Structure of Dream Visions" 255); and Steven Justice ("The Genres of *Piers Plowman*," *Viator* 19 [1988]: 291-306), who ignores the dream vision form and argues that "the *Visio's* pilgrimage to Truth is the search for a genre that will accommodate an authority neither abusive nor idiosyncratic" (291).

[24]Kathryn L. Lynch, *The High Medieval Dream Vision: Poetry, Philosophy, and Literary Form* (Stanford: Stanford University Press, 1988), esp. 46-76. For other recent studies of the dream vision, dealing with Chaucer but not *Piers Plowman*, see Michael D. Cherniss, *Boethian Apocalypse: Studies in Middle English Vision Poetry* (Norman: Pilgrim Books, 1987); J. Stephen Russell, *The English Dream Vision: Anatomy of a Form* (Columbus: Ohio State University Press, 1988); and the fourth chapter of Linda Tarte Holley, *Chaucer's Measuring Eye* (Houston: Rice University Press, 1990). Holley curiously cites Langland—along with Augustine, Bede, Boethius, and the authors of the *Roman de la Rose*—as giving Chaucer "authority" for taking "advantage of the dream vision narrative" (104). For Chaucer's citations of Macrobius, see *The Book of the Duchess* 284-89; *The Parliament of Fowls* 29-112; and *The Nun's Priest's Tale* 3123-26.

Peden has shown, Macrobius's influence actually decreased in the later Middle Ages: "By the xiii century, Macrobius' *Commentary* was not, I have suggested, the familiar source it had once been: the prevailing dream theory in the Schools was Aristotelian, and tended to emphasize the physiological origin and consequent non-significance of dreams."[25] The late medieval recognition that dreams are not necessarily significant means that we should not assume that *Piers Plowman* represents its fiction as a series of dreams in order to underscore its truthfulness and that Will's dreams are unambiguously positive and truth-revealing.[26] The poem's fragmented, directionless, and inconclusive dreams do not resemble the coherent, guided, and progressive dreams of the Macrobian tradition, but suggest the kind of naturalistic explanation developed by the scholastics that closely links the state of mind and passions of the dreamer when awake to the substance of his dream when asleep.[27] And, as we have seen, Will, from his first dream through his confrontation with Anima, is controlled by a *curiositas* that casts doubt on the reliability of his dreams and subverts the validity of dreaming as a source of truth. It would be a mistake, therefore, to assume that in *Piers Plowman* the dreams are unproblematic, that they necessarily represent "a revelation, a higher form of truth."[28]

Critics need to distinguish *Piers Plowman* from medieval dream visions in the philosophical Boethian and Macrobian tradition and

[25]Alison M. Peden, "Macrobius and Mediaeval Dream Literature," *Medium Ævum* 54 (1985): 67.

[26]In his discussion of Chaucer's *House of Fame*, Spearing explains the value of presenting "a literary fiction as a dream," by noting that it allowed medieval poets the opportunity to claim "that a fiction possessed an imaginative truth or validity even though it did not correspond to any literal truth" (*Medieval Dream-Poetry* 74). More recently, Jacqueline T. Miller, *Poetic License: Authority and Authorship in Medieval and Renaissance Contexts* (New York: Oxford University Press, 1986), has questioned the implied authority of the dream for Langland's contemporaries: "It cannot simply be assumed that the dream convention would immediately signify authoritative sanction; rather, it is likely that the choice of this framing device would indicate on the author's part, and perhaps invoke in his audience, an awareness of the very unsolved, ambiguous, and unstable nature of dreams, of interpretation, and of authority" (46).

[27]See Boethius of Dacia, *On Dreams*, trans. John F. Wippel, Mediaeval Sources in Translation 30 (Toronto: Pontifical Institute of Mediaeval Studies, 1987), 68–78, whose explanation of dreams is almost totally naturalistic.

[28]Bloomfield, *Piers Plowman* 11.

even from those in the French allegorical love tradition.[29] There are few if any Middle English works as "biblical" as *Piers Plowman*, a text which, "it could almost be said," to quote David Fowler, "offers itself to us as Scripture, as an extension of the Bible   ."[30] As a radically scriptural poem relating a series of dreams, its understanding of visionary experience is more likely to reflect Augustine's explanation of the modes of *visio corporalis*, *visio spiritualis*, and *visio intellectualis* than Macrobius's categories of *somnium*, *oraculum*, and *visio*.[31] The Dreamer, furthermore, is more likely to be modelled on such prophets and visionaries of the Old and New Testaments as Joseph, Daniel, John, and Paul, than on the classical Scipio and the allegorical Amant. Commenting in *De Genesi ad litteram* on 2 Corinthians 2, Augustine grapples with the various possibilities by which Paul might have seen the third heaven, "whether in the body or out of the body," and in the process discusses two of the most popular Old Testament models who come to figure prominently in medieval discussions of dreams, Joseph and Daniel. These two are cited, as well, by Chaucer in *The Book of the Duchess* (280-83), the *Monk's Tale* (2154-58, 2207-35), and, in a more humorous vein, in the *Nun's Priest's Tale* (3126-35). But, as the convoluted arguments of Chauntecleer and Pertelote make evident, these exempla were just two among many in the long-winded late-medieval debate concerning the significance of dreams, and they were not easy to appropriate to

---

[29]For an opposing view, see Weldon, who argues that the Prologue to *Piers Plowman* initially identifies the poem as a "secular courtly love vision after the manner of the *Roman de la Rose*" (258). Stephen A. Barney, "Allegorical Visions," in *A Companion to Piers Plowman*, ed. John A. Alford (Berkeley: University of California Press, 1988), notes that the French allegorical dream visions "collectively provide the immediate background for the form of Piers, even though none is demonstrably a source" (126); but he also points out that "Practically all the uses of allegory and visions that occur in *Piers Plowman* may be found in the Bible . . ." (120).

[30]Fowler, *Bible in Middle English Literature* 226. More recently, Justice has read the poem as selecting a series of genres, and ultimately moving to "biblical narrative" ("Genres," 305).

[31]For example, the *Visio* of *Piers Plowman* (B Prol.1-7) hardly qualifies as the Macrobian *visio*, which is a plain prophecy of the future that "actually comes true." See Macrobius, *Commentary on the Dream of Scipio*, trans. William Harris Stahl, Records of Civilization, Sources and Studies 48 (New York: Columbia University Press, 1952), 90. For Augustine's categories, see *De Genesi ad litteram* 12.9.20, trans. John Hammond Taylor, Ancient Christian Writers 42 (New York: Newman Press, 1982), 2:189-90.

one's personal experience.[32] There was an understandable reluctance to claim supernatural inspiration for dream and other "prophetic" experience, even though — given the biblical *exempla* — it was heretical to deny the possibility of such inspiration.[33]

Thus, although the status of Joseph and Daniel as divinely inspired visionaries is never questioned, their role as models for fourteenth-century Christians is. *Dives and Pauper*, for instance, after summarizing the usual arguments concerning the various types and potential significance of dreams, cites Joseph and Daniel to explain that it is appropriate to interpret dreams only under specific (and, one assumes, rare) conditions:

> Also it is leful to tellyn þyngys þat ben to comyn be dremys þat comyn be reuelacioun of God ȝif man or woman haue grace for to vndirstondyn is, as Ioseph and Danyel haddyn. But forasmychil as dremys comyn on so many dyuers maner and it is wol hard to knowyn on what maner it comyn, weþer be God or be kende or be þe fend or be ony oþir wey, þerfor it is wol perlyous to settyn ony feyth þerynne, as seyth Sent Gregorie, lib. viii, Moralium, super illud Iob: Terrebis me per sompnia.[34]

When it comes to dreams, *Dives and Pauper*, which is an early fifteenth-century compendium of orthodox common sense, teaches most Christians to follow the advice of Gregory rather than the actions of Joseph and Daniel. Even when the dream is divinely inspired, it is impossible to be certain about its origins without an explicit sign or the divination of an authority of the stature of Joseph and Daniel:

---

[32]The debate between Chauntecleer and Pertelote generally summarizes the various medieval explanations of dreams. See Robert A. Pratt, "Some Latin Sources of the Nonnes Preest on Dreams," *Speculum* 52 (1977): 538–70. Perhaps what is clearest from Chaucer's treatments of dreams, in the *Nun's Priest's Tale*, *The House of Fame* and elsewhere, is the difficulty faced by any contemporary dreamer in determining a dream's meaning.

[33]Even Boethius of Dacia acknowledges that "by divine will an angel or a devil can in truth appear to a person who is sleeping or to one who is ill" (*On Dreams* 75). Bishop Stephen Tempier's condemnation of Aristotelian scholastic propositions in 1277 included the following: "That raptures and visions do not take place except through nature." See *On Dreams* 75, n. 14, and Wippel's introduction, 23.

[34]*Dives and Pauper* 1.43.58–66, ed. Barnum, 1.1:176–77.

DIUES. Be þe same skyl, þou a drem kome of Goddis sonde to helpe of manys soule and in warnynge of myschef comynge he schulde takyn non hede þerto ne settyn no feyth þerynne, for he whot neuyr of whens it comyth.

PAUPER. Withoutyn reuelacoun of God he whot neuyr of whens it comyth, and þerfor whan God sent swyche dremys he schal schewyn to hym þat dremyth þis or to som oþir from whens it comyn and what it betoknyn, as he dede to þe kyng Pharao be Ioseph, and to þe kyng Nabugodonosor be Danyel.[35]

A similar warning is issued by an early fourteenth-century version of the *Somnia Danielis*, a "bok of sweuenyng,/þat men meteþ in slepyng." Although tracing its authority to Daniel — "þat wes prophete of gret pris" who interpreted dreams in Babylon "þurh þe holi gostes myht" — after confidently setting forth the traditional topoi of dream interpretation, it nevertheless carefully warns:

> Of alle sweuenes, þat men meteþt
> day oþer nyþt, when hue slepeþt,
> nomon ne con þat soþe þyng
> telle, bote þe heuene-kyng.[36]

Throughout *Piers Plowman* Will never claims such prophetic authority or divine inspiration, even though he does wonder about the nature of his dreams and their significance.[37] For example, while deliberating on the meaning of his second dream — which, in one of the poem's most enigmatic scenes, concludes when Piers tears Truth's pardon — Will recalls the stories of Daniel and Joseph:

---

[35] *Dives and Pauper* 1.44.37-45, ed. Barnum, 1.1:179.

[36] British Library, MS Harley 2253, fols. 119, 121; ed. Steven R. Fischer, *The Complete Medieval Dreambook: A Multilingual, Alphabetical Somnia Danielis Collation* (Bern: Peter Lang, 1982), 22, 162.

[37] Only at the beginning of his fourth dream does Will even hint that his dream may be divinely inspired: "I lay down longe in this thoght, and at the laste I slepte; / And as Crist wolde ther com Conscience to conforte me that tyme" (XIII.21-22). Lawrence M. Clopper, "The Life of the Dreamer, the Dreams of the Wanderer in *Piers Plowman*," *Studies in Philology* 86 (1989): 261-85, points out that for the Dreamer to assume the prophetic role of judging others requires that he be "trewe," that he have moral authority. "The doubts about the legitimacy of publishing his dreams make vivid the internal conflict that exists within someone who believes himself to be prompted by God and thus to have prophetic vision but who also doubts whether he has the moral authority to make public the faults that he sees in others" (270-71).

Ac for the book Bible bereth witnesse
How Daniel divined the dremes of a kyng
That was Nabugodonosor nempned of clerkes . . .
Daniel seide, "Sire Kyng, thi dremels bitokneth
That unkouthe knyghtes shul come thi kyngdom to cleyme;
Amonges lower lordes thi lond shal be departed."
And as Daniel divined, in dede it fel after:
The kyng lees his lordshipe, and lower men it hadde.
    And Joseph mette merveillously how the moone and the sonne
And the ellevene sterres hailsed hym alle.
Thanne Jacob jugged Josephes swevene:
"*Beau fitz*," quod his fader, "for defaute we shullen —
I myself and my sones — seche thee for nede."
    It bifel as his fader seide, in Pharaoes tyme,
That Joseph was Justice Egipte to loke:
It bifel as his fader tolde — hise frendes there hym soughte.

                                                    (VII.152–67)

These biblical *exempla*, however, are bracketed in such a way that
their experience is distanced from Will's dream experience. For
example, the stories of Daniel and Joseph are introduced by Will's
expression of scepticism towards dream interpretation, in which he
cites Cato's advice and the authoritative teaching of canon law:

    Ac I have no savour in songewarie, for I se it ofte faille;
    Caton and canonistres counseillen us to leve
    To sette sadnesse in songewarie — for *sompnia ne cures*.
                                                    (VII.149–51)[38]

And, after relating the two much-longer *exempla*, Will's summary
response is typically ambiguous, showing that the problem of the
interpretation and significance of dreams remains unresolved: "Al
this maketh me on metels to thynke" (VII.168). By explicitly sum-
moning the traditional biblical *exempla*, yet refusing to associate
Will's dreams with the experience of Daniel and Joseph, the poet

---

[38]It is perhaps significant that Cato's full distich connects the substance of the
dream to the state of the dreamer's mind: "Take no account of dreams, for while
asleep the human mind sees what it hopes and wishes for" (*Distichs of Cato* 2.31, cited
by Schmidt 84, note to line 151). It should be noted that Will cites Daniel as a
prophet in other passages as well, including XV.597–602 and XVIII.108–09a.

avoids claiming any supernatural source for his poem, just as, even after Ymaginatif argues that making books is good *if* they are inspired by the Holy Ghost (XII.101–02), no spiritual inspiration is claimed for Will's "makyng."[39] The juxtapositioning of the Old Testament visionaries with ancient and church authorities denigrating the value of dreams thus problematizes the status of Will's dreams.

To clarify this point it is worth contrasting Will's comment concerning Daniel and Joseph to the conclusion John Gower reaches when he cites the same *exempla* in the *Vox Clamantis*:

> Ex Daniele patet quid sompnia significarunt,
> Nec fuit in sompnis visio vana Ioseph:
> Angelus immo bonus, qui custos interioris
> Est hominis, vigili semper amore fauet;
> Et licet exterius corpus sopor occupet, ille
> Visitat interius mentis et auget opem;
> Sepeque sompnifero monstrat prenostica visu,
> Quo magis in causis tempora noscat homo.
> Hinc puto que vidi quod sompnia tempore noctis
> Signa rei certe commemoranda ferunt.[40]

As A. J. Minnis comments, Gower hereby suggests that his *Vox Clamantis* is composed in the *forma prophetialis* associated with the biblical prophets.[41] Certainly, Gower's allusion to the "angelus bonus" implies that his vision is the result of divine inspiration. In contrast, Will's visions lack an authority figure comparable to Gower's "angelus bonus." Lady Holy Church, who at first appears to

---

[39]As Bowers notes, "Langland felt no deep confidence in the merit of working as a poet" (*Crisis of Will* 192).

[40]*Vox Clamantis* 1.Prol.7–16, ed. G. C. Macaulay, *The Complete Works of John Gower*, vol. 4, *The Latin Works* (Oxford: Clarendon, 1902), 20. Trans. Eric W. Stockton, *The Major Latin Works of John Gower* (Seattle: University of Washington Press, 1962), 49–50: "What dreams may mean is clear from Daniel, and Joseph's vision in his sleep was not meaningless. Indeed, the good angel who is the guardian of the inner man always protects him with vigilant love. And granted that sleep may envelope the outer body, the angel visits the interior of the mind and sustains its strength. And often in a vision during sleep he furnishes portents so that the man may better understand the conditions of the time. Hence, I think that the dreams I witnessed at nighttime furnish memorable tokens of a certain occurrence."

[41]A. J. Minnis, *Medieval Theory of Authorship: Scholastic Literary Attitudes in the Later Middle Ages*, 2nd ed. (Philadelphia: University of Pennsylvania Press, 1988), 168–69.

take the role of such a visionary authority by explicating the significance of the "feld ful of folk" (I.1-9), for example, quickly ceases to explain the meaning of Will's dream. Becoming only one of many competing voices in the dream and only a small part of its confusing experience, she ultimately disappears.

A further contrast between *Piers Plowman* and *Vox Clamantis* is revealing. In contrast to Will's unguided "merveillous swevene" (Prol.11), Gower from the very beginning of his work cites the Apocalypse and directly summons as a guide its "author," the most important Christian visionary, John the Revelator:

> Insula quem Pathmos suscepit in Apocalipsi,
> Cuius ego nomen gesto, gubernet opus.[42]

That a similar invocation is absent in *Piers Plowman* has not prevented critics from attempting to define the poem as an apocalypse and to associate its visionary experience with the Book of Revelation.[43] Yet, the fact remains that, unlike Gower, the author of *Piers Plowman* never calls on John the Revelator as a model, even though John's visionary experience is a rare instance of the divinely sanctioned revelation of "Goddes pryvetee":

---

[42]Gower, *Vox Clamantis* 1.Prol.57-58, ed. Macaulay, *The Latin Works* 22. Trans. Stockton 50: "May the one whom the Isle of Patmos received in the Apocalypse, and whose name I bear, guide this work."

[43]In addition to Bloomfield, *Piers Plowman as a Fourteenth-century Apocalypse*, see Barbara Nolan, *The Gothic Visionary Perspective* (Princeton: Princeton University Press, 1977), 205-58; Joseph Anthony Wittreich, Jr., *Visionary Poetics: Milton's Tradition and his Legacy* (San Marino, Calif.: Huntington Library, 1979), 46; and Mary J. Carruthers, "Time, Apocalypse, and the Plot of *Piers Plowman*," in *Acts of Interpretation: The Text and Its Contexts, 700-1600. Essays on Medieval and Renaissance Literature in Honor of E. Talbot Donaldson*, ed. Mary J. Carruthers and Elizabeth D. Kirk (Norman: Pilgrim Books, 1982), 175-88. More recently, Kathryn Kerby-Fulton, *Reformist Apocalypticism and Piers Plowman*, Cambridge Studies in Medieval Literature 7 (Cambridge: Cambridge University Press, 1990), 79-96, has made the longest and most detailed such argument, although she relies more on examination of early Christian examples than of the poem itself. She concludes inconclusively: "The apocalypse, as the mode of fully developed visionary narrative within the religious tradition, is perhaps the best term we have for describing these qualities and tendencies in *Piers Plowman*" (96). In "The Apocalypse in Medieval Culture: An Overview," I argue against the existence of an apocalypse genre in the Middle Ages. See *The Apocalypse in the Middle Ages*, ed. Richard K. Emmerson and Bernard McGinn (Ithaca: Cornell University Press, 1992), 295-300.

Seynt Iohñ, that was a martyr fre,
on crystis lappe a-slepe lay he,
of hevyn he saw þe preuete,
ꝺꝰꝰꝰꝰꝰ convinio.[44]

Nor, with the possible exception of the "Pocalips" (XIII.90) of the gluttonous master of divinity in the famous banquet scene, does the poem explicitly cite the Apocalypse.[45]

The one New Testament visionary cited in the poem is Paul, but once again Will's relationship to this traditional visionary model is problematic. The reference comes towards the end of Will's climactic vision of the Harrowing of Hell, a powerful revelation of "Goddes pryvetee." Here Christ's explanation of his mercy and righteousness is interrupted by a reference to 2 Corinthians 12:4:

"And my mercy shal be shewed to manye of my bretheren;
For blood may suffre blood bothe hungry and acale,
Ac blood may noght se blood blede, but hym rewe."
Audivi archana verba que non licet homini loqui.
"Ac my rightwisnesse and right shal rulen al helle,
And mercy al mankynde bifore me in hevene."
(XVIII.394-98)

---

[44]"A Song for the Epiphany," lines 9-12, ed. Carleton Brown, *Religious Lyrics of the Fifteenth Century* (Oxford: Clarendon, 1939), 122. This special role is long-standing in Christian poetry. In his *Liber Cathemerinon*, for example, Prudentius describes the "profound . . . secrets" (line 73) that Christ shows John, "That faithful friend of the Master, / Evangelist of the Highest" (lines 77-78). Significantly, Prudentius also notes that, unlike John, "We merit not such visions" (line 117). Trans. M. Clement Eagan, *The Poems of Prudentius*, vol. 1, Fathers of the Church 43 (Washington, D. C.: Catholic University of America Press, 1962), 39-45.

[45]Scholars usually identify the "hir Pocalips" alluded to by Patience (XIII.90) as the *Apocalipsis Goliae*. See Pearsall's comment on C XV.99, *Piers Plowman: C-text*, 250; Schmidt's comment on B XIII.90, *Piers Plowman: B-Text*, 339; and Barney, "Allegorical Visions" 119. But the reference may be to the biblical Apocalypse, since by the fourteenth century it was closely associated with the mendicants—particularly the Franciscans. See David Burr's chapter on mendicant commentaries in *The Apocalypse in the Middle Ages*, ed. Emmerson and McGinn. If Patience's reference is to the biblical Apocalypse, and if Anne Middleton is right that the accompanying "Seint Avereys" (XIII.90) refers to Averroes—who was also often associated with mendicant schoolmen—then Patience here is condemning the friars for their misuse of revealed as well as natural knowledge. See Middleton, "The Passion of Seint Averoys [B.13.91]: 'Deuynyng' and Divinity in the Banquet Scene," *Yearbook of Langland Studies* 1 (1987): 33-35.

The Pauline citation has never been satisfactorily explained. It seems to be a type of "marginal gloss" common in *Piers Plowman*, which presents an opposing viewpoint or commentary on what is happening rather than being part of the narrative or vision.[46] Even if we understand it as such, the reference is curiously out of context, for although the passage is taken from Paul's enigmatic account of his being taken up into the third heaven, in the poem it interrupts a vision that has descended into hell: "I drow me in that derknesse to *descendit ad inferna*" (XVIII.111). Furthermore, it is not clear who speaks the verse. It certainly cannot be Christ. Perhaps it is Will, commenting on his privileged position as exclusive visionary witness to a crucial event in salvation history not even recorded in Scripture.[47] Noting that the third-person verb in the Vulgate (*audivit*) has been put into the first-person (*audivi*), Derek Pearsall comments that the poet "transfers Paul's words, of the man (evidently Paul himself) caught up into the third heaven, to his dreamer, suggesting that he is aware of the limits to which his vision of Christ's promise of mercy can be taken."[48]

But if indeed the Pauline verse is to be understood as spoken by Will, his subsequent actions cast doubt on the extent to which he has understood Paul's words. As the fourteenth-century translation of the passage reads, "[a man] herde pryue woordys þe whiche it is not leefful a man to speke."[49] These "pryue woordys" — the *archana verba* —

---

[46]On the "marginal gloss," see Helen Barr, "The Use of Latin Quotations in *Piers Plowman* with Special Reference to Passus XVIII of the 'B' Text," *Notes and Queries* n.s. 33 (1986): 440–48. Because, as Barr notes, in passus XVIII "more of the Latin quotations are absorbed into the metrical and alliterative structure than in any other place in the poem" (445), the "marginal" element in the quotation is more striking.

[47]The source for the extensive literature of the Harrowing of Hell is the *Descensus Christi ad Inferos*, which was attached to the apocryphal *Acts of Pilate*, perhaps as late as the fifth century. See Constantinus Tischendorf, ed., *Evangelia Apocrypha* (Leipzig: Hermann Mendelssohn, 1876), 389–416. The events are not witnessed in vision, but recorded by Karinus and Leucius, who were among those Christ released from Hell.

[48]Pearsall, commenting on the parallel passage in C XX.438a (*Piers Plowman* 339). Fowler, *Bible in Middle English Literature* 293, cites Pearsall, but suggests that the comment is authorial, expressing "the poet's awareness of 'the limits to which his vision of Christ's promise of mercy can be taken.'"

[49]Margaret Joyce Powell, ed., *The Pauline Epistles contained in MS. Parker 32, Corpus Christi College, Cambridge*, EETS, ES 116 (London: Kegan Paul, 1916), 129. At this point in the text, several Latin verses are first provided in a block, and then translated in a block.

recall, according to Hugh of St. Cher's commentary, the "secretum meum," the things reserved to God described in Proverbs 25, which Anima cites in his condemnation of Will's *curiositas*.[50] They reflect Paul's reluctance to meddle in or even talk about "Goddes pryvetee," so that he refers to himself in the third person and refuses to describe what he has seen in the third heaven. Will, in contrast, awakes shortly after uttering these words and immediately — and for the first time in the poem explicitly — writes about his vision (XIX.1–3). The Pauline reluctance to repeat *archana verba* is forgotten. Furthermore, although R. A. Waldron praises the "climactic power" of the Harrowing of Hell episode and the way in which Will's waking "into everyday life on Easter morning to the reassurance of the Cross and *goddes resurexion* and to the sound of Easter bells" provides "the satisfying finality of a synthesis and an answer to doubt," this waking reassurance is short-lived, for Will almost immediately falls asleep again.[51] Thus the poem suggests that the search for "Goddes pryvetee" may be endless, that the "coveitise to konne" can never be quenched. *Piers Plowman* continues through another two dreams, moving from the triumphal building of Unity to its catastrophic buffeting by Antichrist, ending ambiguously when Will is awakened by Conscience's cry for vengeance and his search for Piers. In its conclusion the only thing that seems certain is Will's capacity to dream again.

Students of *Piers Plowman* have often commented on how the poem does not fit the neat conventions of the dream vision, and David Lawton has recently warned against a simple, unquestioning, generic approach to the poem: "Langland disrupts and disturbs one's formal or generic expectations of the dream-vision as surely as he tampers with, reshapes, or transforms everything else he touches;

---

[50]Hugh of St. Cher, *Opera omnia*, vol. 7, fol. 142v.

[51]R. A. Waldron, "Langland's Originality: the Christ-Knight and the Harrowing of Hell," in *Medieval English Religious and Ethical Literature: Essays in Honour of G. H. Russell*, ed. Gregory Kratzmann and James Simpson (Cambridge: D. S. Brewer, 1986), 66. For a differing view of the Harrowing of Hell scene, which has greatly influenced mine, see M. F. Vaughan, "The Liturgical Perspectives of *Piers Plowman*, B, XVI–XIX," *Studies in Medieval and Renaissance History* n.s. 3 (1980): esp. 130–43. Vaughan contrasts Will with the dreamers in *The Dream of the Rood* and *Pearl*, who "awake to conversion (real or at least intended) and so conclude. Piers, however, goes on to two further dreams, which would seem to posit a continued lack of final conversion on the part of the Dreamer" (143).

and if this is so, the dream-vision cannot be used effectively to unify one's critical discourse about his poem."[52] As we have noted above, other critics continue to understand the poem as a dream vision, sometimes admitting difficulties with its generic inconsistencies, sometimes praising it for extending "the genre to new ways of viewing experience, making it work to represent new formulations of man's relationship to God and of the relationship between ordained and absolute truth."[53] But at what point is a genre extended beyond recognition? The poet's challenge to the genre seems radical and total, not only disrupting expectations, but questioning and perhaps even condemning its very basis, the notion that the dream can serve as a privileged source of knowledge. If, as I argued above, a model for Will's visionary experience should not be sought in the Macrobian and philosophical love tradition of the high Middle Ages, it may also be that even Augustine's archetypal discussion of dream experience in De Genesi is not particularly helpful in understanding Will. That is, just as the poem does not appropriate Augustine's exempla, Joseph and Daniel, as models for Will, it does not appropriate the three modes of visio that Augustine outlines in his analysis of Paul's rapture into the third heaven. These orderly, divinely inspired models and modes are simply not relevant to Will's chaotic dream experience. Instead, it is easier to understand Will if we recognize how his visionary experience, rather than following biblical models, inverts the powerful Pauline model discussed by Augustine in De doctrina Christiana, perhaps the most influential and sustained Christian defense for the value of acquiring and applying knowledge. Comparison of this passage with Will's dreams and especially his response to his experience suggests that Will's thirsting for further visionary experience and his meddling "with makynges" (XII.16), like his "coveitise to konne and to knowe science," are to be condemned.

In De doctrina Christiana, Augustine praises humble Christian teachers and warns against those who wish to be taught only by the Holy Spirit, who prefer visionary experience over mundane instruction. This visionary preference is dangerous as a form of pride and

---

[52]Lawton, "Subject of Piers Plowman" 3.

[53]Lynch, High Medieval Dream Vision 193, commenting on the visions of the narrators in both Pearl and Piers Plowman.

curiositas. We cannot all experience Paul's rapture, Augustine argues, and if we wait until we do, we fall prey to the temptations of the Devil:

> Rather, those things which can be learned from men should be learned without pride. And let anyone teaching another communicate what he has received without pride or envy. We should not tempt Him in whom we have believed, lest, deceived by the wiles and perversity of the Enemy, we should be unwilling to go to church to hear and learn the Gospels, or to read a book, or to hear a man reading or teaching, but expect to be "caught up to the third heaven," as the Apostle says, "whether in the body or out of the body," and there hear "secret words that man may not repeat," or there see Our Lord Jesus Christ and hear the gospel from Him rather than from men. (Prol.5)

Augustine continues, now using Paul as a positive example:

> We should beware of most proud and most dangerous temptations of this kind and think rather that the Apostle Paul himself, although prostrated and taught by the divine and heavenly voice, was nevertheless sent to a man that he might receive the sacraments and be joined to the church. (Prol.6)[54]

These passages serve as an inverted template for the Dreamer's actions not only after Will awakes from his vision of the Harrowing of Hell, but throughout the poem where he arrogantly accosts his various teachers. Thus the reference to 2 Corinthians 12:4 in the vision of the Harrowing of Hell may very well be intended to call to mind Paul's response in order to contrast it with Will's. It reminds us that Will not only appropriates for himself the personal experience that Paul modestly described in the third person, but that he also ignores Paul's example as soon as he awakes by immediately and for the first time explicitly writing down the "pryve" words that should be left unuttered. Furthermore, he continues to confuse the proper response to such visionary experience. Whereas Paul, after being taught by the divine and heavenly voice, proceeded to receive the

---

[54]*On Christian Doctrine,* trans. Robertson 5. Augustine's second example is from Acts 9:3–18, which describes Paul's actions after his vision on the road to Damascus.

sacraments and join the Church, Will, after writing down his vision,
enters church on Easter Sunday but only to fall asleep once again.[55]
Perhaps his intentions are good, since he calls his family to join him
in reverencing the Cross (XVIII.430–31), but the result is yet another
vision:

> Thus I awaked and wroot what I hadde ydremed,
> And dighte me derely, and dide me to chirche,
> To here holly the masse and to be housled after.
> In myddes of the masse, tho men yede to offryng,
> I fel eftsoones aslepe — and sodeynly me mette
> That Piers the Plowman was peynted al blody,
> And com in with a cros bifore the comune peple,
> And right lik in alle lymes to Oure Lord Jesu.
>
> (XIX.1–8)

It is easy at this point to assume that, because here Will dreams of
a Christ-like Piers, his falling asleep is a positive act, and there is no
question that the substance of his dream is a moving revelation of
the history and structure of the Church. But it is imperative to
distinguish this doctrinal substance from the form of its presentation, just as Anima condemns not the doctrine of the Trinity but
endless talk about it. Commenting on Will's dream-within-a-dream
in passus XVI, A. C. Spearing states that "Wille's persistent desire for
kynde knowyng seems to be justified by the outcome of the inner
vision, for what immediately follows is Gabriel's announcement of
the coming birth of Christ."[56] But if we are to understand the nature
of Will's ambiguous dream experience, we must distinguish doctrinal content from dream form. The justification for Will's "persistent
desire for *kynde knowyng*" surely is not yet another dream — however
pious and theologically sound. Such "coveitise to konne," as the
poem repeatedly makes clear, could be justified only by Will's applying his increasing knowledge to his active life. Thus, if Paul shows
that the proper response to a true vision is to remain silent about the
visionary world and to act in the world of everyday experience, Will,

---

[55]On this scene, see David Mills, "The Role of the Dreamer in *Piers Plowman*," in
S. S. Hussey, ed., *Piers Plowman: Critical Approaches* (London: Methuen, 1969), 189.

[56]Spearing, *Readings in Medieval Poetry* (Cambridge: Cambridge University Press,
1987), 243.

by writing rather than practicing what he sees and through his continued need to reenter the dream world, casts doubt on his authority as visionary and on the efficacy of his dreams. His continued dreaming his abdication from the waking world in which one must act in order to do well — and especially his falling asleep during Mass represent the very danger that Augustine admonished Christians to avoid. It is a sort of addiction to visionary revelation, a habit that can only be satisfied through a dream, an arrogant demand to "see Our Lord Jesus Christ and hear the gospel from Him rather than from men." Thus, at the very moment in the poem when Will should put into practical effect the lessons learned from his visions — from their personified and historical presentations of Charity — rather than making an offering and taking part in communion, he falls asleep again.[57] And when he wakes up later (XIX.485), it isn't to take the Eucharist, but once again to write.

Although it is impossible to be sure whether the poem is specifically recalling Augustine's words in De doctrina Christiana, it is clear that Paul provides a model of Christian behavior that challenges Will's. Whereas Paul modestly describes his visionary experience in the third person, Will speaks in the first person; whereas Paul refuses to relate the secret words that ought not to be uttered, Will writes immediately upon waking; whereas Paul's response to visionary experience is to enter church, be taught by man, and take the sacrament, Will enters church to fall asleep rather than take the sacrament. Augustine condemns those who expect to be taught through visionary experience rather than through holy men, yet that is exactly what happens to Will, who heads to church "To here holly the masse," but falls asleep and sees Jesus Christ wearing the arms of Piers. Given the results of Will's curiositas, it is not surprising that the attitude and experiences he represents would be understood by Augustine as potential threats to Christian unity:

---

[57]Vaughan ("Liturgical Perspectives" 143–48) also underscores the serious implications of Will's falling asleep during Easter Mass and suggests that the repeated failure to act on the added knowledge gained through his dreams is an index of how little Will has changed as a result of his visionary experience: "His behavior on Easter Sunday, even though the context has changed for the better, continues to be very like that he exhibited at the poem's opening, with its tension between the outward appearance of religious living and the reality of a flawed, 'vnholy' activity" (144).

. . . the condition of man would be lowered if God had not wished to have men supply His word to men. How would there be truth in what is said — "For the temple of God is holy, which you are" — if God did not give responses from a human temple, but called out all that He wished to be taught to men from Heaven and through angels? For charity itself, which holds men together in a knot of unity, would not have a means of infusing souls and almost mixing them together if men could teach nothing to men.[58]

Perhaps it is for this reason that Will must be instructed in the building of "that hous Unite — Holy Chirche on Englissh" (XIX.330).

Near the beginning of the *Inferno*, after Virgil has told Dante the pilgrim that he is about to be led through Hell, Purgatory, and Heaven, Dante responds:

> Ma io, perche venirvi? o chi 'l concede?
> Io non Enea, io non Paulo sono;
> me degno a cio ne io ne altri 'l crede.[59]

Although for quite different reasons, Will clearly is also not Paul; nevertheless, unlike Dante, he seems unaware of his condition, even near the end of his visionary quest. As is evident throughout the *Commedia*, Dante was troubled by the dangerous implications of his role as visionary, only slowly coming to recognize his responsibility as prophet while receiving warnings — such as the fate of Ulysses in *Inferno* 26 — of the dangers of violating boundaries and prying into the unknown.[60] Yet Will's visionary quest, lacking divine authority, positive guidance, systematic progress, and prophetic results, seems to be motivated by *curiositas*, particularly his desire to pry into "Goddes pryvetee." Even when Will in his inner dream is rebuked by Reason, who tells him to control his tongue (XI.385) and scolds him

---

[58]*De doctrina Christiana*, Prol.6, trans. Robertson 5-6. Augustine again cites Paul: 1 Cor. 3:17.

[59]"But I, why do I come there? And who allows it? I am not Aeneas, I am not Paul; of this neither I nor others think me worthy." *Inferno* 2.31-33; ed. and trans. Charles S. Singleton, *Dante Alighieri: The Divine Comedy*, Bollingen Series 80 (1970; rpt. Princeton: Princeton University Press, 1980), 1.14, 15.

[60]On the sin of Ulysses as *mala curiositas*, see Joseph A. Mazzeo, *Medieval Cultural Tradition in Dante's Comedy* (Ithaca: Cornell University Press, 1960), 205-12. See also Zacher, who describes Dante's Ulysses as "[p]robably the most striking medieval depiction of the curiosus as wanderer" (35).

for his arrogant meddling (*"De re que te non molestat noli certare,"* Ecclus. 11:9 [xi.393]), he doesn't fully understand his problem. Although chastened, the ashamed Will awakes from his inner dream not to renounce his *curiositas* but to bemoan the fact that he has not learned even more:

> Tho caughte I colour anoon and comsed to ben ashamed,
> And awaked therwith. Wo was me thanne
> That I in metels ne myghte moore have yknowen.
>
> (xi.403–05)

Only once in the poem does Will seem to realize that his "lust and likyng" for knowledge must not be pressed. In his conversation with Piers in the vision of the Tree of Charity, Will recognizes that he must ask no further questions after Piers identifies the Tree with the Trinity and gives him a threatening look:

> "And I have told thee what highte the tree: the Trinite it meneth"—
> And egreliche he loked on me, and therfore I spared
> To asken hym any moore therof . . . .
>
> (xvi.63–65)

Otherwise, it is not clear that Will ever realizes the extent to which his visionary experience is motivated by an intellectual *curiositas* that at its best leads only to "makynges" rather than doing well and at its worst allies him to the hated friars. This point is stressed by Ymaginatif, a severe critic and teacher, who associates Will's activity with that of the friars:

> And thow medlest thee with makynges—and myghtest go seye
>   thi Sauter,
> And bidde for hem that yyveth thee breed; for ther are bokes ynowe
> To telle men what Dowel is, Dobet and Dobest bothe,
> And prechours to preve what it is, of many a peire freres.
>
> (xii.16–19)

In other words, Will would rather write (and dream) about Dowel, Dobet, and Dobest than actually do well. Will rather defensively cites Cato for support, but he nevertheless acknowledges the rightness of Ymaginatif's attack: "I seigh wel he seide me sooth" (xii.20).

But if Ymaginatif, the faculty which is crucial not only to dreaming but also "makyng," condemns Will's somatic and poetic activity, it seems impossible to avoid the conclusion that *Piers Plowman* not only undercuts the prophetic status of the Dreamer and the privileging of his visionary experience, but also calls into question the very notion of the dream vision as a revelatory mode and undermines the poem's authority and even its legitimacy.[61] Because Will's "makyng" is based on his dreams — they are a necessary prerequisite to his writing — he must continually fall asleep to pursue his poem. It is not just that, as Bowers notes, Will "simply transcribes his dreams without due regard for their interpretation or inquiry into their trustworthiness," although this is clearly a problem.[62] The critical issue is more profound. Even if the dreams are trustworthy and reveal compelling images of Christian doctrine, even if they are "Full of high sentence" and are interpreted properly, they remain the result of *curiositas*. The "lust and likyng" implied by Will's "coveitise to konne" results in his addiction to visionary experience, his determination to pry into "Goddes pryvetee" and to record *archana verba* "whiche it is not leefful a man to speke."

Certainly David Fowler is correct in identifying some major differences between the A and B versions of *Piers Plowman* as reflecting a shift from the prophetic to the apocalyptic outlook. But if Will as narrator achieves the divine certainty of the Old Testament prophet in the A version, he never achieves the visionary authority of the apocalyptic seer who is called by God, visited by an angel, and instructed into the "pryvetee" of heaven. The problem of *curiositas*, which motivates Will in the B continuation and is explicitly condemned by Anima, is never fully overcome. For as *Dives and Pauper* states, even if a dream leads to virtue, as ultimately Will's dreams should for readers who take his "makynges" seriously, a dream may

---

[61] Although approaching the poem with different questions in mind, Justice also stresses the irresolution of the text and its failure to become *auctoritas*: "And, notoriously, the poem never reaches resolution: the long interpretive pilgrimage of the *Vita* ends on a moment of emphatic deferral. . . . The text cannot make final claims for itself" ("Genres" 305). Clopper ("Life of the Dreamer"), concentrating on Will rather than generic questions, makes a similar point. He notes that the Dreamer is "reckless" in "his assumption of the mantle of prophet, the scourger of his people, for unless he is Dobest and does as he preaches, he condemns himself" (262).

[62] Bowers, *Crisis of Will* 195.

be the first step toward deceit and "couriouste."[63] Thus as readers we
share the danger of preferring Will's intellectual search for Dowel
over actually doing well, of being motivated by an intellectual *curiositas* that is fed by Will's ambiguous dream experience. If Will remains
the earthbound erring human will, then perhaps his "relentless inquisition" is directed at us as readers, just as the poem in its opening
lines challenges us to interpret:

> (What this metels bymeneth, ye men that ben murye,
> Devyne ye—for I ne dar, by deere God in hevene)!
> (Prol.209-10)

---

[63]*Dives and Pauper* 1.45.10, ed. Barnum, 1.1:179.

Conscience, Piers, and the Dreamer in the Structure of *Piers Plowman* B

ELTON D. HIGGS

I N VIEW OF THE REPEATED separate appearances of the characters
Conscience and Piers Plowman in the action and development of
Piers Plowman, it is notable that the two of them do not appear
together until the last two passus (XIX-XX, B-Text; XXI-XXII, C-
Text)[1]; even then, they are together for only a short time before
Conscience is shown at the end of the poem crying out to find Piers,
who has once again disappeared. Nevertheless, the alternating appearances of Conscience and Piers and their interaction with the
Dreamer focus our attention in various ways on major themes of the
poem, all of which are brought to a head in the last two passus. I
believe that this confluence of themes and characters at the end of
the poem is best understood if we see passus XIX and XX (B-Text) as
the last of six sections of *Piers Plowman* which are largely defined by
the presence or absence of Conscience and/or Piers Plowman and by
the reflection of their experiences in the unfolding of the Dreamer's
visions.

These six sections may be outlined as follows:

Section One — Prologue — passus IV
Section Two — passus V-VII

---

[1] I shall use the B-Text as my primary point of reference in this paper, and unless
otherwise stated all citations of *Piers Plowman* will be from *The Vision of Piers Plowman*, ed. A. V. C. Schmidt (London: J. M. Dent & Sons, 1978). Citations of the C-
Text will be from *Piers Plowman: An Edition of the C-text*, ed. Derek Pearsall (Berkeley
& Los Angeles: University of California Press, 1979).

Section Three— passus VIII—XII
Section Four— passus XIII—XV
Section Five— passus XVI—XVIII

There are large areas of congruence between the structure outlined above and the two traditional ways of describing the structure of *Piers Plowman*: the *Visio/Vita* (or *Vitae*) and the eight (or ten) dreams.[2] Sections one and two in my structural description coincide with dreams one and two and the *Visio*. Section three begins the *Vita/Vitae* and is congruent with dream three. Section four begins with dream four and goes up to the beginning of the dream-within-a-dream in dream five. Section five starts with this dream-within-a-dream and goes through dream six. Section six corresponds to dreams seven and eight. The partial incongruence of my sections four and five to the dream structure of the B-Text may be seen as reflecting the radical differences at this point between the B-Text and the C-Text revision. I would like to think that my suggested divisions of the poem both reinforce its basic dream structure and provide a perspective on the development of its themes which aids in understanding both of the longer versions, in spite of the differing boundaries of some of the dreams in the B- and C-Texts. I believe that the six sections are (as Alford [31] says of the dreams) "firmly embedded in the text itself" in both versions, although I have confined myself to commenting only on the B-Text.

Important patterns of thematic development in the poem coincide with the six sections I have identified, and Conscience and Piers Plowman have complementary but distinctively different functions in defining the structure and the themes of the poem and in reflecting the development of the Dreamer. Conscience and Piers appear twice each before they come together in the last section; the first appearance of each one entails open conflict with forces rebellious against God and order, and in each case the conflict is to a large extent unresolved. The second appearance of each one presents a spiritualization of his character and a movement toward an idealized solution: Conscience allies himself with Patience, and Piers ex-

---

[2]For a survey of these traditional structures, see John A. Alford, "The Design of the Poem," in *A Companion to Piers Plowman*, ed. John A. Alford (Berkeley: University of California Press, 1988), 30–31.

pounds on the Tree of Charity and is embodied in the Passion of
Christ. Set between these paired appearances of Conscience and
Piers is the crucial episode (section three) in the visionary pilgrimage
of Will the Dreamer, in which he also makes a turn toward the
acceptance of spiritual, supra-rational answers to the questions he
has thus far been raising only in human terms and demanding to
understand according to his simplistic conception of *kynde knowynge*
(e.g., passus I.138-44).[3] By the end of the poem we realize that what
theoretically-oriented Conscience needs is to be confronted with the
practical difficulties of living a virtuous life in a sinful world, as
depicted in the section on Patient Poverty. That is why the Dreamer
identifies so closely with Conscience, because he must learn the same
lesson.[4] Piers, on the other hand, concentrates in the beginning on
the spontaneous *actions* of Doing Well which spring from his moral
instincts, and he must be brought to deal with the mysteries of
theology (e.g., the Trinity and the Incarnation). Whereas Conscience's rather smug "right thinking" must be tempered by the im-
preciseness of living in a sinful world, Piers's unstudied practice of
simple virtue in such a world has to come to terms with the seeming
paradoxes of divine thinking.

    In the light of this contrast between Conscience and Piers, we can
see why *Piers Plowman* depicts only a temporary union between
them, followed by another separation. Their interaction within the
poem reflects the struggle of fallen mankind to Do Well (depicted to
a great extent in the character of Conscience), which could have no
lasting effect until God had made a uniquely powerful entry into the
sinful world (depicted in the evolution of Piers Plowman/Christ);
but the very purpose of that entry was to create a spiritual watershed
and a new point of reference, not a perpetually intrusive and "magic"
cure-all. Mankind must, consequently, endure the limited success of

---

[3]See Mary Clemente Davlin, "*Kynde Knowyng* as a Major Theme in *Piers Plowman*
B," *RES* 22 (1971): 1-19, where she notes that the Dreamer manifests a perverted
desire for "the detached, objective knowledge of the encyclopedist" (5).

    [4]I have focused in a previous article on the Dreamer's "refusal to participate in the
world he is so willing, self-righteously, to criticize" ("The Path to Involvement: the
Centrality of the Dreamer in *Piers Plowman*," *Tulane Studies in English* 21 [1974]: 2).
This point of view was recently echoed by Steven F. Kruger, "Mirrors and the
Trajectory of Vision in *Piers Plowman*," *Speculum* 66 (1991): 84-91, esp. 87.

God's kingdom on earth until Christ shall come again (i.e., until Piers Plowman is united again with Conscience).

At the center of the theology in *Piers Plowman* is the necessity of aligning one's will with God's in order for good to be accomplished. Mankind must run the course of its struggle to Do Well (maintaining a good Conscience) until the end of the human drama of free will. Assurance of the efficacy of that struggle, however, is embodied in the historical drama in which God Himself (Christ/Piers) acted out the achievement of victory through suffering. It is only in loving patience that fallen humans can submit to God in their poverty and need, accepting the Pardon that first sternly defines mankind's moral indebtedness, and then (by divine paradox) becomes the instrument of grace by which it is paid.[5]

This, then, is the broad outline of the argument I wish to make. Let us now see in more detail how the six sections of *Piers Plowman* I have postulated are defined by the stages of development in Conscience and Piers and the parallel progress of the Dreamer.

Section One: Conscience vs. Lady Meed

The Prologue of *Piers Plowman* presents a world full of hucksters, hustlers, and unrepressed scoundrels. Those in positions of authority are depicted ambiguously (see Prol.100–216), and whatever order there is seems to be overshadowed by the rough-and-tumble of competitive human energy. This is a picture of fallen human society, with all of its indulgence and exploitation of petty fleshly desires and appetites. In passus I Lady Holy Church appears to Will with instructions about curbing these appetites and abiding within the bounds of true need, which she defines as "vesture from chele thee to save, / And mete a meel for mysese of thiselve, / And drynke whan thou driest" (I.23-25). Her memorable aphorism, "Al is nought good

---

[5]Pamela Raabe, *Imitating God: The Allegory of Faith in Piers Plowman B* (Athens and London: University of Georgia Press, 1990), p. 147, incisively comments on the purposeful paradox of the Pardon: "[T]he pardon does not express conflict; rather it expresses the resolution of conflict through paradox, since there is no Dowel without faith, and no pardon without Dowel. Piers tears the pardon when the priest fails to read Dowel as the faithful works of love that alone save the soul."

to the goost that the gut asketh" (I.36), summarizes well the principle of Patient Poverty which is developed at length later in the poem. But Will wants to know how such a minimalist approach to human experience can deal with the political and economic complexities of the world, specifically "the moneie of this molde that men so faste holdeth" (I.44). Lady Holy Church replies with the first of several important references in the poem to the Latin *reddere*, to pay or render, using the words of Jesus in the Gospel story of the loaded question addressed to him about whether godly people ought to pay taxes to a godless power. He replies: " '*Reddite Cesari*,' quod God, 'that *Cesari* bifalleth, / *Et que sunt Dei Deo*, or ellis ye don ille' " (I.52–53). The next two lines make clear that the realm of earthly order, imperfect though it may be in its fallen state, is under Reason and Kind Wit (associated later with Conscience, it should be noted: III.284–85) and must be respected and supported. Most of the rest of Holy Church's instruction to Will (I.61–209) has to do with the disorder and rebellion of Lucifer in contrast with the perfect order of love in Christ, who is the embodiment of the Truth-in-Love sought by the Dreamer and available to him through innocent (not prideful) "kynde knowynge" (I.142–45).[6]

The introduction of Lady Meed in the poem emphasizes that she is the progeny of False, and the altercation between her and Conscience shows the inherent incompatibility between her amoral fickleness and his uncompromising commitment to moral and social order. It is appropriate that in this initial conflict Conscience should be matched against a materialistic foe, since later the purification of his character entails the embracing of Patient Poverty. In passus II, we see Meed lending herself to all the evils of excess that Holy Church had warned Will against, until the King has her arrested and brought to court for examination (II.199–239). When the King proposes that she and Conscience marry, Conscience objects vehemently against the corruption brought about by the misuse of Meed, and he absolutely refuses to be associated with her (III.118–69). In spite of her appeals that money is necessary to oil the machinery of

---

[6]Hugh White, *Nature and Salvation in Piers Plowman* (Cambridge [Eng.]: D. S. Brewer, 1988), 34–35, 54–59, sees "kynde knowynge" as experiential, in contrast to the more purely intellectual nature of Kind Wit, and therefore more efficacious in the development toward salvation depicted in the poem.

war and civil government (III.175-229), Lady Meed is completely
put down when Reason is called in to bolster Conscience and the
King embraces the two of them together to be his chief counselors
(IV.171-96). The social order established as the province of these
partners represents an equilibrium toward which, in the opinion of
many of Langland's contemporaries, the rationality of man naturally
guides him,[7] even though he is able to implement it only imperfectly.
The association of Conscience and Reason with moral uprightness
lays the groundwork for the confessions of the Seven Deadly Sins in
the next section.

Section Two: Piers and the Pardon

After the confessions of the Seven Deadly Sins begin in passus V,
Conscience and Reason disappear as Repentance takes over; and
when the Sins have done with their confession, Piers Plowman
comes on the scene to guide the repentant pilgrims to the shrine of
Truth, providing they will help him to cultivate his half-acre first
(V.537ff; VI.1-6). This complex episode, which ends with the much-
discussed pardon-tearing scene at the end of passus VII, places the
figure of Piers in an earthly frame of reference that corresponds with
the earthly concerns of Conscience in section one. Several of Piers's
actions echo the insistence of Lady Holy Church and Conscience on
conduct which contributes to social order: his initial directions on
how to reach Truth (an applied approach to salvation through the
Ten Commandments: V.560-84); his management of workers and
loafers on his half-acre; and his identification of the social actions
expected of those who wish to be included in the Pardon sent by
Truth. Although the function of Piers as supplier of food is endowed
with spiritual as well as physical meaning, Piers's immediate concern
in the plowing of the field is with the same kind of well-ordered
society that Conscience and Reason wanted the King to establish.
    Piers seems to be secure in his attempts to institute order until a
priest asks to interpret his Pardon for him. On looking at it, the
cleric exclaims, "I kan no pardon fynde / But 'Do wel and have wel,

---

[7]See White 6-10.

and God shal have thi soule,' / And 'Do yvel and have yvel, and hope thow noon oother / That after thi deeth day the devel shal have thi soule!' " (VII.111–14). Piers's abrupt tearing of the Pardon in the B-Text has, of course, raised consternation in the poem's readers for some time.[8] We need to be concerned here only with the fact that Piers takes a radical action showing his "tene" at the priest's impugning the integrity of his pardon, while at the same time turning away from seeing his service to God as a contribution to social order. In sum, Piers becomes more concerned with personal salvation than with taking care of the world. The quarrel between Piers and the priest awakes the Dreamer and sets him to puzzling about the relative value of dreams, pardons, and good works. Whatever dreams are worth, the logical dilemma that Will faces about the relationship of a pardon to good works is clear: How can the answer to man's sinfulness be both a matter of pardon from God and a matter of man's earning some right to salvation? A pardon implies a need that goes beyond what one deserves, and salvation by good deeds implies that pardons are irrelevant.[9] It is a corollary to this quandary that sets Will on the path that occupies him in section three: If Doing Well is required, what quality and quantity of good deeds are necessary to meet the requirement?

As was noted above, such subtle niceties do not concern Piers. Obviously confident in his own good motives, he opts out of the dilemma by determining to engage himself in the most spiritual activity he can find; he will "cessen of [his] sowyng" (VII.118) and devote himself to "preieres and . . . penaunce" (VII.120), trusting God to supply his food, and presumably that of others as well, since

---

[8]Two well-articulated but contrasting views of the Pardon are Robert Adams, "Piers's Pardon and Langland's Semi-Pelagianism," *Traditio* 39 (1983): 367–418; and Denise N. Baker, "From Plowing to Penitence: *Piers Plowman* and Fourteenth-Century Theology," *Speculum* 55 (1980): 715–25. Another notable explication of this scene (with a survey of criticism) is in Samuel A. Overstreet, "Langland's Elusive Plowman," *Traditio* 45 (1989–90): 278–97.

[9]For recent comments on the tension between grace and works in the poem, see Adams's previously cited article, "Piers's Pardon," and his "Mede and Mercede: the Evolution of Economics of Grace in the *Piers Plowman* B and C Versions," in *Medieval English Studies Presented to George Kane*, ed. Edward Kennedy, *et al.* (Woodbridge: D. S. Brewer, 1988), 217–32. See also Baker, "From Plowing to Penitence," and Samuel A. Overstreet, " 'Grammaticus Ludens': Theological Aspects of Langland's Grammatical Allegory," *Traditio* 40 (1984): 251–96. Baker's emphasis on the necessity of grace in the poem most clearly reflects my own view.

he is retiring from the farm. It is not clear at this point, either to us or to the Dreamer, whether Piers has made the right choice, nor what are the implications of the argument between him and the priest. Piers must join Conscience in retiring from the scene for a bit while Will wanders around probing the complexities of Doing Well.

Section Three: Will's Third Dream

Section three of *Piers Plowman* (passus VIII-XII) coincides with the third dream of Will, including the waking passage before it and the enclosed dream-within-a-dream. This portion of the poem has received wide attention as a turning point in the action,[10] and it is pivotal also in the interpretation I am presenting of the structure and the major themes of the work. Although this section is obviously important in its own right, I shall deal only briefly with it here to show its function as a fulcrum on which are balanced the paired, sequential appearances of Conscience and Piers. In the first stage of this section, the Dreamer is earnestly searching for an intellectually satisfactory answer to the question of "What is Do-Well?" The more he pursues it, however, the more complex it becomes, quickly expanding into a question of the distinction between Do-Well, Do-Better, and Do-Best (VIII.79). After he has been instructed by Thought, Wit, Study, Clergy, and Scripture, Will exclaims in frustration, "This is a longe lesson . . . and litel am I the wiser! / Where Dowel is or Dobet derkliche ye shewen" (X.369-70). But Will's problem lies in the way he has asked the question, expecting an answer that makes sense and is practicable in purely earthly terms: "Where . . . Dowel dwelleth" (VIII.13, 78); "How Dowel, Dobet, and Dobest

---

[10]See John Burrow, "The Action of Langland's Second Vision," *Essays in Criticism* 15 (1965): 247–68; Joseph A. Longo, *"Piers Plowman* and the Tropological Matrix: Passus XI and XII," *Anglia* 82 (1964): 291–308; Mary Riach, "Langland's Dreamer and the Transformation of the Third Vision," *Essays in Criticism* 19 (1969): 6–18; Elizabeth Salter and Derek Pearsall, eds., *Piers Plowman* (Evanston, Ill.: Northwestern University Press, 1967), 40, *et passim*; Kruger 74–95; James F. G. Weldon, "The Structure of Dream Visions in *Piers Plowman," Medieval Studies* 49 (1987): 254–81; Joseph Wittig, *"Piers Plowman* B. Passus IX-XII: Elements in the Design of the Inward Journey," *Traditio* 28 (1972): 211–80. My own previous article ("The Path to Involvement"), referred to above, also gives special significance to the third dream (15–24).

doon among the peple" (VIII.112). In this approach he reflects the attempts to define and maintain earthly order which were undertaken by Conscience and Piers in the first two sections. Scripture roughly points the way for Will when she scorns him and accuses him of pursuing knowledge but neglecting to learn about himself (XI.1–3). This rejection propels Will into a deeper dream, wherein he first abandons himself to unbridled pleasure, then encounters the bitter end of such behavior when Fortune forsakes him; finally, he is forced by Reason, Kind (a figure of God Himself), and Imaginative to confront the shallowness and vulnerability of criticizing others without examining himself. His final encounter before waking out of the inner dream is an argument with Reason in which he presumes to oppose his own perception of proper order to that of God (XI.368–402).

As Will awakes from the third dream and meditates on what he has seen, concerning both the disorder of the world of mankind and the perfect order of God (XIII.1–18), he especially puzzles over the enigmatic quotation and interpretation of I Peter 4:18 with which Imaginative concluded his instruction of the Dreamer: "*Salvabitur vix iustus in die iudicii; / Ergo — salvabitur!*"; that is, "The just shall scarcely be saved — therefore, they shall be saved!" (XII.279–80; the emphasis is on *vix* — "scarcely" — in C XVI.21–23). It was a strong statement, designed to refute the suggestion of Will that virtuous people before the coming of Christ, such as Solomon and Socrates, must be assumed by orthodox doctrine to be unsaved (XII.275–77). Will has shown an unflagging determination to get answers to his questions which are consistent and understandable according to human reason and intellect, and Imaginative's answer to him in this case is that since even the righteous, in human terms, are only *barely* saved, it must be clear that salvation depends on God's sovereign will, and not on conformity with some conception of order that mankind can fully comprehend. As it is put in the C-Text, no one is saved "bot *vix* helpe" (C XVI.23). In accordance with the usual pattern in Will's waking and dreaming, he falls asleep and dreams again because he has reached the limit of his ability to work things out in the waking state. In his next dream, he encounters one of the most amazing scenes in the poem, the dinner party of Conscience.

The function of the third section of *Piers Plowman* in the structure I have outlined is to provide in the experience of the Dreamer a transition between the physically oriented questions and answers emphasized in the first two sections and the more spiritual principles focused on in the next two passus, in which once again Conscience and Piers will play key roles.

Section Four: Conscience, Patience, and Haukyn

As the Dreamer sleeps again and enters into his fourth dream, he is obviously gratified by Conscience's invitation to dinner ("ther com Conscience to conforte me that tyme" [XIII.22]), and he looks forward to enjoying his hospitality. However, more distinguished guests than Will have been invited, and Will and Patience (who is admitted as a beggar) end up being placed at a side table (36) and fed rather austere spiritual fare (52–57), while a more honored guest, the "maister" (a friar, accompanied by his assistant), gorges himself on rich physical food (40–42, 60–63). Will is indignant at the advantage enjoyed by the friar and is ready to reproach him for his hypocrisy and his insensitivity to social inequity; but both Patience and Conscience restrain him, and Conscience invites the learned friar and another guest, Clergie, to expound on the definition of Dowel. Both of their answers are governed by theoretical reason, except that Clergie in his humility points to Piers Plowman (XIII. 123–29) for a kind of answer which he considers outside his capability, that is, an approach that stresses the oneness of the three "Do's" rather than their separate identities. This deference to Piers anticipates that when he comes on the scene again, he will speak with more certainty and authority than he did when last seen, and that there will be an added dimension to his character that goes beyond merely managing a social order to keep the world working and adequately fed. At this point, however, it is Patience who supplies this new focus on the key to Doing Well/ Better/Best — that is, Love.

For Patience, learning is Do-Well, teaching is Do-Better, and loving one's enemies is Do-Best (XIII.136–39). And the power in the latter is not that it imposes certain behaviors to enforce a worldly order, but that it effects a spiritual transformation — love casts out fear (XIII.163; I John 4:18) — and brings peace between warring parties (XIII.158–72). Although this seemingly naive statement evokes derision from the friar, it is the catalyst for Conscience's decision to go on pilgrimage with Patience. Even Clergie is sceptical about the advisability of this course of action, but Conscience justifies it by telling Clergie that "Me were levere, by Oure Lord, and I lyve sholde, / Have pacience parfidiche than half thi pak of bokes!" (XIII.200-01). Clergie (who represents the study of Scripture and theology) promises to be there for Conscience when he has need of him, after "Pacience have preved thee and parfit thee maked" (XIII.214).

The way in which Patience can "prove" Conscience is shown in the next several scenes, which conclude section four and introduce section five. Several interlocked themes and figures are developed in this part of the poem: Patient Poverty (with the Latin refrain, *Pacientes vincunt* — "The patient conquer"), Charity, the ambiguity and peril of this world's goods, and the necessity of penitence. Piers Plowman is increasingly referred to, and another character, Haukyn, seems almost to be a parody of Piers's transition from earthly manager to spiritual guide.

Haukyn ("*Activa Vita*") leads a frenetic life and in many ways a contradictory one. He is thoroughly involved in the world, but he has sensitivities which make him uncomfortable in it. As a "waferer" he is part of the food supply, as was Piers Plowman, and he is well-known and even depended upon in the community. Moreover, he supplies not only ordinary food but wafers for the Mass as well. On the other hand, he is much soiled by his contact with the world, as is seen in his dirty coat covered with the stain of sins. Conscience urges him to confess and be absolved of his sins, and there ensues another confession scene, which ends with a revealing conversation between Haukyn, Conscience, and Patience.

Replying to Conscience's question of why he allowed his coat to get so dirty, Haukyn pleads that such soiling is unavoidable, since he is completely enmeshed in the normal activities and vicissitudes of the world:

> And kouthe I nevere, by Crist! kepen it clene an houre,
> That I ne soiled it with sighte or som ydel speche,
> Or thorugh werk or thorugh word, or wille of myn herte,
> That I ne flobre it foule fro morwe til even.
>
> (XIV.12–15)

Conscience proposes to rescue him through the conventional steps of penance (contrition, confession, and satisfaction) and says that these are equivalent to Do-Wel, Do-Better, and Do-Best (XIV.16–28). Patience, however, goes a step beyond this rational and systematic solution and promises the repentant Haukyn that if he will but depend on God for the support of his life, he need not involve himself in the world that has so soiled him in the past. He can lead a life that stays strictly within the bounds of need and is governed by Patient Poverty and Love (XIV.29ff). The food that Patience would supply is "a pece of the Paternoster—*Fiat voluntas tua*" (XIV.49), that is, "Thy will be done."

Here the switch from the order of human reason to the spiritual order is explicit, and it is reinforced by two other Latin tags that resonate throughout the last half of the poem: "*Ne soliciti sitis*" and "*Pacientes vincunt*" (XIV.34). The first one ("Be not anxious [what you shall eat]") comes from the Sermon on the Mount (Matt. 6:25, Luke 12:22) and was used previously in the poem by Piers Plowman when he forsook his plowing to devote himself to penance (VII.127); the second one ("The patient conquer") was first invoked by Conscience when he called on Patience to comment on Do-Well (XIII.134) and is used afterward three times by Patience (XIII.171; XIV.34, 53) and twice by Anima (XV.267, 596). It should be noted that "*Fiat voluntas tua*" is also put forth again by Anima in XV.179 as the spiritual sustenance which is sufficient for those who are voluntarily and patiently poor.

Through the rest of passus XIV, Patience carries on with his discourse on Patient Poverty as a product and concomitant of Charity. In so doing, he fulfills the objective of perfecting Conscience, as was anticipated by Clergy when they parted from each other (XIII.214). Although we see nothing more of Conscience in this section, it is clear that he is under instruction from Patience, and when he reappears in passus XIX (section six), he is ready to accept, along with Piers Plowman, the more radical spiritual approach to establishing God's order that is spoken of by Patience here. Patience's main points are these: (1) The poor have an advantage over the rich in that they can plead that having been deprived on earth they have the greater claim on the joys of heaven (XIV.104–216). (2) The Seven Deadly Sins have less of a hold on poor people than on the rich, since the poor have less leisure and fewer resources to indulge in sin

(XIV.217-72). (3) Several proverbs about poverty show that poverty enforces temperance, decreases temptation, and takes away the fear of losing worldly goods (XIV.273-319). To summarize, Patient Poverty (which can include the two sons of a generous rich person) allows one to participate in the Charity by which alone true order is brought to this fallen and imperfect world. Haukyn, seeing how far he is from the experience of Patient Poverty and Charity, weeps mightily for his sins to end this episode (XIV.320-32).

The last scene in section four (passus XV), which is initiated by the beginning of Will's fifth dream, presents a body of instruction by Anima, whose discourse is dominated by an exposition on Charity and by fulminations against the abuses practiced by the clergy. Will, still reflecting the insistence on having unambiguous answers which he (as well as Conscience and Piers) manifested in the first half of the poem, is challenged by Anima for his pride. "Thanne artow inparfit," says Anima, "and oon of Prides knightes! . . . . It were ayeins kynde . . . and alle kynnes reson / That any creature sholde konne al, except Crist oone" (XV.50, 52-53). It is not mere knowledge that is needed by mankind to solve its problems, says Anima, but Charity, which is characterized by complete reliance on the same "*Fiat voluntas tua*" (XV.179) that was offered as food by Patience (XIV.49). Moreover, continues Anima, no one will come to know Charity except through help from Piers Plowman, who has the advantage of perceiving "moore depper / What is the wille, and wherfore that many wight suffreth" (XV.199-200). What Will the Dreamer really needs, then, is to relinquish his own will (his lust for knowledge and intellectual mastery) and instead to take for his satisfaction the will (*voluntas*) of God, which, as Anima begins to reveal, is mediated by Piers/Christ. Anima is the first in the poem to indicate the merger between Piers and Christ as he expands on the uniqueness of Piers's ability to lead people to Charity:

Therfore by colour ne by clergie knowe shaltow hym nevere,
Neither thorugh wordes ne werkes, but thorugh wil oone,
And that knoweth no clerk ne creature on erthe
But Piers the Plowman — *Petrus, id est, Cristus.*

(XV.209-12)

The comments of Anima on the sins of clerics are not particularly well-focused, but at several points they deal with the damage done to the order of society by church leaders who, rather than being in the mold of Patient Poverty and Charity like Piers/Christ, are corrupted by both their greed and the improper support they receive from tainted sources. Anima lauds those such as the Desert Fathers who were wholly dependent upon God for their sustenance (XV.269-306), and he advises secular rulers that the best thing they can do to reform the church is to make sure that clerics have no living except their legitimate tithes (XV.551-67). As Lawrence Clopper points out in a recent article, the poem shows great concern about friars, in particular, who in their begging went beyond their minimal needs.[11]

It is appropriate, then, that Anima ends his discourse (and section four) by reinvoking the theme words, *"Pacientes vincunt"* (XV.598). This has been a wide-ranging section, carrying us and the Dreamer all the way from Conscience's dinner, where Patience turns out to be the most important guest, to the last appearance of Piers Plowman, who will be used to outline the covenants of God with mankind, the spiritual answers to physical problems.

Section Five: The Apotheosis of Piers

After all of Anima's instruction, Will is still not clear on the meaning of Charity, so Anima introduces the "Tree of Charity" (XVI.4-9) to offer further enlightenment. In the last two sections of *Piers Plowman* (passus XVI-XX), characters and symbols merge with almost bewildering rapidity and complexity. The Tree of Charity (XVI.1-99) provides yet another embodiment of the spiritual love already presented by Patience and Anima, and with its three props it anticipates an exposition of the Trinity (XVI.181-253), which blends into   a
brilliant merger of several trinities of characters and qualities at the end of passus XVI and the beginning of XVII. First there are Abraham, Moses, and the Samaritan (who later blends with Jesus/Piers), a trio which corresponds to the covenantal triad of Patriarchy, Law,

---

[11]Lawrence M. Clopper, "Langland's Franciscanism," *Chaucer Review* 25 (1990): 54-75.

and Grace; these, in turn, are subsumed by the theological triad of
Faith, Hope, and Love and bolstered by another exposition of the
Holy Trinity (XVII.126–253). The characters of Abraham and Moses
merge into the more abstract representations of Faith (XVI.173–79)
and Hope (XVII.1–24) and then are transformed into the priest and
the Levite of the Gospel parable of the Good Samaritan (XVII.49–
64); in the replay of that parable the Samaritan first plays his expected part, and then he becomes Love (XVII.89–125) to complete
the triad begun by Faith and Hope, before finally merging with
Piers and with Christ. Piers Plowman is the key figure in section
five, beginning its action as caretaker of the Tree of Charity and later
blending with the character of the Samaritan (Love) and with both
the suffering and the triumphant Christ.

The essence of the Tree of Charity is Patience ("Pacience hatte the
pure tree"—XVI.8) and the tenor of its meaning is embodied in
submission to God's will. Consequently, Will the Dreamer's hunger
for the fruit of the tree (XVI.10–11, 73–74) shows that he is now
willing to partake of the same kind of spiritual nourishment as that
recommended by Patience, "*Fiat voluntas tua.*" The food imagery[12]
becomes increasingly important as the poem works toward its end,
relating not only to the Dreamer (particularly his striving to be fed
in the Eucharist—XIX.1–3, 386–93; XX.1–5), but functioning also in
the use of the tree's fruit in the scheme of redemption (XVI.75–96;
XVIII.28–35), the thirst of Christ for souls (XVIII.359–73), and the
spiritual cultivation of the land by Piers in establishing the church
(XIX.264–319). All of these allegorical uses of food imagery emphasize the transition that has taken place in the poem from attention to
the purely physical nature of mankind's deficiencies to emphasis on
his need to be fed spiritually.

The last passus in section five (XVIII), brings us to the climax
toward which the poem has been building all along: the Incarnation,
Passion, and Triumph of Christ. The metamorphosis of Piers is now

---

[12]Jill Mann, "Eating and Drinking in 'Piers Plowman'," *Essays and Studies* n.s. 32
(1979): 26–43, comments on the interactive literal and figurative uses of food and
drink in the poem. One of her most perspicacious observations is that there is a
parallel between the way human hunger supersedes all other considerations (as in
the arguments of Need in passus XIX) and the overriding thirst of Christ in XVIII.
363ff. "which legitimates the suspension of the letter of the law that would leave
mankind in damnation . . ." (43).

complete, as he and the Samaritan become one with each other and with Jesus, preparing for the "jousting" in Jerusalem, the battle of Christ with the Devil (XVIII.10–35). Jesus's right to plunder Hell is justified in the "Four Daughters of God" debate (XVIII.110–229), where the redemptive value of Jesus's death, argued by Mercy and Peace, is shown to compensate for the requirements of Righteousness and Truth. Jesus completes the Harrowing of Hell, and the Dreamer awakes from his sixth dream to call his family together and reverence the cross on which Jesus died. The next passus (XIX) begins section six with Will's attempt to participate in the Mass, but he sleeps again and calls on Conscience to guide him once more.

Section Six: The Synthesis

And so, once again, we come to the confluence of themes and characters at the end of the poem. The connector between all of the patterns and themes which finally converge in passus XIX and XX (especially Conscience, Piers Plowman/Christ, plowing and pardon, patient poverty, social and spiritual order) is the Dreamer, whose attempts at detached intellectual exploration are finally relinquished in this last section as he joins Conscience and Piers Plowman in the Barn of Unity.[13] At the beginning of this section, Will's question about Jesus/Piers (XIX.9–11) initiates a discourse from Conscience on the implications of Christ as Conqueror, during which he delivers the final definitions in the poem of Do-Well, Do-Better, and Do-Best, all attached to stages of Jesus's ministry on earth. Although he was born into the world from royal lineage and was worshiped by angels and the Magi, Jesus "Was neither kyng ne conquerour til he [comsede] wexe / In the manere of a man, and that [b]y muchel sleighte" (XIX.97–98). As he exercised these "sleightes," or skills, in his ministry, he achieved Do-Well, Do-Better, and Do-Best. The key to the difference in the three degrees of virtuous action lies in the scope of their effect. Do-Well (symbolized by turning the water to

---

[13]Elizabeth Kirk, *The Dream Thought of Piers Plowman* (New Haven and London: Yale University Press, 1972), 183, notes that the recurring patterns in the last passus, "in one way or another, merge the Dreamer's individual and idiosyncratic experience into a larger, corporate pattern." See also Alford 58–61.

wine at Cana) was primarily for the benefit of Mary, his mother, to convince her of his true nature; this deed identified him as the son of Mary—a human, but by miraculous birth (XIX.108-23). The next level, Do-Better, was achieved by his miraculous healings and other deeds that were for the physical benefit of the multitudes among whom he walked. To these he was known as the son of David, showing his right to the throne of Israel as the one who fulfilled the messianic prophecies (XIX.124-39). Do-Best is manifested when the triumphant Christ (now identified, we may assume, as the Son of God) gives authority to Piers Plowman to grant forgiveness to those who "pay what they owe" ("*redde quod debes*") to Piers's pardon (XIX.183-94).

This pardon is essentially the same as the one sent by Truth in passus VII and is described in much the same terms: when Christ comes again as judge, he will send "The goode to the Godhede and to greet joye, / And wikkede to wonye in wo withouten ende" (XIX.198-99). In this context, however, Piers has been enlightened and empowered by Christ so that he understands and can administer the pardon in the light of the Incarnation and all of its redemptive effects. It is therefore precisely appropriate for Grace and the Holy Spirit to be introduced at this point as the manifestations of divine power that enable mankind to meet the requirement of "paying what they owe." When the pardon was introduced in the earlier scene, the emphasis was on law-keeping, not grace; it was in the era of Moses/Hope, not of the Samaritan/Christ/Love. Piers, as Christ's Vicar on earth, has become the chief minister of the new covenant of Love, a ministry embodied ideally in Peter, the first pope, the rock on which the church was considered to have been built.

The task of Piers/Christ at this point, however, is not to bring the struggle between good and evil to its final end; the divine visitation of the Incarnation has made a radical change in the way fallen humans relate to God, but it is Conscience who is left to guard and marshal the defense of the Barn of Unity, Holy Church. Jesus did not himself remain on earth after his resurrection, but ascended to be with his Father until the time for him to come again at the consummation of all things, the Day of Judgment. He left behind his Holy Spirit and the gifts of Grace to enable Conscience and all who pay Piers's pardon to fight against the power of Antichrist and his allies.

Conscience is therefore a principal figure in the founding of
Christ's kingdom, the society of the saved, which is once again
represented in the planting and cultivation of a field; but this time
the basis of the food supply is clearly spiritual. The seed sown is
supplied by Grace to Piers and consists of the Four Cardinal Virtues, prudence, temperance, fortitude, and justice. "Thise foure
seedes Piers scw, and siththe he dide hem harewe / With Olde Lawe
and Newe Lawe, that love myghte wexe / Among thise foure vertues, and vices destruye" (XIX.311–14). The Old Law of Moses,
which supplied the only foundation for interpreting the pardon first
given to Piers, has now been consecrated to serve along with the
New Law of Christ to cultivate the virtues appropriate to the concerns of Conscience. One's debt to Piers's pardon may now be paid
in the coin of love through grace, which renders true contrition,
confession, and satisfaction meritorious because of the grand payment of the debt of sin by Christ. But one's contact with His redemptive body and blood must be maintained by participating in the
Eucharist, emblem of the ongoing divine food produced by the Tree
of Charity.

After the House of Unity has been built to hold the harvest of
Piers's plowing and to protect his followers, Conscience tells Christian people how they are to be nourished while standing against the
siege by Pride and his allies:

> "Cometh," quod Conscience, "ye Cristene, and dyneth,
> That han laboured lelly al this Lenten tyme.
> Here is breed yblessed, and Goddes body therunder.
> Grace, thorugh Goddes word, gaf Piers power,
> Myght to maken it, and men to ete it after
> In helpe of hir heele ones in a monthe,
> Or as ofte as thei hadde nede, tho that hadde ypaied
> To Piers pardon the Plowman, *redde quod debes*."
>   (XIX.386–93)

What is being urged here by Conscience reflects both his and Piers
Plowman's newly acquired spiritual wisdom. Conscience is not
merely arguing rational morality (what might be called the observance of natural law), but instead is inviting people to do what
Haukyn did: acknowledge their spiritual poverty and submit to the

penance prescribed by Patience, so that they can eat of the true food of God, the "blessed bread" of the Eucharist (which corresponds to Patience's "*Fiat voluntas tua*").[14] This is the continuing confirmation of the New Covenant of Christ, in the establishment of which Piers's initial simple goodness has been transformed and given meaning through the New Adam (Christ), the embodiment of the mystery of God's love.

As it was noted in the prologue to this paper, the complementary pilgrimages of Conscience and Piers and the Dreamer, though they cover vast distances, are not shown in their ultimate completion. Thus we find the last temptation of the Dreamer becoming the catalyst that separates Conscience and Piers Plowman once again and produces the plaintive cry in the last lines of the poem. This temptation to Will is delivered by the somewhat puzzling character of Need, introduced at the beginning of passus XX, berating and browbeating Will for not following the example of the special plead-ers at the end of passus XIX who reject Conscience's instructions.

> Coudestow noght excuse thee, as dide the kyng and othere—
> That thow toke to thy bilyve, to clothes and to sustenaunce,
> Was by techynge and by tellynge of *Spiritus Temperancie*,
> And that thow nome na moore than nede thee taughte,
> And nede ne hath no lawe, ne nevere shal falle in dette. . . .
> So Nede, at gret nede, may nymen as for his owene,
> Withouten conseil of Conscience or Cardynale Vertues—
> So that he sewe and save *Spiritus Temperancie*.
>
> (XX.6–10; 20–22)

Just as Conscience and Piers have both had to be freed from being bound too closely by their commitment to social order, so the Dreamer has been brought from a simplistic desire for uncompli-cated answers to a realization that both the problems and their solutions in a sinful world are far beyond rational or moral simplic-ity. This last temptation for Will is in its subtlety reminiscent of the

---

[14]Joseph Wittig, "The Dramatic and Rhetorical Development of Long Will's Pilgrimage," *Neuphilologische Mitteilungen* 76 (1975): 52–76, emphasizes the centrality of the theme of submission to God's will in *Piers Plowman*, the main lesson of which, he says (65), is that the will of God is sufficient and must become, in patient endurance, the individual's will (*fiat voluntas tua*).

temptations put before Jesus by the Devil (see Matt. 4:1-11); like
them, it uses misapplied truth to argue the permissibility of what, in
the situation at hand, would be sinful.[15] Need says first that mere
deprivation of the basics of life justifies whatever means are used to
sustain life; and then he cites the life of poverty endured by Jesus
and his disciples as proof that they embraced the principles he is
advocating. In other words, he is trying to convince Will that the
doctrine of Patient Poverty, which is at the center of Patience's
instruction to Conscience, can be interpreted to justify looking only
at one's *own* need, without regard to any of the other vital spiritual
principles of the poem: Charity, *fiat voluntas tua*, and *redde quod debes*.
Need flies directly in the face of Conscience's authority by elevating
Temperance to primacy among the Cardinal Virtues, whereas Conscience has clearly designated Justice as the chief of the four
(XIX.408-09). Need reveals the speciousness of his own argument by
criticizing the other three Cardinal Virtues for the very radical qualities that constitute their moral strength (XX.23-33). It is significant
that when Will's distress at the onslaught of Need sends him into
another dream (his last), the first scene he secs is that of Antichrist
turning Piers's crop of truth upside down and sowing falsehood in its
place so as to "spede mennes *nedes*" (XX.51-55; italics mine). This
thrust of the attack of Antichrist is reinforced by subversive friars,
whom Need is later partly responsible for getting into the House of
Unity against Conscience's better judgment. Need's subtle arguments directed toward Conscience at that point once again run
counter to the main lessons that have been learned in the poem.

With the coming of Antichrist, the assault on Unity is launched in
earnest, and the Dreamer must finally bring together in his experience the different but related lessons which have been learned with

---

[15]Robert Adams, "The Nature of Need in *Piers Plowman* XX," *Traditio* 34 (1978):
273-301, explains Need's radical arguments to the Dreamer as reflecting both
Langland's apocalyptic outlook (293, 296-99) and the Dreamer's vulnerability to
specious justifications for his unorthodox behavior (287-88). He contends that
while Need's advice to Will may be granted as equivocal, his remarks to Conscience
should be taken as more straightforward. Clopper, on the other hand, sees the
arguments of Need in both cases as reflecting a radical Franciscan polemic against
friars who "beg solicitously and for more than they need" (56); he agrees with
Adams that Conscience's rejection of Need's advice has disastrous results and that
Need reinforces the idea of Patient Poverty (pp. 65-67). Obviously, both Adams
and Clopper view the character of Need more positively than I do.

such difficulty by Conscience and Piers. Although Conscience and Piers have both had a change of direction away from purely human answers and toward spiritual solutions, they have been led along different educational paths. The development of Conscience represents the divine enabling of that residue of moral light in human minds that glimmers forth even in a fallen world. Conscience, much more than Piers, is a moral *theorist*: he relishes debate, as is seen in the argument with Meed and in the theological discussion of Do-Well (passus XIII) at his dinner with the friar, Clergy, and Patience. Conscience's development in the poem shows that for fallen man, reason (though necessary and desirable) is not sufficient to maintain order in the world or to achieve salvation.[16] The natural end of Conscience's education was his recognition that to live virtuously is to conduct a long, steady battle against an evil that requires more than reason to conquer it; he must learn to have patience with God's methods, and especially with His timetable. The natural end of Piers's education, on the other hand, was for him to embrace and become the instrument of a radical infusion of the divine precept of redemption, and that is why he ultimately becomes the body of Christ in the Incarnation. The Dreamer needed both the lesson of loving patience in the midst of imperfect mankind learned by Conscience and the lesson of Truth mediated only by divine grace (the Incarnation — the embodiment of all theology and moral virtue) which is at the center of Piers Plowman's development.

This final step in the Dreamer's education does not come without stress, however. As Piers called earlier on Hunger to come to aid him in controlling his workers, Conscience now calls on Kind to come to his assistance. It is obvious here, as it was in the previous passage where the Dreamer encountered Kind, that we are not

---

[16]White 1–34, sees only temporary associations of Kynde Wit with Conscience and Piers Plowman up through the end of passus VIII (B-Text), showing that even the best that mankind can do according to the light of natural reason is not the answer to his plight. He observes that "at the very end of the poem, Conscience is alone without Kynde Wit, being the only thing able, it seems, to continue the search for Piers, the only human resource which remains effective to the last in the battle against evil" (23). James Simpson, "From Reason to Affective Knowledge: Modes of Thought and Poetic Form in *Piers Plowman*," *Medium Aevum* 55 (1986): 18, also notes that Conscience rejects rational worldly wisdom (*scientia*) to go off with Patience.

seeing merely Nature as an agent of God, but God Himself.[17] The
defenders of Unity supplied by Kind do not seem at first to be very
positive for mankind, for they are agents of mortality—diseases,
Death, and Old Age (xx.80–99). Nevertheless, unlike the uncon-
trollable Hunger called in by Piers, these avengers sent by Kind are
bound by his precise purpose and strategy (xx.106–09). This purpose is specifically seen in the reaction of Will to the ravages of Old
Age, who mockingly deprives him of hair, hearing, and sexual po-
tency (xx.83–198), bringing Will finally to the point of complete
submission to God as he calls on Kind to deliver him and beseeches
his counsel. The answer Kind gives him is again a summary of what
had to be learned by Conscience and Piers:

> "Lerne to love," quod Kynde, "and leef alle othere."
> "How shal I come to catel so, to clothe me and to feede?"
> "And thow love lelly, lakke shal thee nevere
> Weede ne worldly mete, while thi lif lasteth."
>
>   (xx.208–11)

Will at last "pays what he owes" through sincere penance
(xx.212–13) and enters into Unity. He now sees the battle from
inside the fortress, and from that perspective he describes the last
movement of the poem.

Now, however, the subtle assault of Need is directed toward Conscience. The friars brought to Conscience's attention by Need represent a direct threat to the key action necessary to people's "paying
what they owe" to Piers's Pardon: they abort the process of penance.
When the friars answer Conscience's cry for help because of "in-
parfite preestes and prelates of Holy Chirche" (xx.229), Conscience
rejects them at first because "thei kouthe noght wel hir craft"
(xx.231). Need pops in again to offer to Conscience another subtle
perversion of the doctrine of Perfect Poverty by arguing that friars
seek for "cure of soules" (xx.233)—for which Need seems to admit
they are not qualified—because they are deprived of a regular living
and make a pious fetish of poverty and begging (xx.234–41). Need's
answer to the problem, then, is to let them alone—by way of punish-

---

[17]See White 60–88.

ment, he implies, but actually, it will be seen, so that they can be a Trojan horse used against Conscience and the virtues he defends.

Conscience's response to Need's observation and advice is unexpected: he laughs (XX.242), and then he invites the friars in for a conference. He evidently sees the problem with them as similar to his own former short-sightedness, for he admonishes them:

> [L]yveth after youre reule.
> And I wol be youre borugh, ye shal have breed and clothes
> And othere necessaries ynowe—yow shal no thyng lakke,
> With that ye leve logik and lerneth for to lovye.
>
> (XX.247–50)

Francis and Dominic, he continues, gave up everything to become holy in love (252), not (he implies) to gain prestige or honor; their poverty was endured willingly and sincerely and had no taint of self-promotion. But their successors have left such simplicity behind and try, while maintaining a clever fiction of virtuous poverty, to become scholars and theologians. Conscience has been led subtly by Need to focus on remedying the problem of the friars by funding them sufficiently so that they no longer have an excuse to beg, and by curbing their numbers. Neither of these measures, however, will eliminate the damage done by the friars, for the problem lies precisely in their exercising the hypocrisy taught them by Need. Envy feeds the problem by sending the friars to school to be intellectual game-players and glossers (XX.273–76) who are thus better equipped to follow the example of their undercover advocate, Need.

So it is that Conscience makes himself vulnerable to Friar Flattery's disastrous incursion into Unity. And so it is also that, in spite of what he has learned in the course of the poem, and in spite of his brief companionship with Piers Plowman, he is in danger of being overwhelmed by the forces of evil. We have come a long way since the Field of Folk in passus I, and we have seen amazing developments in the characters of Conscience, Piers Plowman, and the Dreamer, whose cumulative complementary experiences provide a basic structure of the poem. But whatever insights have been given us and them, we are yet in the fallen world where the struggle goes on and the will of God is still being worked out.

As the poem reaches its end, the anguished plea of Conscience

shows that the battle is complicated by Conscience's being left to
fight it without the direct aid of Piers Plowman:

> "By Crist!" quod Conscience tho, "I wole bicome a pilgrym,
> And walken as wide as the world lasteth
> To seken Piers the Plowman, that Pryde myghte destruye,
> And that freres hadde a fyndyng, that for nede flateren
> And countrepledeth me, Conscience. Now Kynde me avenge,
> And sende me hap and heele, til I have Piers the Plowman!"
> And siththe he gradde after Grace, til I gan awake.
>
> (XX.381–87)

The Dreamer awakes this final time, it seems, to join with Conscience in dealing the best way he can with a world that is repeatedly
in rebellion against God.[18] The hypocritical poverty of the flattering
friars stands as a symbol of the stubborn resistance of the sinful
world against submitting to the penance of Grace that makes effective the Pardon of Piers, and against being satisfied by the divine
sustenance of *fiat voluntas tua* which was so beautifully uncloaked by
Patience. The B-Text author surely focused accurately on the ambiguity of Need in the last passus, for as he illustrated throughout *Piers
Plowman*, only by accurately assessing the difference between true
and false need and true and false satisfactions is there hope of meeting the requirements of *redde quod debes*.

---

[18]Míċeál Vaughan — "'Til I gan Awake': The Conversion of Dreamer into Narrator in *Piers Plowman* B," *The Yearbook of Langland Studies* 5 (1991): 175-92 — sees no
real enlightenment in the Dreamer until this final waking, through which he at last
breaks out of the spiritual slumber which has bound him thus far even in the waking
periods between dreams.

The Idea of Alliterative Poetry:
Alliterative Meter and *Piers Plowman*

DAVID LAWTON

T HE PURPOSE OF THIS PAPER is to supplement work I have published on the meter of Middle English alliterative poetry, and
particularly of *Piers Plowman*,[1] by taking account of the studies of
Hoyt Duggan[2] and proposing certain generic constraints. It therefore entails a brief but detailed statement of a debt: the difference
Duggan has made to my work as co-editor, with Ralph Hanna III, of
The Siege of Jerusalem. It is worth looking at the large number of times
we have followed either a suggestion by Duggan or the implications
of his system, and at the few times we have not, because it is in these
detailed editorial decisions that the value of Duggan's work has im-
pressed itself upon me, and my response to it—broad agreement,
with several areas of minor but significant disagreement—has been

---

[1]David A. Lawton, "Alliterative Style," in *A Companion to Piers Plowman*, ed. John
A. Alford (Berkeley/Los Angeles/London: University of California Press, 1988),
223-49; "Middle English Unrhymed Alliterative Poetry and The *South English Legendary*," *English Studies* 61 (1980): 390-96.
[2]Hoyt N. Duggan, "Alliterative Patterning as a Basis for Emendation in Middle
English Alliterative Poetry," *Studies in the Age of Chaucer* 8 (1986): 73-105; "The Shape
of the B-Verse in Middle English Alliterative Poetry," *Speculum* 61 (1986): 564-92;
"The Authenticity of the Z-Text of *Piers Plowman*: Further Notes on Metrical Evidence," *Medium Ævum* 56 (1987): 25-45; "Notes toward a Theory of Langland's
Meter," *Yearbook of Langland Studies* 1 (1987): 41-70; "Final *-e* and the Rhythmic
Structure of the B-Verse in Middle English Alliterative Poetry," *Modern Philology* 86
(1988-89): 119-45; "The Evidential Basis for Old English Metrics," *Studies in Philology* 85 (1988): 145-63; "Langland's Dialect and Final *-e*," *Studies in the Age of Chaucer*
12 (1990): 157-91; "Stress Assignment in Middle English Alliterative Poetry," *JEGP*
89 (1990): 309-29.

tested. Although the paper therefore proceeds by means of detailed work on alliterative poetry of the formal type, its focus, as befits its occasion, is *Piers Plowman*, for this is the poem that has sometimes made me doubt the potential for universal application of an approach such as Duggan's to Middle English unrhymed alliterative poetry, and remains the stress-point for Duggan's system.

As Duggan has always recognized, matters of meter here have an importance that is historical as well as theoretical: what is at stake is one's sense of what kind of writing/s Middle English alliterative poetry really was, and where it/they came from. An evident conflict between Duggan's work and mine arose partly from different terminology of description and partly from the different models, especially of provenance, with which we approached our work. That further conflict is inappropriate is apparent to me not only in the usefulness I have found in Duggan's conclusions but also in my conviction that his method of coming at questions — meticulous quantitative analysis assisted by logical skills — surely deserves support, and may eventually yield results to supplant any current differences of opinion. However, Duggan's work in its present state already has theoretical implications, not all of them overt in Duggan's writing, that are not yet and may never be susceptible to measurement. In response to these, I shall propose a possible view of *Piers Plowman* that would run counter to the trend of both Duggan's work and my own, one that might reinstate its separation — in kind, in intention, and so inferentially in meter and perhaps geographically — from other Middle English alliterative poems. That is why the title of this paper refers to "the idea of alliterative poetry." The intertextuality of its reference, with an eye to the controversy aroused by James L. Kugel's attack on standard views of meter in the Jewish Bible in *The Idea of Biblical Poetry*,[3] provides further insight into questions of alliterative meter and *Piers Plowman*.

---

[3] James L. Kugel, *The Idea of Biblical Poetry: Parallelism and Its History* (New Haven and London: Yale University Press, 1981): see below, pp. 167.

Duggan's system

It might be argued that Duggan's system hardly needs restating. Its series of metrical rules, all of them presented as running counter to a prevailing orthodoxy, have been published in a large number of contexts over a period of years during which his output has come to resemble a demonstration of formulaic variation in a literate context such as he espouses. One can only look forward keenly to the publication of the book in which all comes together with the unique mass of evidence he has assembled. For Duggan's importance lies partly in the moment in which his work began, and the intelligence with which he seized it. Questions of Middle English unrhymed alliterative meter badly need quantitative analysis, based not only on received texts from printed editions but also on the testimony of multiple manuscripts in the cases where such testimony exists: *Piers Plowman*, the nine manuscripts of *The Siege of Jerusalem*, the two manuscripts of *The Wars of Alexander* and *The Parliament of the Three Ages*. Duggan saw that the preparation of computer data-bases, made widely available in the technology of the personal computer, allowed for far more systematic analysis of these witnesses than currently existed. He prepared a data-base of "almost 13,000 lines taken from fifteen unrhymed long-line poems" ("Alliterative Patterning" 76), of which he analyzed the syntax as well as the meter — taking up, and brilliantly extending, major work by R. A. Waldron and R. F. Lawrence applying to Middle English the transference of Parry's and Lord's model of oral-formulaic composition into literate contexts.[4] Thus Duggan's conclusions are really the first on the meter of Middle English alliterative poetry to be supported by large-scale quantitative analysis on computer (though Waldron's pioneering thesis, on what Lawrence was to call "grammetrical" molds, is amazingly well supported by large-scale analyses he did by hand). Duggan has proved to be well-suited to such modes: his work is characterized by a mastery both of detail and of logic.

Some reservations might be expressed at once. While the sample

---

[4]Ronald A. Waldron, "Oral-Formulaic Technique and Middle English Alliterative Poetry," *Speculum* 32 (1957): 792–804 (based on Waldron's admirable University of London thesis); R. F. Lawrence, "Formula and Rhythm in *The Wars of Alexander*," *English Studies* 51 (1970): 97–112.

is impressively large, it falls far short of the length of the alliterative corpus: given the speed of change in personal computing, it would have been possible only three or four years later to have worked comfortably with a much expanded base. Duggan is aware of this, and has considered variant readings of *The Siege of Jerusalem* (unfortunately, not the whole text) and *The Parliament of the Three Ages*; he now shows strong signs of leading an attempt to make real systematic inroads into the text and meter of the *Piers Plowman* manuscripts, which will be his most important work to date. The number of whole poems he entered is small, and most of these are of the size of *St Erkenwald* or, at most, *The Parliament*; only one of the really long poems (over 1000 lines) was entered in its entirety, and this was of course *The Wars of Alexander* (5806 lines) in its two manuscripts, which Duggan was engaged in editing with Thorlac Turville-Petre.[5] The usefulness of his work is apparent at once in their edition, which could scarcely be better; but it is not a poem that raises strongly the issues about which Duggan is now most dogmatic, such as possible disjuncture between stress and alliteration. If we only had *The Wars* to go by, no metrist need have raised the problem of "*Piers Plowman*" lines. This is a danger in all computer analyses: the data are based on models which are predisposed to support the interpretation of the data, so that the circularity of more evidently subjective interpretation is not, after all, entirely avoided. That said, Duggan has been generous in providing data to all enquirers, and his data-base remains by far the best for this purpose ever assembled. Its usefulness is far from exhausted, and Duggan's extension of it promises to continue to break important new ground.

As first presented, some of his conclusions were surely not in conflict, as he claimed, with "most published scholarship" ("Alliterative Patterning" 79). Propositions such as the irrelevance to the meter of the notion of the foot, that "the line is made up of two distinct half lines divided by a caesura" (77), and that of these the a-verse allowed for three metrical prominences whereas the b "is rather

---

[5]Their edition has since been published as EETS, SS 10 (1989). Turville-Petre provides a valuable editorial statement in "Editing *The Wars of Alexander*," in *Manuscripts and Texts: Editorial Problems in Later Middle English Literature*, ed. Derek Pearsall (Woodbridge: D. S. Brewer, 1987), 143–60.

more difficult to determine" (77) were hardly revolutionary. His major innovations were the following:

(i) the suggestion that the only alliterative pattern allowed by the poets was *aa/ax*;

(ii) the proposition that "stress and alliteration coincide" (77)—that is, they do so invariably;

(iii) his use of syntactic frames and the notion of a shared "metrical grammar" (78) to offer detailed determinations about metrical and unmetrical b-verse types and a "hierarchy of word classes" (78) determining "which words may appear in metrically prominent positions" (78).

To these he was to add, in contradiction of his own earlier views,

(iv) that the "*Piers Plowman*" line operated similarly to other alliterative poems in applying (i) to (iii).

I should say at once that the greatest benefit I have derived from Duggan's work, as will become clear, is from (iii), his detailed anatomy of b-verses metrically, semantically and syntactically. I remain unsure of (iv), as, it seems, does Duggan, whose pronouncements on *Piers* lack the dogmatism of the rest. Intuitively, I distrust it, and the evidence of the manuscripts, with which I have worked for some years, does not seem to me unequivocally supportive—unlike Duggan's presentation of *The Wars of Alexander* or *The Siege of Jerusalem* or *The Parliament of the Three Ages*, where Duggan has a truly remarkable piece of evidence. Where multiple manuscripts exist, and there is a reading in conflict with Duggan's rules, such deviation fails to win unanimous support from all manuscripts. This is the strongest of all supports for Duggan's work, and it is one that writers dissenting from him have signally failed to explain away.[6]

In the case of (i), the prevalence of *aa/ax*, Duggan has already accepted a-verses that scan *aaa*, and he makes a further exception in the case of vocalic alliteration—so his rule sounds more absolute than it is. The essay advancing this principle follows J. P. Oakden in discounting the contrary evidence of more than twenty *aa/xa* lines in

---

[6] See Thomas Cable, "Middle English Meter and Its Theoretical Implications," *Yearbook of Langland Studies* 2 (1988): 47–69.

the sole manuscript, Cotton Nero A x, of *Sir Gawain and the Green Knight*. All these lines make reasonable sense, and Duggan's support for Oakden in contradistinction to "a conservative editor" is questionable, since it involves his by no means unconservative acceptance of common authorship of the poems of the Cotton Nero manuscript, without proof or discussion (and silently elides one of the arguments against common authorship, metrical variation).[7] Nevertheless, the rule is sound for *The Siege of Jerusalem*, for *The Destruction of Troy*, and for *The Wars of Alexander*, all of which are related.

When I began my work on alliterative poetry as a graduate student of Elizabeth Salter and Derek Pearsall at York, I argued for what is in effect now Duggan's position against Professor Pearsall, who at that time, I suspect for my instruction, maintained a form of stress-levelling or resolution. Duggan's support for three-stress *aaa* a-verses has therefore encouraged me. But the difference between his early experience and mine has caused a misunderstanding. When Duggan pronounces his rule on stress and alliteration, he has in mind mainly b-verses and the argument that in *Piers Plowman* unstressed syllables are occasionally raised to metrical prominence; I have in mind mainly a-verses, and the possibility that alliteration may offer too many metrically prominent syllables to be carried by normal phrasal stress.

There are grounds, in any case, for suspecting that statement (ii) — on the invariable coincidence of stress and alliteration — may itself be rhetorically overstated; at least, Duggan's (and Turville-Petre's) view is cast in terms that work for *The Wars of Alexander* but may require some adaptation for the unrhymed alliterative corpus as a whole. If Duggan means — as on *Piers* he seems to mean — that wherever there is an apparent conflict between alliteration and stress which is plausibly authorial rather than scribal in origin, alliteration can be taken as modifying normal prose-rhythm and conferring stress, then the discursive absolutes "alliteration" and "stress" become somewhat flexible elements: the prescription becomes, at most, a guide to performance. Elsewhere, on the other hand, the formula-

---

[7]"Alliterative Patterning" 74-75, and n.3, citing J. P. Oakden, *Alliterative Poetry in Middle English* I (Manchester: Manchester University Press, 1930), 261-63, and "The Scribal Errors of the MS Cotton Nero A.x.," *The Library* 4th series, 14 (1933-34): 353-58.

tion becomes a rule that words without lexical stress or semantic prominence cannot be raised to alliteration — which is a proposition I and most other commentators accept as true of all formal alliterative poetry. In a recent paper ("Stress Assignment"), Duggan rephrases the rule in terms of the lexical stress of individual words: alliteration does not normally fall anywhere but on the stressed syllable of the word. Again, I should always have accepted this (with Duggan's own valuable proviso, that if a word has two acceptable but different stress-patterns, some but not all alliterative poets may for convenience use either), yet here find my work cited as a contrary view. It may be that differences in handling lexical and phrasal stress — the stress of the individual word and what happens to it as it competes for semantic prominence within the phrase — have been a source of unnecessary disagreement between us. At any rate, I strongly endorse Duggan's conclusion: "My intuition . . . is that it is Langland alone who writes b-verses in which stress and alliteration do not coincide. But we must do more work before we can be sure which is the case."[8]

I now want to show how we found Duggan's system valuable in important practical ways, editing *The Siege of Jerusalem*, and how one might still arrive at a different view from his or mine of the meter of *Piers Plowman*.

---

[8]"Stress Assignment" 328 (1990), with its implicit revision of the views advanced in "Notes toward a Theory of Langland's Meter" (1987). Duggan's revision of his views is a proper response to the issues and interpretation of evidence. I have revised my views in a similar way, not least in response to Duggan's work, so there would be little purpose served in considering in detail the various disagreements with my work that he has articulated. There is some appearance of spasmodic skirmishing: when Duggan thought *Piers* unlike any other unrhymed alliterative poems, I was cited as an example of "the contrary argument" ("The Shape of the B-Verse" 528, n.27), and it seemed a trifle hard that when he otherwise completely changed his mind, I was again cited as one who had reached "a diametrically opposed conclusion" ("Notes toward a Theory of Langland's Meter" 52-53). However, I should take some blame for initiating such skirmishing in "Middle English Alliterative Poetry: an Introduction," in *Middle English Alliterative Poetry and its Literary Background*, ed. David Lawton (Cambridge: D. S. Brewer, 1982), 5-6, with what I now consider a regrettably dismissive mention of Duggan's essay, "The Role of Formulas in the Dissemination of a Middle English Alliterative Romance," *Studies in Bibliography* 29 (1976): 265-88.

Editing The Siege of Jerusalem: *Metrical Emendations*

Ralph Hanna and I have completed the text of our edition of *The Siege of Jerusalem*, but it is not yet fully revised for publication.[9] The information I offer here is therefore provisional, and may vary somewhat, though I doubt significantly, in the final version of the printed edition.

Moreover, the information is offered without Ralph Hanna's checking, and he is therefore not responsible for any mistakes that may appear. I apologize to readers who find themselves faced with more detail than they ever desired. Given the nature of Duggan's work and our use of it the evidence cannot readily be relegated to an appendix. (However, the argument is summarized on pp. 157–59).

We have agreed with emendations proposed by Duggan in the case of 35 b-verses, in our lines 48, 62, 78, 106, 127, 133, 134, 187, 197, 264, 343, 432, 510, 513, 537, 575, 590, 679, 708, 710, 712, 743, 840, 923, 929, 932, 1134, 1138, 1172, 1219, 1221, 1228, 1236, 1327 and 1337; and we have followed his lead in refraining from emendation on metrical grounds in lines 85, 586, 1131 and 1150, which Duggan shows to be metrical in spite of their apparent contravention of other rules. Since all 39 cases are specifically presented in Duggan 1986 and Duggan 1988, there is no need for fuller discussion here. All are to do with Duggan's construction of metrical and unmetrical b-verse types, and all the emendations involve the addition or deletion of one syllable in order to conform with these types. The most common recurrent type is the addition of -(e)n to the infinitive or the third person plural form, present tense or preterite, of verbs. Since final -*e* is not available in the dialect of the poem, emendation is unavoidable. Another common type is infinitive with *[for]to* rather than copy text *to*. We have used Duggan's rules to

---

[9]The edition will be published by Colleagues Press, probably in 1994. It is edited from the nine manuscripts: **L** (Bodleian Library Laud Misc. 656); **P** (Princeton University Library Robert Taylor ms.); **A** (BL Additional 31042 – Thornton); **V** (BL Cotton Vespasian E xvi); **Ex** (Exeter, Devon Record Office 2507); **U** (CUL Mm. v 14); **D** (Lambeth Palace Library 491, part 1); **E** (Huntington Library HM 128); **C** (BL Cotton Caligula A ii, part 1). We have consulted the earlier edition, by Kölbing and Day, EETS, OS 188 (1932), and the edition of lines 521–724 by Thorlac Turville-Petre in *Alliterative Poetry of the Later Middle Ages: An Anthology* (London: Routledge, 1989). Line references in our edition will vary upwards by up to 4 lines from those of other editions.

determine what seems to us clearly authorial *ilk a* in place of scribal *eche* or *eche a* (as in 1167b, 1187b).

Our confidence in Duggan's conclusions on these matters can be gauged by our desire to apply them consistently — as, for example, in 710b, *topsailes walten*, where the adverbial *-es* form is not followed in the edition by Thorlac Turville-Petre. One or two instances, at most, seem to us worthy of further study: we are not certain whether *bale* in 187b, *hem bale [for]to wyrche*, may have historical final *-e*, in which case L would be metrical, or what may be said further in favor of the *hapax* L reading, *regnance* (which would have to be trisyllabic), rather than the PUDC reading *realte* preferred by Duggan and so far followed by us in 510b.

On several occasions, our pursuance of Duggan's principles has led to emendations on our part not suggested by Duggan (for example, *dryueþ* for L *drof* in 56b; *þe fals [for]to mete* in 555b, following PAD and Turville-Petre rather than LE *to*; 675b, where we emend to create a metrical line, as in 959b or 686b, where we read *kirnel[e]s* rather than LPA *kirnels* — and Kölbing-Day; Turville-Petre). These number 20 instances: 30b, 56b, 526b, 555b, 556b, 641b, 675b, 686b, 793b, 939b, 959b, 989b, 1023b, 1062b, 1072b, 1097b, 1234b, 1269b, 1276b, 1295b. On a further eight occasions, we have preferred a reading other than that suggested by Duggan which is nevertheless grounded in Duggan's system: 108b, 128b, 144b, 212b, 379b, 399b, 411b, and 1267b (*pulsched vessel*, where Duggan suggests *pulisched* for b-verse metricality; *pace* Duggan, we take *vessel* to be an uninflected plural, in which case it forms an adjective-noun syntactic frame in which according to Duggan /x/x is allowable). These additional emendations offer extensive further support to the justice of Duggan's system; again, all relate to matters of one syllable in the b-verse.

The system provides assistance to the editors in cases such as 1276b, *[þer]no freke wanted*, where *[þer]* is omitted in LAVUDC and Kölbing-Day: it would seem here that some scribes perceived problems with the off-verse, which is too short, though the solution, we think, is to supply the redundant *[þer]* from L1274, attracted to a sequence of þ-words in that context.

In 1062, Duggan provides the key to sifting the variants. L characteristically misses an impersonal verb-form and supplies *to go wher he wolde*; PA, with support from VUD, present the alternative *to go wher hym beste lykede*, and metricality determines our strong preferred reading, *to go wher h[ym lyke]de*. As well as this sort of applicability, the system also proves invaluable in posing a metrical choice, as in 978b, of *at wille* or *at my wille*, which might confirm the authorial form of the past participle as L's disyllabic *taken* or as *tan(e)*, which is the form allowed by AVUDEC. The extensions of the system confirm its value.

Duggan's b-verse typology also enables editors to reconstruct copy text errors: as in 181b, *seide þe kyng* + *þan* (PAUD vs. L: . . . *riche þan*) and 182b, *worþy þe* + *tille* (PA vs L . . . *to telle*); or to support copy text against errors in other manuscripts, as in 199b, *grete god þanked*, where PAUD fear that the reading is unmetrical and add an extra syllable, whereas in fact the final *-e* of *grete* is sounded because the form is adverbial.

There are of course other places at which we have emended *metri causa*, and without doubt Duggan is a factor in our preparedness to do so, but the changes owe nothing directly to his system. I can think of only one place at which we are in sharp disagreement with him, line 642, *Geten girdeles and ger, gold and good stones*, where Duggan's preferred UDEC reading (his line 638) is scribal, a secondary effort at smoothing the line. In any case, his rejection of the L reading as unmetrical ("Alliterative Patterning" 96) is evidently countermanded by second thoughts ("Authenticity" 34–36), which seem to accept such b-verse structures.

Given the weight of Duggan's work, it is hardly surprising that all the evidence I have offered so far is to do with the b-verse. The last example, however, line 642, raises questions of alliterative structure and is hyper-alliterative. We accept this, but not a lack of alliteration from the *aa/ax* standard. For this reason we were tempted to emend the universally attested form of line 583, *Saue an anlepy olyfaunt at þe grete gate*, to a standard *aa/ax* by reading *at þe [aþel] gate* in the b-verse; but we conclude that *at* here takes stress, like *with* in 436, *þer waspasian was with princes and dukes*. These are *"Piers Plowman"* type lines. In line 1237, we cannot accept L's reading: *& þan þey deuysed hem & vengaunce hit helde*, which lacks adequate alliteration except in a dialect such as that of *Piers Plowman* with þ/v crossrhyme. Our provisional solution reads *þey* as a remnant of something like *þe vylayns*, but there are some objections. The preponderance of lines with *devisen* in the *Gawain*-group and *The Wars of Alexander* alliterate on /d/, not /v/; this may have inspired UD's substitution *auised*, which alliterates on /v/. We wondered whether more radical reconstruction was required, as in something like: *And þan þe [douth] deuysed hem & [her dome] hit helde*. But there was in the end sufficient evidence for v-rhyme on *devisen* for us to favour a different reading: *& þan þe [vilayns] deuysed hem & vengaunce hit helde*. The line follows a scribal supply in LUDEC, accepted by Kölbing-Day, *& haplich was had away how wyst I neuere*, which we reject altogether as vacuous and unmetrical. On alliterative patterning, therefore, our conclusions agree largely with Duggan's. On word-stress, they probably do so as well, as with the stress on the alliterating first syllable of *conceyued* in line 108. More difficult is our reading for line 344b, *[& what] ʒe coueyte wolde*, where the supply of *wolde* as in L's reading *ʒif ʒe coueyte wolde*, appears to be a less than compelling anticipation of the first word of the following line, but there is no other evidence for a second b-verse stress.

Line 344 stands on its own in our typology, however. There are three possible *"Piers Plowman"* lines where we favor an explanation of the deviation from metrical and alliterative norms in terms of textual corruption rather than authorial license. They are, in order,

line 436: *þer waspasian was with princes and dukes*;
line 797: *bot Waspasian þe wile wel ynow knewe*;
line 1175: *Eleuen hundred þousand Iewes in þe mene whyle*.

To take the last first, the archetypal version is a *Piers* line with vowel/h crossrhyme, rhyming on *in* in the b-verse — a rhyme which is unlikely to be original, and probably conceals the loss of a form such as *euenwhile* later in the line. The rhyme on *wel* in 797 is a little less suspect, but the line is feeble; unfortunately, non-L alternatives — PAUEC *of þe wer*; D *of werre wele* — for *wel ynow* have all imported it from the quatrain's end, line 800a. Line 436 also presents an absence of alternatives, but seems to us highly corrupt.

In brief, then, our edition will lend support to Duggan's view of the *aa/ax* standard, to the likelihood that alliteration in this poem was not designed to fall on unstressed syllables, and, above all, to the correctness of Duggan's characterization of the structure of the b-verse, including syntactic frames. I should add that we have found no evidence in all the variants of deliberate authorial revision or sustained scribal rewriting: to this extent our work supports a model of textual corruption rather than one of scribal participation, though I do not wish to advance this observation as a basis for generalization.

To this evidence for the usefulness of Duggan's work I add the following observations:

(1) Emendation to achieve b-verse regularity must always bear in mind that spelling systems are graphemic, not phonemic; scribes may spell trisyllabic words as if they were disyllabic, and vice versa, without intending to determine pronunciation. There is no automatic need or licence to emend orthographic forms as if they were infallible guides to pronunciation.

(2) Duggan's work so far relates almost entirely to b-verses, and provides little help with a-verses. This is not a fault, but it might be expected to operate as a check on the claims Duggan makes for the universality and scope of his conclusions. Particularly, it is inherently strange that in this account a-verses and b-verses operate differently. According to Duggan, b-verses are syllable-counted and a-verses are not. The disparity requires to be analyzed and conceptualized further.

(3) Duggan reads his evidence as demonstrating that alliterative poets counted the syllables of the b-verse, and for practical purposes we have found this to be a safe enough premise for editors. Yet the differences of reading generated by his analyses of b-verse types are almost all of the order of only (plus or minus) one syllable; and I wonder whether an analysis in terms of duration rather than number, time rather than syllables, might prove just as accurate, and allow common terms for describing a-verse and b-verse.

(4) If in fact Duggan's insistence on not counting the syllables of the a-verse is correct, we have a marked peculiarity in the alliterative unrhymed line in Middle English, driven forward from the beginning of the a-verse by its alliteration and pulled up in its b-verse by syllabic (and other) constraints. This may impact on the question of metrical provenance. Given a difference of measurement between a-verse and b-verse and a habit of counting syllables only at the end of a line, there may yet be a need to look at other models, including patterns we may not associate with poetry at all, such as *cursus* patterns (which only operate at the end of a clause, in order to mark

its termination).[10] There is still room for thinking of unrhymed alliterative poetry as a kind of metrical prose.

(5) Duggan's conviction is that his system re-opens matters of provenance. I think it does. Duggan himself associates the complexity of the metrical system he describes with its antiquity: "whether one has recourse to the recently much despised notion of oral tradition or to a theory of lost manuscript witnesses to a written tradition, it is very difficult to account for the metrical evidence discussed above without reference to a very long tradition of composition in essentially this form."[11] Theories of meter do indeed call upon hidden histories, and Duggan is right to make his public. The terms of discussion, however, require rethinking; a brisk positivism enters the discussion from the moment Duggan proclaims that "recent students have got it wrong," and one question must be whether the terms leading him to this sort of statement are not overly reductive — especially in a context where the common task is interpreting a lack of evidence. In the first place, what is the justification for looking for a single answer?

(6) The desire to describe a single phenomenon is strong in Duggan and, in subtler ways, in his colleague Turville-Petre. Both seem more comfortable than I am with a premise that one model and one explanation will meet most if not all occurrences. I have already noted Duggan's treatment of the 28 aa/xa forms in the Cotton Nero text of *Gawain*. Consistently, Turville-Petre asks: "If an editor of *Sir Gawain and the Green Knight* were to conclude that the poem was written within the same alliterative and rhythmic constraints as the *Wars*, and that the only surviving manuscript had thus been subject to a considerable degree of scribal interference, what should s/he do about it?"[12] It is a fair and provocative question, and I shall return to it; but in the absence of relevant controls, a sympathizer may yet be led to wonder what sort of data would inspire the question without also supplying the answers. In such approaches, we are back with one choice, an Alliterative Revival or an Alliterative Survival, yet without any confidence that we are not dealing with plurality and diversity, both of metrical practice and of origins. These are the issues that come together in Duggan's recurrent question: what is the relation of *Piers Plowman* to formal alliterative poems?

---

[10]For further references, see my first published article, "Gaytryge's Sermon, *Dictamen*, and Middle English Alliterative Verse," *Modern Philology* 76 (1978–79): 329–43, which treated such possible relations, albeit tentatively.

[11]For this and the other Duggan reference in this paragraph, see "Final -*e*" 145.

[12]Turville-Petre, "Editing *The Wars of Alexander*" 160.

Piers Plowman *and the Form of Prophecy*

Duggan's metrical discoveries led him to conjecture about provenance, "a very long tradition of composition in essentially this form"
("Final -*e*" 145). His receptiveness to oral-formulaic theory and its
adaptations to literate contexts has made him more prepared than
most recent scholars to think again in terms of oral tradition; and in
these linked respects his views are a timely corrective. Those of us
who have tended to underplay oral potentiality have been reacting
against the use of oral tradition as a universal and patriotic explanation in earlier scholarship: German, and then R. W. Chambers's
argument for the continuity of English prose. Chambers in effect
postulated that alliterative meter at the Norman Conquest behaved
like Hereward the Wake, and stayed alive in hiding through the
support of the people.[13] Countering such arguments has led in turn
to another kind of elision, and Duggan is right to bring oral tradition
back into play.

It will take more debate, however, to bring the terms of the question into focus. Duggan's view is based on a metrical analysis of
certain areas of poetic practice, mainly alliterative patterns and the
structure of the b-verse, and may need to be supplemented for the
purposes of research into origins, at least with an account of the a-
verse and stylistic comparison of prime features in such a manner as
to show differences to set beside those areas of metrical practice
where poets can now be shown to agree. It is necessary to ask what
the force is of "essentially" in Duggan's claim ("a very long tradition
of composition in *essentially* this form"), and how we accommodate
the changes from Old English to Middle English alliterative poetic
practice in this account: it has always seemed too conveniently in
accord with Chambers to talk of them as morphologically inevita-

---

[13]R. W. Chambers, "On the Continuity of English Prose from Alfred to More
and his School," EETS, OS 191a (1937), reprinted from his introduction to EETS,
OS 186 (1932); see my discussion of this and related issues in "Alliterative Style"
244–46.

ble.[14] I have already objected that Duggan's view may be reductively unitary, where I and others have thought increasingly in terms of diversity.[15] In the present state of knowledge and debate, it may be best to agree in general terms that all the evidence we have examined in the past for what most persist in calling "the origins of the alliterative revival" needs systematic re-examination, allowing more generously than in recent times for possibilities such as oral transmission and composition. But I should want to insist that such research will continue to deal not just with unrhymed alliterative long lines but with a variety of metrical forms, and with prose.

It may be that whatever continuities of practice we find may be more spatial than temporal in character, that what matters most is how alliterative traditions are transmitted in particular places. Turville-Petre's fine work leads the way here.[16] An example is the relationship claimed for nearly a century between *The Destruction of Troy* and *The Siege of Jerusalem*, especially in storm sequences. Huchown-style theories ascribing these to common authorship or to borrowing in one or other direction have never commanded universal assent, and have been countered by the formulaic school with the explanation that both draw on a common stock of formulaic language and may therefore be unaware of each other's existence.[17] Yet there is a sustained quality to the resemblances that has continued to intrigue some of us. From Nicolas Jacobs's demonstration of the relation between storm passages in *The Destruction of Troy* and its Latin source, Guido's *Historia Destructionis Troiae*, it seemed plausible

---

[14]Margaret M. Roseborough Stobie, "The Influence of Morphology on Middle English Alliterative Poetry," *JEGP* 39 (1940): 319–36. Duggan is more sympathetic to this sort of suggestion; indeed, he needs it for his school of oral poets whose work he supposes to have influenced the writers of the Middle English alliterative poems we possess.

[15]See my essay, "The Diversity of Middle English Alliterative Poetry," *Leeds Studies in English* 20 (1989): 143–72.

[16]Thorlac Turville-Petre, "Some Medieval English Manuscripts in the North-East Midlands," in *Manuscripts and Readers in Fifteenth-Century England: The Literary Implications of Manuscript Study*, ed. Derek Pearsall (Cambridge: D. S. Brewer, 1983), 125–41, and "The Lament for Sir John Berkeley," *Speculum* 57 (1982): 332–39.

[17]See my "Middle English Alliterative Poetry: An Introduction" 5 and 126, n.13, citing George Neilson, *Huchown of the Awle Ryale* (Glasgow: MacLehose & Sons, 1902), and Nicolas Jacobs, "Alliterative Storms: A Topos in Middle English," *Speculum* 47 (1972): 695–719.

to infer that the alliterative sea-storm topos is Latinate and patterned on Guido—in which case it also seemed reasonable to restate, though as a special case, the notion of borrowing from it in *The Siege of Jerusalem*. In fact, it turns out that both types of explanation may be needed; certainly, it is no longer a question of a sharp choice between them.

The first piece of new evidence was Turville-Petre's brilliant discovery that there is an acrostic ranged across initial letters of the books of *The Destruction of Troy* identifying its translator as one John Clerk (or John, clerk?) of Whalley.[18] The second piece of evidence is Ralph Hanna's and my judgment that the authorial dialect of *The Siege of Jerusalem* belongs at or near Bolton Abbey in Yorkshire—eight miles or so from Whalley. These combine to suggest very strongly that in the case of *The Destruction of Troy* and *The Siege of Jerusalem* we are dealing with a local school of composition, and that its practice in both poems reflects the local importance of particular models, here Guido's *Historia*. And I see no reason why we should not have to allow for a series of such local and broadly parallel developments in the explanations of provenance we may offer: the *Gawain*-manuscript provides another example, more obvious if we did not conceal it under the automatic presumption of common authorship.

In such local growths, both unity and diversity may be necessary assumptions: they produce what may reasonably be described as "essentially the same" metrical form, but different subsidiary models may nevertheless make for important differences. In the case of the poems of Cotton Nero A x, we have such a difference from other unrhymed poems in the unequivocal evidence of the interaction between rhymed and unrhymed models in *Pearl* and the bob-and-wheel of *Gawain*. That interaction is both metrical and stylistic: the influences it shows testify to one source of the lexical richness of this group, with relations like the Harley Lyrics. The fact is that these differences point to nuanced differences in transmission: in the *Gawain*-group, these poems come with different stylistic and metrical affiliations from other poems composed in broadly the same form, and the more we come to know about other groupings, the more complex is our sense of the diversities of transmission likely to be-

---

[18]Turville-Petre, "The Author of *The Destruction of Troy*," *Medium Ævum* 57 (1988): 264–69.

come. It would be truly surprising if the different influences are not reflected in some metrical and/or stylistic differences, and if the model we have fails to show them, this may be an argument for the need to refine the model itself. The logical force of such differences is what makes me resist, for the moment, Turville-Petre's and Duggan's sense that 28 apparently good lines in *Gawain* may need emendation because they do not conform to the rules applicable elsewhere—especially since their pattern, *aa/xa*, is just the pattern to show some influence from poetry with end-rhyme.[19]

Local differences among various groups of alliterative poems may mark not only different lines of transmission but also different kinds of interest, themselves provenance-related, in the use of alliterative meter. Questions about the meter of many poems may need to be set in this expanded framework: most usefully, *Piers Plowman*. Here the traces of ancillary models that may be implicated in transmission are multiple. Rhymed poetry plays a part, in short-line (*Debate Between the Body and the Soul*) and long-line types (*The Simonie*, *The South English Legendary*). So do homiletic writings of many sorts, and above all what the format of the poem on the page faithfully reflects: Latin writing, devotional, academic, legal and biblical. I am suggesting that these may not simply illustrate a difference in genre or literary purpose, but that they may be the signals of a distinctive local provenance.

The evidence from late Old English is not unambiguous, but it hardly supports a view that unrhymed alliterative poetry was altogether a healthy practice in all parts of the country at the time of the Norman conquest: the Chronicle poem for 1065, for example, is feeble. There is also, of course, no shortage of evidence for the assimilation of poetic practices into the construction of alliterative prose such as Ælfric's or Wulfstan's, and for the continuity across the verse/prose boundary of what Norman Blake helpfully characterized as "rhythmical alliteration."[20] It is one of the ironies of Chambers's position that he chose to cite alliterative poetry as a parallel continuity from Old English when he was doing much to provide another

---

[19]See above, pp. 151–52 and 159. See also my "Larger Patterns of Syntax in Middle English Unrhymed Alliterative Verse," *Neophilologus* 64 (1980): 604–18, for the difference made by end-rhyme.

[20]N. F. Blake, "Rhythmical Alliteration," *Modern Philology* 67 (1969–70): 118–24.

vehicle, prose, that might have conveyed a good deal of alliterative practice into Middle English. In recent years we may have stressed this alternative far too exclusively, as Duggan urges; but if there is any virtue in a model of locally different patterns of transmission, then this remains one possible type. All we know about the general area of the production of *Piers Plowman* — which corresponds to the general area in which Old English homiletic prose was preserved and in which it can be seen to have decomposed into a series of other forms, verse and prose — tallies with the major differences in affiliated model. *Piers Plowman* may demonstrate a transmission from Old English poetic practice in which prose and poetry were already mixed. It implies a function for Middle English alliterative poetry in which the construction of a homiletic voice or voices may be more important than metrical virtuosity (though I have no wish to present these as polar opposites). The function is valued across a range of alliterative poems, as in the homiletic passage at the end of *The Parliament of the Three Ages*; it is not unique to *Piers*. But there is no knowing at the present whether its appearance elsewhere is influenced by *Piers* itself or, equally probable, marks a supplementary model that may have been active in transmission. Not all such models will have made for metrical precision.

Possibilities such as this have presented themselves in my work for several years, not least in my edition of *Joseph of Arimathea*.[21] The sole copy of this work, in the Vernon manuscript, presents certain highly unusual features: it is written in prose format, but with a punctuation system that marks verses, and is wildly irregular in its alliterative patterning. In attempting to explain these features, I made a tentative suggestion that failed to win universal assent: that the Vernon copy might show a poem in the process of composition, lacking its final alliterative reworking. There is no need for this proposal to involve drastic and discrete states of revision: Barry Windeatt's view of the composition of *Troilus* is similar, and simply supposes fluctuating stages in a continuum during which the demands of meter and source are accommodated.[22] I retain an agnostic attitude towards this possibility, but that contrasts with the certainty

---

[21] *Joseph of Arimathea*, ed. David Lawton (New York: Garland, 1983).

[22] Geoffrey Chaucer, *Troilus and Criseyde: A New Edition of "The Book of Troilus"*, ed. B. A. Windeatt (London: Longman, 1984), 36.

of subsequent refutations. Duggan, for example, briskly expressed the doubt (consistent with an oral-formulaic hypothesis) that alliterative poets ever composed in any such way (by means of something like a prose first draft), and ascribed the state of the Vernon copy to textual corruption, comparing *Joseph* to the state of *Chevalere Assigne* as it occurs uniquely in Cotton Caligula A ii ("The Shape of the B-Verse" 567, n.3).

This may well be right. Duggan's rules empower a drastic re-editing of *Joseph*, and perhaps it ought to be done as an enterprise in conjecture. The rules will work if one judges that this is the right place to apply them: but is it? There is no doubt about the case of *Chevalere Assigne*: it is thoroughly corrupt, it occurs as the work of a scribe who tampers with alliteration, often but not consistently by removing it, and it can probably be usefully re-edited as an essay in conjectural emendation mainly in accord with Duggan's rules. This would be an interesting extension of the editing of *The Siege of Jerusalem*, and the scribe's handling of that text would be the major comparison and control (a control which is needed in order for the editor to anchor conjecture). It is the obvious analogy to make with *Joseph*, and it is one that I carefully considered from the start. Yet the principle of economy, if too hastily invoked, would itself become a foundation for illogic. The Vernon scribe is not at all like the Cotton scribe: he seems at home with alliterative poetry, and has copied *Piers* as the item immediately preceding *Joseph*. In fact, the inclusion of *Joseph* may derive at least partly from a desire to continue with alliterative work, and might even show a link with *Piers* in transmission. If so, the scribe's different format may testify to a different understanding of form.[23]

As it seems to me, we cannot discount the possibility that on the available evidence (or lack of it) *Joseph* may be an example of a different kind of alliterative writing from the formal poetry of the "alliterative revival." There is no need to see a relative looseness as a sign of an earlier date: the differences can all be accommodated in

---

[23]Of course, if the scribe had merely acquired an already corrupt copy of *Joseph*, his understanding would count for little. But this is not what the evidence of the source leads one to think. The irregular writing of the English text is often relatively close translation. Conversely, occasional passages of more regular writing mark drastic elisions from and abbreviations of the source. The balance of probability is that the Vernon copy is a decent record of a redactor's program.

the model of different local provenances for alliterative writing, as outlined above.[24] It may also be that understanding of the form of *Joseph* cannot be separated from understanding of its subject. In the edition I characterized this in terms of the conversion of pagan rulers, but I can perhaps rephrase that in terms more immediately relevant to *Piers Plowman*: prophecy.

The importance of prophecy to *Piers* has been explored by several scholars, from Morton Bloomfield on. David Fowler has considered biblical sources and parallels, and in his essay in *A Companion to Piers Plowman* Stephen Barney makes shrewd and stimulating sugges-tions.[25] At about the same time A. V. C. Schmidt was making simi-lar comments about *Cleanness*.[26] A recent study by Theodore L. Steinberg considers the issue at length, and does much to fore-ground it in *Piers* studies, though problems of focus, definition and concept remain.[27] Most helpful in considering these are general works on prophecy, not least the proceedings of the 1986 Harvard conference on "Poetry and Prophecy" published in 1990 in a book of that name, with the significant subtitle: "the beginnings of a literary tradition."[28] The primary reference is to the prophetic books of the Jewish Bible; but in this context the idea of prophecy is hardly separable from a Christian reading of the Jewish Bible that turns it

---

[24]Duggan makes a similar point in "Alliterative Patterning" 102, n.39.

[25]Morton W. Bloomfield, "Joachim of Flora: A Critical Survey of his Canon, Teachings, Sources, Biography, and Influence," *Traditio* 13 (1957): 249–311, and *Piers Plowman as a Fourteenth-century Apocalypse* (New Brunswick, NJ: Rutgers Univer-sity Press, 1961); David Fowler, *The Bible in Middle English Literature* (Seattle: Uni-versity of Washington Press, 1984); Stephen A. Barney, "Allegorical Visions," in *A Companion to Piers Plowman* (n.1 above), 117–33. See also R. K. Emmerson, "The Prophetic, the Apocalyptic, and the Study of Medieval Literature," in *Poetic Prophecy in Western Literature*, ed. Jan Wojcik and Raymond-Jean Frontain (Cranbury, NJ: Associated University Presses, 1984), 40–54.

[26]". . . the basic mode of *Purity* is less akin to that of scholastic theology than to that of Biblical prophecy: it aims less to persuade than to challenge": A. V. C. Schmidt, "*Kynde Craft* and the *Play of Paramorez*: Natural and Unnatural Love in *Purity*," in *Genres, Themes and Images in English Literature from the Fourteenth to the Fifteenth Century*, J. A. W. Bennett Memorial Lectures, Perugia, 1986 (Tubingen: Gunter Narr Verlag, 1988), 105–24, esp. 124.

[27]*Piers Plowman and Prophecy: An Approach to the C-Text* (New York and London: Garland, 1991).

[28]*Poetry and Prophecy: The Beginnings of a Literary Tradition*, ed. James L. Kugel (Ithaca and London: Cornell University Press, 1990). See also Stephen Geller, "Were the Prophets Poets?" *Prooftexts* 3 (1983): 211–21.

into the Old Testament and so renders most of the book prophetic, in a looser sense, of its fulfilment in the New. This reading shifts prophecy from its meaning of "speaking for" (God, morality) to one of "speaking about and in anticipation of" (God, morality, future events). The Jewish Bible is read as a privileged vision of a Christian future, and becomes the model for reading that future as it extends beyond the reader. Therefore it inaugurates a literary tradition, a tradition that produces *Piers Plowman*. The question is to what extent the form and meter of *Piers* express that tradition as well as a more limited alliterative one.

To ask this question is not, as it may appear, to mix evidence of form with evidence of genre. For they are inseparable, not just in the nature of *Piers* but also in that of prophecy. It is the prophetic tradition that writes itself into literary consciousness as the high style of the Bible, as its most elevated or poetic utterance, such as is found in the Psalms or much of Isaiah or the Song of Songs. And in using the word "poetic" here I call up a keen controversy about what James L. Kugel has called "the idea of Biblical poetry." Were these more elevated portions of the Hebrew Bible designed to be metrical? This has been a common view among Biblical scholars since Lowth in the eighteenth century, and influences a strange typographical habit of verse format for the generally prosaic renderings of modern translations. Kugel traces its origin in Jewish Alexandrian commentary and its pervasive influence in the Christian tradition, and objects to the idea strongly. He does so on two sorts of grounds: formal, given the failure to find a metrical description of the "rules" by which such writing proceeds; and moral, his desire to reject anything that feeds a notion of the Bible as literature.[29]

Kugel is also the editor of the volume of essays on prophecy that I have cited, and his introduction makes clear how linked the formal and generic issues are. The literary tradition prophecy inaugurates is that of poet as prophet, but there is an accompanying ambivalence about the notion of human craftsmanship. If prophecy is poetry, it is not just poetry — for poetry is human work. If prophecy is the word of God, it is not poetry, whatever the formal similarities. The Sibyl, not the Lord of Hosts, speaks in hexameters. Yet the elevation of

---

[29]See n.3 above, and my discussion of Kugel's views in my *Faith, Text and History: The Bible in English* (Charlottesville: University Press of Virginia, 1990), 69–70, 78.

language is a sign of God's presence or sanction. Therefore prophecy is like poetry, and transcends it.

This begins to sound a lot like the persistent mulling over good and bad poetry in *Piers Plowman*. Do Kugel's twin preoccupations apply? Can we speak of "the idea of alliterative poetry" in a manner parallel to Kugel's "idea of Biblical poetry," a use of craft in which there is both ambivalence and ambiguity? Ambiguity, because its formal qualities defeat discriminations, albeit historically variable ones, between verse and prose. Ambivalence, because the presence of human workmanship signified by meter compromises the divinity of its voice. Poetry is Will's work. Moreover, this is a work written at a time when the "poetic" quality of Hebrew is represented in the careful prose periods of the Vulgate, so that it is conveyed by rhetorical patterning of various kinds but primarily by clause-endings. *Piers Plowman* is written from a cultural desire to render into English the style of the Bible, to be, if not Bible translation, then at the least a substitute for it. Alliterative writing is the English mode of (Latinate) prophecy. Unlike Hebrew prophecy, it has a demonstrable metrical structure. But what we know about that meter at the moment emphasizes constraints of clause-ending, the b-verse, and may indicate a looser, less formal attitude to metrical constraints (the coincidence of stress and alliteration) in the line as a whole. Could this constitute a deliberate departure from strict meter in order to satisfy the text's own distrust of it? Or does it show instead the trace of a different and local provenance in which alliterative writing registers the prophetic impulse from Old English homilies onwards?

In the end I do not see how we can consider the meter of *Piers Plowman* without asking such questions as well. That is why this essay has moved out from its more technical base. I propose that we need to bring together two different types of scholarship. Generic scholarship, such as Steinberg's, which speaks relatively hazily of the poem's "disjunctive style" (90), desperately needs a more precise technical focus. Metrical scholarship will have to consider voice as well as meter if in fact, as the role of prophecy suggests, both are integral to and related in the enterprise of the poem.[30] Prophecy has formal ramifications. Form too has prophetic consequences.

---

[30]Very few scholars move with equal confidence between these two fields. David Fowler, as one who does, is a rare resource.

Piers Plowman:
Indirect Relations and the Record of Truth

PRISCILLA MARTIN

T HIS ARTICLE GREW OUT of a paper, "Indirect Relations: The
Misty Syntax Of *Piers Plowman*," in which I examined the com-
parisons suggested by the grammatical analogy in C between good
grammar and good living and considered whether similar moral
implications could be drawn from the syntax of the poem.[1] When I
tried to analyze the syntax, I found it strangely elusive. One of the
poet's many sardonic comments on misuse of language haunted me:
"Thow myȝtest bettre meete myst on Maluerne hilles" (B Prol.215).[2]
My critical strategies felt equally futile. Yet the mistiness of the
syntax seemed functional to the mystery of the poem. Dame Study
admits: "Ac Theologie haþ tened me ten score tymes; / The moore I
muse þerInne þe mystier it semeþ, / And þe depper I deuyne[d] þe
derker me [þouȝte]" (B X.185–87), but she attests to the profundity,
not the obscurantism, of the subject. This paper will also start from
the grammatical analogy but will develop it in rather different direc-

[1]Delivered at Fifteenth Annual Conference of the Medieval Association of the
Pacific at the Claremont Colleges, February 18–20, 1982. The *Piers Plowman* ses-
sions were organized by David Fowler. The section on gender was presented as a
paper at the Twenty-Second International Congress on Medieval Studies at Western Michigan University, Kalamazoo, May 7–10, 1987.
[2]Except where I note otherwise, quotations from *Piers Plowman* are from *Piers
Plowman: The A Version*, ed. George Kane (London: Athlone Press, 1960); *Piers
Plowman: The B Version*, ed. George Kane and E. Talbot Donaldson (London:
Athlone Press, 1975); *Piers Plowman by William Langland: An Edition of the C-text*, ed.
Derek Pearsall, York Medieval Texts, second series (London: Edward Arnold,
1978; Berkeley: University of California Press, 1979).

tions. After considering the passage in C, I shall turn to one grammatical feature and one syntactical feature of *Piers*: gender and its influence on personification; direct and indirect speech and the thematic contrasts between some examples of each. Finally I shall consider the problems and significance of "relationships" in the verbal detail and larger organization of the poem.

The Grammatical Analogy

Piers Plowman is such a very strange poem that it is difficult to answer the question "What is it about?" However, there are two replies that are rather different in kind, which are perhaps inadequate and yet which are both evidently correct. First, it is about the Dreamer's own question to Holy Church in the first passus, "How can I save my soul?" Holy Church answers the question immediately with the orthodox Christian teaching which, as she emphasizes, he ought already to know, but the poem does not close here. It explores the implications of the question and the answers to it, the nature of the narrator who can ask such a question, and the contexts in which the standard Christian answers may not seem so obvious as the Church insists. This is, in one sense, the subject of *Piers Plowman*.

The second reply is "It's about language itself," about the problems of conducting this enquiry in the inadequate, approximate, accommodated language of the fallen world, about the status and usefulness of the poem and about the author/narrator's fitness as poet and person to compose a work on this subject. "How can I talk about saving my soul?" The two questions interlock because an attempt to answer the first raises all the difficulties inherent in the second. The treachery of language mirrors the instability of the fallen world.

The poet focuses explicitly on the connections between ambiguous or incorrect uses of language and sinful dishonest behavior. He sees the proper understanding and use of language as vital to salvation. The importance of sound teaching in the verbal arts is stressed in the marriage of Study to Clergy and in the repeated defenses of learning given to the sceptical dreamer: without it the doctrines of the Church could not be transmitted or the sacraments celebrated. The doctrine of the Trinity is supported by God's use of the plural form in Genesis 1:26: *"Faciamus."* Christ wrote in the dust and saved the life of the woman taken in adultery, figuring the crucial role of the clerkly skills for Christian salvation. Patience's riddle, which encapsulates Dowel, opens with a statement of faith in the value of language and the power of its rules:

> Kynde loue coueiteþ noȝt no catel but speche.
> Wiþ half a laumpe lyne in latyn, *Ex vi transicionis*,
> I bere þer, [in a bouste] faste ybounde, dowel . . . .
>
> (B XIII.150–52)

In his demonstration that the Latin phrase should be rendered as "by the power of transitivity," R. E. Kaske discusses the concept of grammatical *regimen*, developed in the thirteenth century.[3] He quotes a thirteenth-century author who explains how the term *"regere"* is used of grammar by analogy with its use in *"natura"*: *"Sicut in natura illud dicitur regere aliud, quod non sinit illud deviare, similiter in arte illa dictio dicitur regere aliam, que non sinit illam poni in alio casu vel genere vel numero"* (38; Blanch 235).

Individual words come under close scrutiny. Sometimes a word is illuminated by an understanding of its etymology: Anima explains that "heathen" is derived from "heath" ("Heþen is to mene after heeþ and vntiled erþe" [B XV.459]). Sometimes the behavior of sinners is seen as a denial of the true meaning of their name. The word "cardinal" is derived from *"cardo,"* the Latin for "hinge": there are four virtues "[t]hat Cardinals ben called and closynge yates / There [crist is in] kyngdom, to close and to shette, / And to opene it to hem and heuene blisse shewe" (B Prol.104–6), but it is implied that "þe Cardinals at court þat kauȝte of þat name" (B Prol.107) are notoriously unworthy of such power; later a "lewed vicory" (B XIX.409) is quite unable to apply the word to any virtues and understands it only of mighty parasites: "I knew neuere Cardynal þat he ne cam fro þe pope, / And we clerkes, whan þei come, for hir comunes paieþ, / For hir pelure and palfreyes mete and pilours þat hem folweþ"

---

[3] "'*Ex vi transicionis*' and Its Passage in *Piers Plowman*," *JEGP* 62 (1963), 32–60; reprinted in *Style and Symbolism in Piers Plowman* ed. Robert J. Blanch (Knoxville: University of Tennessee Press, 1969), 228–63. See also Cynthia Renée Bland, "Langland's Use of the Term *Ex vi transicionis*," *Yearbook of Langland Studies* 2 (1988): 125–35.

(B XIX.413–15). In the confession of the Deadly Sins Coueitise claims that verbal ignorance and confusion caused him to commit theft rather than make amends: "I wende riflynge were restitucion for I lerned neu*ere* rede on boke" (B V.235). The personification allegory assumes an authority in the name itself, which, early in the poem, causes intense anxiety about the polysemous quality of Meed or reward.

The first vision deals with the problem of Meed, the question of what constitutes just payment and the economic ordering of society. It centers on the definition of the word "Meed." The character Meed is superficially attractive and claims to stand for the healthy circulation of clean money, for just payment honestly rendered for valuable service, for the reward proffered by a generous lord to his loyal followers. Conscience exposes her as standing only — or equally — for bribery and corruption. Meed, he claims, is exploiting the ambiguity of her name and arrogating to this word the meanings which would be properly expressed by the term "mesurable hire" (B III.256).

In the C-Version the poet makes some important additions to the speech in which Conscience analyzes the nature of Meed. He apparently coins the term "mercede," in distinction to "meed," for the concept of just monetary payment. He also adds the long passage in which the different operations of "meed" and "mercede" are illustrated by the "grammatical analogy" (C III.332–405). This is not the only occasion in *Piers Plowman* in which a painstaking attempt to clarify an issue leaves it more deeply enshrouded in mist, and I am not sure that I understand this passage in detail. However, the general thesis is fairly clear: right and wrongful payment may be compared respectively with direct and indirect relationships in grammar. There are several illuminating discussions of the passage and the commentary in Pearsall's edition is very helpful.[4] Nobody, however, succeeds in clearing up all the ambiguities. As far as possible, I shall avoid repeating previous accounts and shall concentrate

---

[4]Pearsall 78–82. And see also John A. Alford, "The Grammatical Metaphor: A Survey of Its Use in the Middle Ages," *Speculum* 57 (1982): 728–60; Margaret Amassian and James Sadowsky, "Mede and Mercede: A Study of the Grammatical Metaphor in 'Piers Plowman' C:IV.335–409," *Neuphilologische Mitteilungen* 72 (1971): 457–76; Mary Carruthers, *The Search for Saint Truth: A Study of Meaning in Piers*

on the implications of the terms "direct" and "indirect" relationship. Two grammatical relationships are used as examples. The first is that of an adjective and the noun it qualifies: these are in direct relationship when they agree in "kind" (gender), case and number. The second example is that of antecedent and relative pronoun: these too are in direct relationship when they agree in gender, case and number. Derek Pearsall reminds us in his note to the passage (78–79) that here indirect relationship need not be a solecism ("The man to whom I spoke"), but the text does not explicitly make this point. Characteristically, the poet expresses a rule in terms so strict that we must consider exceptions and extensions.

The king asks for some help with this terminology. Conscience responds with definitions and examples of direct and indirect relationship. Direct relationship, "[r]elacoun rect," is a "record of treuthe . . . / Folowynge and fyndynge out þe fundement of a strenghe, / And styfliche stande forth to strenghe þe fundement . . ." (C III.343–45). In Pearsall's translation: "Direct relation is a remembrance of and witness to truth, reflecting in its nature the firm foundation of concord, and acting to strengthen that foundation." So correct grammar is an analogue of the divine ordering of the cosmos and in employing it we collaborate with God's harmonious purpose.

Pearsall expands the term "record" to "remembrance and witness," emphasizing the cognitive, ethical and legal aspects of the term. It is a standard explanation of grammatical relationship, "a record of what has gone before," but it is rich with further connotations. It is also a legal term: the *MED* (s.v. -record(e- n. 5.a) gives as one definition "a written account of legal proceedings kept as conclusive evidence" and notes (5.c) the expression "place of record" for a court. This sense of "record of treuthe" reinforces the legal sense of "relacoun rect": according to John A. Alford's glossary of legal diction in *Piers*, "relacioun" is "in law, the action of relating or narrating (an

Plowman (Evanston: Northwestern University Press, 1973), 18, 82–83; A. G. Mitchell, "Lady Meed and the Art of *Piers Plowman*," The Third Chambers Memorial Lecture (London: H. K. Lewis, 1956)—reprinted in Blanch, 174–93; Daniel Maher Murtaugh, *Piers Plowman and the Image of God* (Gainesville: University Presses of Florida, 1978), 48–50; and J. A. Yunck, *The Lineage of Lady Meed: The Development of Medieval Venality Satire*, University of Notre Dame Publications in Mediaeval Studies 17 (Notre Dame: University of Notre Dame Press, 1983).

account, plea, report, etc.)."[5] The "record of treuthe" reminds us of the historical basis of Christianity and the duty of the Christian to bear witness to it. The concept is central to Christian society and to the individual Christian. Penitence, like history, depends on memory: "whan I make mone to god *memoria* is my name" (B XV. 26), says Anima, the soul. The poem itself aspires to be a record of truth; imagination and memory are linked.[6] After the vision of the Harrowing of Hell Will attests: "I awaked and wroot what I hadde ydremed" (B XIX.1). Direct relationship in grammar both enables and is an instance of the record of truth.

Pearsall uses the term "concord" to translate the noun "strenghe," presumably because "concord" has a secondary sense in Modern English, as "strenghe" (*vis*) has in Middle English. This clarifies the passage for the modern reader but sacrifices the wordplay by which the verb "strenghe" in the next line emphasizes the reciprocity of act and paradigm. (Various other features of the lines — the alliteration of "folowynge," "fyndynge," "fundement," and "styfliche," "stande," "strenghe," the modulation of the participles into the main verb, the chiasmus in juxtaposed lines of "fundement" and "strenghe" — suggest first the obedient agreement of language correctly used, then its active role in maintaining our awareness of its structures.) The grammatical analogy appeals to the medieval love of system and correspondence, ideas of harmony which Christianity inherited from classical philosophy. In Pythagorean and Platonic thought, the universe is an orderly creation of the Divine Mind or Logos, comprehensible in terms of the laws of music and mathematics. Christianity enshrines in the opening of St. John's Gospel the idea of the Logos or Verbum as an image of God. During the medieval period the transmission of the word of God through a written medium, the growth of monasticism with its commitment to copying and exegesis, the connection of the love of learning with the love of God and

---

[5] *Piers Plowman: A Glossary of Legal Diction* (Cambridge [Eng.]: D. S. Brewer, 1988), 130. See also his entry on "recorden," 127–28.

[6] Morton W. Bloomfield, *Piers Plowman as a Fourteenth-Century Apocalypse* (New Brunswick: Rutgers University Press, 1962), 170–74, and Carruthers 101, closely connect *vis imaginativa* and *memoria*. This connection or identification is questioned by Britton J. Harwood, "Imaginative in *Piers Plowman*," *Medium Ævum* 44 (1975): 249–63, and John M. Bowers, *The Crisis of Will in "Piers Plowman"* (Washington: Catholic University of America Press, 1986), 160–61.

the fact that literacy was largely confined to the clergy invest the laws of language with numinous power. To the thirteenth-century author quoted by Kaske grammar has *vis*, can be said to *regere* and is to be understood as operating analogously to nature. People learn related truths from the book of God and the book of Nature.

The analogical habit of thought is fundamental to *Piers Plowman*. Drawing on the venerable tradition of correspondences between the various parts of the cosmos, the poet supports his argument with *exempla*: he adapts the fable of the belling of the cat to topical use; the swimmer and the non-swimmer in the Thames "prove" that learning is conducive to salvation; the rich man is like the peacock, magnificent but earthbound. He dramatizes typology, the study of analogies between the Old and New Testament, in the characters of Abraham and Moses who symbolize Faith and Hope and prefigure the priest and the Levite in the parable, inadequate without the Samaritan/Charity/Christ. The belief that humanity is created in the image of God is vital to the theory of salvation. That likeness is affirmed in the Incarnation and ratified in the Atonement. At the great climax of the poem Christ harrows Hell and redeems humanity from the devil on the basis of their common human nature: "I in liknesse of a leode, þat lord am of heuene, / Graciousliche þi gile haue quyt" (B XVIII.356–57). Human society mirrors divine. Christ the King has the power, like an earthly king seeing a condemned man, to reprieve from sentence of death and tells Satan that his likeness to humanity makes the exercise of that power natural: "I were an vnkynde kyng but I my kynde helpe" (B XVIII.398).

The concept of society as a system of direct relationships is an attractive one. It confers on a large society some of the warmth and closeness of a small one, attempting to knit together disparate elements with strong family ties. It postulates as the norm Piers's fellow-feeling with the wastrels ("my blody breþeren for god bouȝte vs alle" [B VI.207]), the earthly version of Christ's promise of mercy at the Harrowing of Hell: "to be merciable to man þanne my kynde [it] askeþ, / For we beþ breþeren of blood" (B XVIII.375–76). Conscience's first example of a direct relationship is a social one, the true laborer and the good master, which allegorically suggests the hope of the Christian soul for its heavenly reward. Family relationships and their verbal aspects may also be seen in these terms: the son should take his father's surname since he is in direct descent from him.

Contracts, such as marriage, involve an acceptance of all their clauses, for good or ill, not a selective and partial agreement. There is a political implication, an established concept of right relations in the kingdom: the king is entitled to demand of the *comune* that they follow him, provide for him and give him counsel; they in turn require from him law, love and *leaute*.

These bonds and analogies have a theological foundation. The relation between God and man, as Conscience explains in his grammatical figure, should be like a direct relation between antecedent and relative: man agrees with Christ in "kind"—"gender" in the grammatical analogy, "nature" in the theological exposition— through the Incarnation. More obscurely, man is also said to agree with God in case, through belief in the Church, and in number through the resurrection of the body, the remission of sins and life everlasting with Christ (presumably these three articles of faith reflect the Trinity). God is both antecedent and substantive; man should "agree" with God like an adjective which correctly qualifies a noun.[7] But at the end of this passage there are several bold and paradoxical reversals: the Lord "coueytede oure kynde and be kald in oure name . . . / And nyme hym in to oure noumbre now and eueremore" (C III.401-2). Christian theology is both the foundation of the laws of nature and an affront to reason. In incarnating himself as man God covets another nature, adopts another name and, though infinite and eternal, limits himself to our number now and for ever, in time and eternity. The grammatical terms shift likewise and God becomes the adjective, man the noun seeking the three correct kinds of agreement in the three persons of the Trinity, the "thre trewe termisones" (C III.405), his end in all senses.

The moral vocabulary that the grammatical analogy associates with direct relations is "lele," "styfliche," "holy," "hardy," "trewe" and "rihte trewe," "resonable," "ryhtful custume." Conscience suggests that direct relationships are truthful, rational, stable, reliable, traditional, sanctified by both human and divine law.

---

[7]Alford ("Grammatical Metaphor" 758) comments on agreement in case and number: "Just as case is a sign of grammatical function, so the king and the church serve to indicate the functions of our political and spiritual lives . . . . Lack of concord, either with Christ or with secular authority, means the multiplicity of separate wills."

Indirect relationships, by contrast, are described as a sort of rebellious promiscuity or irresponsible detachment:

Indirect thyng is as ho-so coueytede
Alle kyn hynde to knowe and to folowe
And withoute cause to cache and come to bothe nombres;
In whiche ben gode and nat gode to graunte here neyþer will. . . .
So indirect is inlyche to coueyte
To acorde in alle kynde and in alle kyn nombre,
Withouten coest and care and alle kyn trauayle.

(C III.362–65, 370–72)

Indirect relation is, like the Dreamer himself, accused of wanting knowledge of all kinds of kind. It is also wanting to follow every kind of kind. This may suggest, for example, the disloyalty many of the poet's contemporaries perceived in the migrant worker who will move to a new master for higher wages. Or it may hint at the unbridled and undiscriminating promiscuity of which Meed is accused, even at — if "Alle kyn kynde" suggests a multiplicity of species and genders — polymorphous perversity. Conscience initially describes Meed as "tikel of here tayl . . . / As comyn as þe cartway" (C III.166–67); it becomes clear that anyone who weds Meed will be a cuckold (C III.157–61); "þe comune calde here queynte comune hore" (C IV.161). After Reason's climactic speech denouncing Meed, "al ryhtful recordede þat Resoun treuthe sayde" (C IV.151), a collocation of some of the words that described direct relationships. Like a direct relationship in grammar, Reason produces in denouncing Meed a rightful "record of treuthe" confirmed and remembered by the righteous. Yet some of the terms explaining indirection anticipate the closing description of the Incarnation in which God covets the kind and number of humanity.

I find III.364–65 perplexing. Villainous indirection is apparently analogous to a word prepared unreasonably to agree with both singular and plural forms. Pearsall comments: "Indirect relation makes a chaos of concord, since it seeks to grasp everything to itself: in terms of grammar, it seeks relationship on the basis of all genders and both numbers. This is confusion, the more so because it confounds the one aspect of the relation that is proper . . . . To refuse the claims of *mede* is good, but in a way not good (365) since there is always some degree of direct relation or entitlement. . . ." As I understand it, a word which is willing to attach itself to either a singular or a plural form is bound to apply itself correctly sometimes. This quality, however, makes it not figuratively partly good but more deeply depraved because it obscures the correct understanding of concord and allegorically further befogs the dense moral confusion of life. If it *always* behaved wrongly, its impropriety would be easier to identify and condemn. The fact that indirect relationship in grammar is sometimes correct, as when the case of a noun or pronoun in the main clause is different from that of a relative pronoun in a subordinate clause, contributes to the flexibility of the analogy.

Just as "case" can be violated in its grammatical sense, it can, punningly, be abused in its general meaning of "situation" and perhaps also in its legal sense. This is appropriate to the legal setting of the dispute about the nature of Meed and the plea brought by Peace against Wrong. It is lawyers who are condemned in that haunting image in the Prologue: "Thow my3test bettre meete myst on Maluerne hilles / Than gete a mom of hire mouþ til moneie be shewed" (B Prol.215–16). At the end of the *Visio* it is they who are granted the least share in the pardon from Truth. There is possibly some play on "case" and "cause," which may have led to some scribal confusion between the words: this would further link the ungrammatical with the unlawful and irrational. Indirect relation is "withoute cause," "nat resonable," "inparfit," "vnstedefast." In short, indirect relationship in grammar is one of the many ways in which language is infected by and expresses the deceptive, ambiguous, untrustworthy, inharmonious nature of this fallen world. The issue is further complicated by the fact that, as we observed earlier, some indirect relationships are grammatically correct.

However, if indirect relations are misty, the theory of direct relations shines with a deceptive clarity. Like various other doctrines affirmed in *Piers Plowman* this grammatical blueprint may prove too simple and static to accommodate the unruly behavior of the poem's teeming world within its prescriptions. In *Chaucer, Langland and the Creative Imagination*, David Aers suggests that Langland draws traditional diagrams of Church and state which are contradicted by his picture of a complex, fluid and energetically changing society and its "unstable relationships."[8] Perhaps these linguistic paradigms are similarly abstract and archaic. There are, I think, serious objections to the grammatical figure itself. First, while it purports to elucidate the English word "meed" by an analysis presented in English, it is based on Latin grammar. The king confesses that it is alien to him: "Knowen y wolde / What is relacion rect and indirect aftur, / Thenne adiectyf, and sustantyf, for Englisch was it neuere" (C III.340–42). Perhaps we are meant to understand a hermeneutic gap between the two. Latin is often used in *Piers* as the vehicle of revelation, the language of the celestial and incorruptible, English as the vernacular of the earthly and approximate.[9] Secondly, the use of Latin grammar to explain or prescribe English usage was becoming even less appropriate, because English was changing. Two of the linguistic features prominent in Conscience's explication of concord — case and gender — were dying out in later Middle English. It was, indeed, a period at which the idea of linguistic "correctness" was particularly difficult to realize. Instead of one correct inflection, there were now merely alternative possibilities. The grammatical analogy may indeed, applied more descriptively, be a vivid metaphor for a fluid and experimental society or for an ethical system which recognizes that circumstances alter cases.

Gender

The grammatical analogy seeks to demonstrate that proper personal, economic and spiritual relationships correspond to correct agreement between words and improper relationships to solecism. In Latin nouns and adjectives should agree with each other in number, case and gender. In the grammatical analogy Conscience gives no examples of agreement in gender and the word he uses synonymously with "gendre" (C III.394) is "kynde," which serves the purpose of his argument in its larger and more usual sense of "nature":

---

[8](London: Routledge & Kegan Paul, 1980), 6.
[9]See E. Peter Nolan, "Beyond Macaronic: Embedded Latin in Dante and Langland," *Acta Conventus Neo-Latini Bononiensis: Proceedings of the Fourth International Congress of Neo-Latin Studies*, ed. Richard J. Schoeck, Medieval and Renaissance Texts and Studies 37 (Binghamton: CEMERS, 1985), 539–48.

"He [humanity] acordeth with Crist in kynde, *Verbum caro factum est*" (C III.355). In this section I shall argue that the original gender of terms in Latin exerts little influence in *Piers Plowman* and that the sense of grammatical gender, which had virtually died out of English by this period, is unstable or even arbitrary in the personification allegory of this poem.[10]

There is a tendency in English language, literature and visual art for a personified abstraction to be female if the Latin word which it translates or from which it is derived is feminine. This may be somewhat counteracted in Middle English if the original gender of a native word was not feminine. But the influence of Latin was reinforced by that of French, in which feminine nouns derived from Latin usually retain their gender. Favorite literary texts in Latin and French supplied notable female allegorical figures, such as Philosophy in Boethius's *Consolatio* and Reason in the *Roman de la Rose*, "dame Resoun" (*RR* 5149) as she is called in the Middle English translation.

Chaucer, who translated the whole of the *Consolatio* and at least part of the *Roman*, follows European tradition in his female personifications of the feminine *Fama, Fortuna, Voluntas, Pax, Patientia, Fides* and *Natura*. He hypostatizes Fame and Fortune as the familiar capricious goddesses. In the Garden of Love in *The Parliament of Fowls* we find the female characters "Wille," the "doughter" of Cupid (214), "Dame Pees" (240) with "Dame Pacience" (242) at the door of the Temple of Venus, and presiding over the debate the "noble em-

---

[10]Morton W. Bloomfield — in "A Grammatical Approach to Personification Allegory," *Modern Philology* 60 (1962–63); repr. *Essays and Explorations: Studies in Ideas, Language and Literature* (Cambridge, MA: Harvard University Press, 1970) — remarks: "Historically, in English, we find a curious phenomenon. As personification came into the literature on a vast scale, the language was at the same time undergoing a process of neutralization by which many masculine and feminine nouns were becoming neuter. Personification in English had to contend with neutralization in the common and public language. Whether this struggle made personification more or less attractive to English writers, given the general poetic tendency to violate grammar, I cannot say . . ."(*Modern Philology* 165; Blanch 249).

As I noted above, this section was completed before the publication of Helen Cooper's recent essay on the topic, "Gender and Personification in *Piers Plowman*," *Yearbook of Langland Studies* 5 (1991): 31–48

peresse" Nature (319). Good faith is also an "emperice" (55) in the short poem "The Former Age."[11]

Piers Plowman also uses some stock female characters and confrontations. There is the dispute between the Four Daughters of God in B xviii and the opposition of Holy Church to Meed in the Visio. Holy Church, the bride of Christ, belongs to the tradition of noble female abstractions, such as Victory and Justice, and female mentors, such as Philosophy. The contrast between Holy Church and Meed, truth versus error, stern simplicity versus seductiveness, has analogues in other tableaux of opposed female figures, such as Sacred and Profane Love or the Church and the Synagogue.

Most of the personifications in Piers Plowman, however, that are derived from Latin feminine nouns or traditionally personified as female are masculine. The central character, Will himself, is in one aspect Voluntas. But he is male and he plays (however imperfectly) the masculine roles of clerk, husband and father. There are other masculine characters whose Latin names are feminine: Conscience (Conscientia), Reason (Ratio), Imaginatif (Vis Imaginativa), Anima, Patience (Patientia), Peace (Pax), Truth (Veritas) Faith (Fides), Hope (Spes), and Kynde (Natura). Conscience and Reason, closely associated in the poem, are male characters and play some specifically masculine roles: Conscience is a knight and Reason a preacher. Faith and Hope are both masculine and in the multi-leveled allegory of the Samaritan represent the male characters of Abraham and Moses and the priest and the Levite of the parable. "Truth" and "Kynde" are both used as masculine names of God. In the allegory of the castle Will is told that "Kynde haþ closed þerInne, craftily wiþalle, / A lemman þat he loveþ lik to hymselue" (B IX.5-6). When he asks who Kynde is, he is told: "Kynde . . . is creatour of alle kynnes [beestes], Fader and formour" (B IX.26-27). All the Deadly Sins are masculine with the exception of Pride, Pernel Proud-heart, though their Latin names are feminine: Luxuria, Invidia, Ira, Avaritia, Gula, Accidia.

Some characters are variously personified with different genders in different episodes. For example, Anima is feminine in the allegory of the castle, a romance motif adapted to Christian homiletic, but

---

[11]Quotations from Chaucer are from The Riverside Chaucer, ed. Larry D. Benson (Boston: Houghton Mifflin, 1987).

masculine in the long conversation with Will in B passus XV. At any rate, the masculine pronoun is used, though this strange tongueless and toothless creature with so many names, masculine and feminine in gender, seems amorphous and sexless.[12] Charity, the feminine *caritas* in Latin, is a "chapman" at B Prol.64 and implicitly embodied by Christ in the episode of the Samaritan (B XVII). But the virtue is feminine at B V.621 as a servant of Truth: "Charite and Chastite ben hi[r]e chief maydenes." The fact that a dozen manuscripts read "hise" for "hire" in this line suggests some authorial vacillation or scribal uncertainty about the gender of Truth in this passage. Peace is masculine in the *Visio* when he represents the peace-loving citizen injured by Wrong (B IV.78–103), but feminine at B V.622 as another maidservant of Truth and feminine in B XVIII as one of the four Daughters of God.

This instability of gender is one of many instabilities in *Piers* — of narrative, setting, genre, and argument — which contribute to our sense of a shifting dissolving landscape and a continually renewed search for understanding. The poet does not seem to be following a program, preconceived in every detail, but to have a habit of ready personification, as if an idea promptly embodies itself in a character apt for the moment but provisional and adaptable. "Tomme trewe-tonge-tel-me-no-tales-/ Ne-lesynge-to-lau3en-of-for-I-loued-hem-neue*re*" (B IV.18–19) and "Dame werch-whan-tyme-is" (B VI.78) are scarcely more than their names, minimal characters who appear and disappear because Truth or Industry could be envisaged quite differently at another turn of this kaleidoscopic poem. The "correctness" and consistency assumed in the grammatical analogy to be so self-evidently desirable that they present a model of good Christian behavior are quite at odds with the poet's own linguistic practices.

Direct and Indirect Speech

Conscience confines himself, in the analogy distinguishing between "mede and mercede," to grammatical agreement between words. I should like now to consider the contrast in *Piers Plowman*

---

[12]In *Piers Plowman as a Fourteenth-century Apocalypse*, Bloomfield ignores the masculine pronoun and refers to Anima as "she" (72, 121).

between one type of syntactical direction and indirection, direct and indirect speech. I do not know of any contemporary theoretical discussion of this distinction and direct speech is not highlighted by quotation marks in Middle English scribal practice. However, it seems to me that reported speech and direct address function rather differently from each other in *Piers Plowman*.

The subject of direct speech (or "mimesis") has been recently discussed a good deal in relation to the novel. Colin MacCabe, for example, argues that the "classic realist text" sets up a "hierarchy of discourses" and privileges the narration (diegesis or meta-language) over the dialogue: "The text outside the area of inverted commas claims to be the product of no articulation, it claims to be unwritten. . . . Whereas other discourses within the text are considered as materials which are open to re-interpretation, the narrative discourse functions simply as a window on reality."[13] By contrast, the work of James Joyce negates such hierarchy and his hostility to quotation marks is symptomatic: "The absence of a meta-language in Joyce's work is evident in his refusal, a refusal which dates from his earliest writings, to use what he calls 'perverted commas' "(MacCabe 14). Perhaps the absence of quotation marks in Middle English manuscripts is a preconstructive virtue. Direct and indirect speech are differentiated in *Piers Plowman* but insofar as there is a hierarchy of discourses in the poem it is the reverse of Joyce's: direct speech is privileged.

The first example of each in all three texts occurs in the vision of the folk on the field in the Prologue. Both concern false speech or abuse of speech. In all three the first example of direct speech is the quotation from St Paul condemning foolish talk and jesting: "þat poule prechiþ of hem I dar not proue it here; / *Qui loquitur turpiloquium* [is] luciferis hyne" (A Prol.38–39); "That Poul precheþ of hem I [dar] nat preue it here; / *Qui loquitur turpiloquium* is luciferes hyne" (B Prol.38–9); "That Poule prechede of hem preue hit y myhte; / *Qui turpiloquium loquitur* is Luciferes knaue" (C Prol. 39–40). The first indirect speech in all three versions is an example of the abuse of language. A and C present a false preacher who traffics in phony confession:

---

[13] *James Joyce and the Revolution of the Word* (London: Macmillan, 1978), 15, 16.

þere prechide a pardoner as he a prest were;
Brouȝte forþ a bulle wiþ bisshopis selis
And seide þat hymself miȝte assoile hem alle
Of falsnesse of fastyng & of auowes broken.
(A Prol.65–68)

The equivalent passage in C (Prol.66–69) is virtually identical. The false pardoner also appears in the B Prologue (68–71) but the first example of reported speech is by false palmers:

I seiȝ some þat seiden þei hadde ysouȝt Seintes;
To ech a tale þat þei tolde hire tonge was tempred to lye
More þan to seye sooþ, it semed bi hire speche.
(B Prol.50–52)

I would not want to argue that *every* example of indirect speech in the poem is morally flawed. However, there is a tendency for direct speech to bear immediate witness and to carry a particular kind of authority. Some moments of high drama and significant presence are signaled by direct speech. Piers himself irrupts into the poem without introduction in direct speech: " 'Peter!' quod a Plowman, and putte forþ his hed" (B V.537). The redeemed Trajan suddenly appears to prove that he has been saved: " 'Ye? baw for bokes!' quod oon was broken out of helle" (B XI.140). The first direct speech in the profoundest vision of the poem bears witness to the presence of the Lord and the coexistence of the Dreamer's and the original Palm Sunday: "Thanne was feiþ in a fenestre and cryde 'a! *fili dauid!*' " (B XVIII.15). The closing lines of the poem modulate from the direct and passionate speech which ends the last dream, Conscience's anguished resolve to seek Piers Plowman, to Will's flat and non-committal report of it: "And siþþe he gradde after Grace til I gan awake" (B XX.386).

   Direct speech has a tendency to take on a life of its own.[14] Angry words leap autonomously in the confession of Wrath: " 'þow lixt!' and 'þow lixt!' lopen out at ones" (B V.163). Here direct speech is personified (or possibly metamorphosed into Kafkaesque insect life). In the same passus Sloth is sharply wakened by an animated text:

---

[14]*Piers* does not, however, go as far in this direction as Chaucer in *The House of Fame*, when the eagle explains:

"*vigilate* þe veille fette water at his eiȝen / And flatte it on his face" (B v.442-43). A few lines later it is reified: at the end of the confessions of the Deadly Sins, "Roberd þe Robbere on *Reddite* loked / And for þer was noȝt wher[wiþ] he wepte swiþe soore" (B v.461-62). The ten commaundments are places on the route Piers recommends to the pilgrims and verses from Scripture are served as courses in the banquet at Clergy's house.

Some of the respect for direct speech can be attributed to the special status of the actual words of Scripture. David Lawton describes the "obvious aspect of the poem on the page: a dialogic and macaronic poem in which the 'English poem' that is the standard topic of criticism is intersected throughout by quotations from the discourses of authority in the language of power, Latin" and comments on the "special quality of the intertextuality of *Piers Plowman*, in which the 'other discourses' are mainly the non-fictional discourses of social and intellectual power as opposed to other literary discourses as in Chaucer."[15] In passus I Holy Church refers the questioning Dreamer to the answers of the Bible and supports her instruction of him with Scriptural quotation: "Go to þe gospel . . . þat god seide hymseluen / . . . '*Reddite Cesari*,' quod god, 'þat *Cesari* bifalleþ, / *Et que sunt dei deo*' . . ." (B I.46, 52-3); "I do it on *Deus caritas* to deme þe sothe" (B I.86); "Iames þe gentile [Ioyned] in hise bokes . . . *Fides sine operibus mortua est*" (B I.185, 187); "þise [ben wordes] writen in þe [euaungelie]: / '*Date & dabitur vobis*, for I deele yow alle.' " (B I.200-1); "Forþi I seye as I seide er by [siȝte of þise] textes: / Whan alle tresors ben tried treuþe is þe beste" (B I.206-7). The relationship between text and gloss sometimes appears in the poem as a distinction between direct and indirect speech. This may express or account for the poet's suspicion of those who "[g]losed þe

Whan any speche ycomen ys
Up to the paleys, anon-ryght
Hyt wexeth lyk the same wight
Which that the word in erthe spak,
Be hyt clothed red or blak;
And hath so verray hys lyknesse
That spak the word, that thou wilt gesse
That it the same body be,
Man or woman, he or she.
(*HF* 1074-82)

[15]"The Subject of *Piers Plowman*," *Yearbook of Langland Studies* 1 (1987): 1-30. Quotations are from page 6.

gospel as hem good liked" (B Prol.60). The most dramatic crux in
the poem is presented as a clash between text and gloss: at the
beginning of passus VII Truth "purchaced . . . a pardoun" (B VII.3)
for Piers and his heirs, nearly a hundred lines follow which purport
to be a paraphrase of it, then Piers unfolds the document and it
proves to consist of two lines of Latin which the priest cannot recognize as a pardon. Their angry dispute about it wakes Will into
prolonged anxiety about whether the pardon is valid and the dream
meaningful. The final waking section of the *Visio* functions as an
indeterminate gloss on the dream. The problems it raises seem hu-
manly insoluble and the vexed Dreamer finds comfort only in the
words of Scripture: "þe book bible bereþ witnesse" (B VII.157) of the
prophetic dreams of Joseph and Daniel; Christ's promise "*Quodcum-
que ligaueris super terram erit ligatum & in celis*" is "[a leef of] oure bileue"
(B VII.181–81a).

Yet even such divinely authoritative texts seem to lose their power
to direct in the misty world of *Piers Plowman*. In passus I Holy
Church expounds the basic teaching of Christianity and supports it
from Scripture but the Dreamer's search continues for many passus,
the poet's through three versions and Conscience leaves the Church
at the end of the poem. David Lawton provides a suggestive double
account of the failure of Holy Church to conclude the poem in the
first passus: "On one level, . . . that of narrative, the dreamer fails to
attend a long, fine and doctrinally sound gloss from an authoritative
glossator, Holy Church, encapsulating all the poem's orthodox theology. To listen to reason would foreclose the poem: there would be no
more call for narrative fiction. On another level, that of discourse,
the first explanation is insufficient. The rejection of an authorized
gloss throws the text, together with its subject (for text and subject
are reciprocal), into a ceaseless questioning of received ideology"
(15). In Lawton's terms the dreamer's discourse is the text, the
speech of Holy Church for all its direct quotation from Scripture is
the gloss. The heuristic narrative of the Dreamer, far from constituting a "position of dominance," has the authenticity of a direct utterance *in via*.

The form of the poem itself presents a curious and challenging
relationship between direct and reported experience. The dreams,
we are to believe, are more "real" than the "real" world. Here Will is
privileged to perceive the meaning of *aenigma*. Here he becomes a

direct witness of the events of Christ's life and death. Yet the truths must be indirectly recorded by the narrator in his imperfect waking life. The poet must compose his poem and disseminate it through the contingencies and indirections of manuscript transmission, oral performance and silent reading, biassed and fallible memory. How can its meaning and reception be controlled? In the A-Text even Will's faithful reproduction of the terms of Truth's pardon to the merchants becomes involved at once in the double-dealing area of profit and reward: "For he co[pie]de þus here clause þei [couden] hym gret mede" (A vIII.44). The "copying" of Truth's "clause" should be a perfect example of direct relation but it is soon implicated in the indirections of meed.

Relationships

Some of the difficulties of *Piers Plowman* are caused or com-pounded by a lack of obvious and direct relationships between lin-guistic units. We are sometimes puzzled by free-floating phrases whose logical connections with their context are unclear. They may be susceptible to different or even opposite interpretations according to the views taken of this relationship. For example, at the opening of the poem, we are told that the narrator is dressed "as an heremite, vnholy of werkes" (B Prol.3). Are we to understand that he is like other hermits unholy, or unlike other hermits unholy, or looks like an unholy hermit without being unholy or a hermit? Holy Church asks him: "sone, slepestow? sestow þis peple . . . ?" (B I.5). The different possible allegorical senses of sleep have been listed by Ro-bertson and Huppé, who seem confident about which to select on any particular occasion, but I do not see how we can determine which applies here or whether sleep is to be taken *in bono* or *in malo*.[16] Holy Church may be rebuking Will: "Are you asleep, so obtuse that you cannot see how these people are living?" Or she may be inspir-ing him: "Are you asleep, receptive to a prophetic vision, so that for

---

[16]D. W. Robertson, Jr., and Bernard F. Huppé, *Piers Plowman and Scriptural Tradition* (Princeton: Princeton University Press, 1951): "Holy Church's question, 'sone, slepestow?' is intended to suggest allegorically Will's state of sinful ignorance in his approval of the corruption of the Folk of the Field" (37).

once you can see them acutely?" The ambiguity depends as much on the unexpressed relationship of the two questions as on the rival interpretations of "sleep." The most violent and vexing of these problems occurs when Piers tears the pardon "for pure tene" (B vii.119). Piers's anger has been variously interpreted as directed at himself, at the priest, or at the pardon, with quite different consequences for our view of the relationships between Piers's old life and his new, between Piers and the priest, between Piers and the pardon, between the pardon and Truth. In the grammatical analogy Conscience describes the "direct" monarch as standing firm in his impartiality, like a fixed landmark between the territories of different lords. This is an image of "relacoun rect," definite and unbending, which appeals to the poet of *Piers Plowman*, perhaps because it is an ideal he finds difficult to realize. These phrases do not suggest any such neutrality. They are obviously polemical in their import but we cannot see what their position is. They incline but we cannot tell definitively in which direction.

Relationships between larger units of the poem show similar ambiguity. It is often difficult to determine how juxtaposed passages relate to each other, and such passages tend to be areas of dispute. Does the introduction of the king in the Prologue herald a sketch of a good or a bad society? Are the lunatic, the goliard and the angel agreeing or disagreeing with each other? Why does Piers resolve to "cessen of [his] sowyng" (B vii.122) when, at the opening of the same passus, Truth told him to "taken his teme and tilien þe erþe" (B vii.2)? What is the relationship among Dowel, Dobet and Dobest?

Some of the doubts about the problematic figure of the narrator focus on his relationships or lack of them. He is rarely seen in "direct" relationships. At the triumphal climax of the poem, after the vision of the Harrowing of Hell, we hear him call his wife and daughter to go to church with him, to be united with him in the community of the faithful, living and dead (B xviii.425–31). But this is exceptional. When Will's marriage is mentioned elsewhere in the poem (which is not often), the inadequacies of the relationship are emphasized: in the "autobiographical episode" (C v.1–104) Will is implicitly criticized for his failure to provide for his wife; at the end of the poem their sexual relationship fails as the Dreamer and the world grow older and love and loyalty become faint in the

Church. In the autobiographical episode and elsewhere Will comes under suspicion for not having a proper job, a clear connection with the rest of society. In as far as he has a recognized occupation, he is blamed for not performing adequately the prayers for his benefactors, a lack of true relationship to his employers, and is suspect for claiming in C V to be a contemplative when he is not a member of a religious community. Within the dreams Will often has difficulty in recognizing or identifying his interlocutors, even when they are aspects of himself. In the waking episodes he is usually alone: at the opening of the *Visio* he is introduced as a kind of hermit or a pseudo-hermit; by its close we have seen with him the field full of folk, the panorama of all man's work on the half-acre, the analysis of the whole of his society, but Will wakes from the vision in isolation again "[m]eteles and moneyles" (C IX.297) on Malvern Hills.

A similar detachment is condemned and summed up in a grammatical term in the description of Hawkin's sinfulness: "so singuler by hymself [. . . / Was noon swich as hymself] . . . / Yhabited as an heremyte, an ordre by hymselue . . ." (B XIII.282–84). His coat is soiled with many sins and he has no other. Conscience suggests to him how he could cleanse it with contrition, confession and satisfaction and protect it forever: "Shal neuere myste bimolen it ne moth after biten it" (B XIV.23).[17] This line is presumably based on the counsel in Matthew 6:19: "Nolite thesaurizare vobis thesauros in terra, ubi aerugo et tinea demolitur," a passage evidently in the poet's mind since it supplies the next text, "*Ne solliciti sitis*" (B XIV.33a). In this adaptation, if the reading is correct, "myste" replaces the biblical rust. To this poet, notorious for his obscurity, lack of clarity is a major threat in the spiritual life. His image of redemption is of bright sunshine dispelling clouds and rain: "*Clarior est solito*

---

[17] I quote from Skeat's edition (B XIV.22). Kane and Donaldson give the line as "Shal neue*re* [myx] bymolen it, ne mo*þ*e after biten it" and cite 10 manuscripts which read "myst." John A. Alford, "Haukyn's Coat: Some Observations on *Piers Plowman* B. xiv 22–7," *Medium Ævum* 43 (1974): 133–38, argues that mist is a more appropriate threat to the cloth of Haukyn's coat than rust and that *aerugo* had, by transference from effect to cause, extended its meaning to "mildew." Alternatively, as Mícéal Vaughan has suggested to me, the poet may have been incorrectly deriving *aerugo*, "rust," from *aer*, "air," rather than *aes*, "copper."

post maxima nebula phebus . . . / 'After sharpe shoures', quod pees, 'moost shene is þe sonne; / Is no weder warmer þan after watry cloudes' " (B XVIII.408a-10). Yet this vision of eternal serenity is expressed through the most familiar symbol of earthly changefulness. Like other images of perfection in *Piers*, it dissolves into the mist and mutability of the waking world.

Manuscript Illustration of Late Middle English Literary Texts, with Special Reference to the Illustration of *Piers Plowman* in Bodleian Library MS Douce 104*

DEREK PEARSALL

MEDIEVAL LITERARY SCHOLARS have become increasingly aware in recent years of the importance of returning to the manuscripts of literary texts as a way of recovering important historical contexts for those literary texts. The tyranny exerted by "the critical edition" is beginning to be recognized, as manuscripts previously dismissed from consideration as "degenerate" or "corrupt" reveal, on closer inspection, unsuspected complexities in the processes of authorial composition, recomposition and revision. The activities of interfering, meddling and improving scribes, though not part of the author's text, reveal ways in which that text was understood and

---

*This essay was first presented as a lecture at the Kresge Art Museum of Michigan State University in May 1988. I was most grateful to Dr. Kathleen Scott on that occasion for allowing me to borrow her complete collection of slides of MS Douce 104 for the purpose of preparing the talk. Dr. Scott has now completed a detailed analysis of the pictures in MS Douce 104, "The Illustrations of *Piers Plowman* in Bodleian Library MS. Douce 104," *Yearbook of Langland Studies* 4 (1990): 1-86. She deals with format, style and selection of illustrations, and provides a descriptive catalogue of all the pictures, with comment on textual reference and information on iconographic analogues, where available. She kindly let me see a copy of this study in draft form, and this has enabled me to avoid some mistakes I would otherwise have made; the approach that I take in this essay does not overlap much with hers and in some ways, I hope, may complement it. It may be appropriate to add here that a complete facsimile of Douce 104 is to be published in 1993 by D. S. Brewer (Cambridge [Eng.]), with introductory material by Pearsall and Scott. In references to the illustrations in MS Douce 104 in the following pages, the folio number is accompanied by a citation of the number of the illustration in Scott's catalogue in *YLS*.

interpreted, and constitute an early and intimate form of literary-critical close reading. The methods of manuscript compilers and anthologists, who seem at first to be throwing texts together indiscriminately, may suggest, on closer analysis, that different kinds of choice were being made which need to be historically understood if we are not to impose modern notions of genre on medieval literary texts. Study of layout, format and decoration gives an insight into the ways in which medieval poems were understood to exist and to be read, whilst the study of the excerpting, abridging and paraphrasing of long poems enables us to understand what were thought to be the important elements in those poems.

But one of the most tempting fields of inquiry is the study of those manuscripts where pictures are provided to illustrate a narrative text, especially a narrative text written by a near-contemporary. The cherished dream is that through the study of these pictures we may gain some insight into a near-contemporary and culturally relevant understanding of a work of literature, such as we rarely have access to. An artist, even if an understanding of his pictorial vocabulary is itself a matter of historical recovery, will surely offer us an immediacy of imaginative response to the significance of a literary text which will enhance our understanding in a unique way. Whether this cherished dream is any more than an illusion will emerge, I am sure, in the brief survey of the subject I am about to offer, and the particular analysis of the pictures in Bodleian Library MS Douce 104. This is a manuscript of the C-Text of *Piers Plowman*, upon which it seems particularly appropriate to offer some remarks in the present volume.

The first results of the kind of survey I propose are not, it must be admitted, very promising. If one is hoping for evidence of an intelligent and interesting response to literary narrative on the part of these manuscript illustrators, one is most frequently disappointed. French Arthurian prose romances, for instance, are amongst the narrative texts most frequently illustrated, but the illustrations are generally uninformative. They are usually done, as Alison Stones has shown, by the lesser artists of the *atelier*, and draw upon a repertoire of stock motifs that are applied with little discrimination

to the narrative.[1] Scenes of mêlée, of siege, of meeting and departure, of procession, of court ceremonial, are dotted about the manuscripts, but more, it seems, with the intention of providing visual
relief and variety, or of punctuating the narrative in a visually convenient way, than of providing a visual commentary on the interpretation of the narrative.

The *Roman de la Rose* is another extensively illustrated secular
narrative, but again the interpretation of the narrative offered by the
illustrations is of limited interest. There is usually heavy concentration of illustration in the scenes portraying the figures painted on the
outside of the garden-wall, such as Avarice, Wrath, Old Age, Poverty and Envy, but the reasons for this are practical as much as
anything: first, illustration always tends to be heavier in the earlier
part of a manuscript, for the same reason that apples always tend to
be rosier on the front of a fruit stall; second, the scenes themselves
are paintings, and therefore lend themselves to illustration; and
third, models are readily available in the portrayal of the Seven
Deadly Sins in penitential treatises such as the *Somme le roi*. There
have been attempts to argue from the pictures in illustrated manuscripts of the *Roman de la Rose* that the lover's pursuit of the Rose was
from the first viewed with systematically sardonic irony by the earliest readers of the poem, and that the intention of its authors is to be
similarly construed as a witty and amusing exposé of *fole amour*.[2] But
this view of the poem, whatever its intrinsic merits, can only be
supported from manuscript illustration by a wilful neglect of work-
shop practice. The pictures simply will not bear the weight of such
an interpretation; furthermore, they were most often painted by
illustrators who made extensive use of pattern books and stereotyped
models and who were given their instructions by a production super-
visor who had at most read the text very cursorily. Lesley Lawton, in
her excellent essay on the illustration of late medieval secular texts,

---

[1]M. Alison Stones, "Secular Manuscript Illustration in France," in Christopher
Kleinhenz, ed., *Medieval Manuscripts and Textual Criticism*, North Carolina Studies in
the Romance Languages and Literatures 173 (Symposia, No.4) (Chapel Hill: University of North Carolina Department of Romance Languages, 1976), 83–102.

[2]John V. Fleming, *The Roman de la Rose: A Study in Allegory and Iconography* (Princeton: Princeton University Press, 1969).

gives some examples of pictures based on a hasty and imperfect reading of the text, or on a complete misunderstanding of it.[3]

The opportunity of finding in pictures derived from such sources an interesting visual commentary on the text will be seen to be severely limited. One might want to turn to more pragmatic explanations of the use of such pictures, as ways for instance of enhancing the value of a book, and making it more of a prestige possession, a conspicuous object of consumption, as well as a thing of beauty in its own right; or as ways of helping the reader to find his way about a book by giving a swift reminder of its story. The usefulness of pictures in this latter role will not be undervalued by those who have tried to find a particular episode in a manuscript or series of manuscripts of a long poem without text-divisions like the *Roman de la Rose*. Beyond this, there is the considerable interest of studying the illustrative program of a work such as the *Roman* or the *Divine Comedy* in a series of manuscripts stretching over two centuries or so, not so much as a way of understanding the poem in its original historical context but as a way of seeing the misunderstandings to which it was subject as its allegory fell out of fashion or as the matter of the poem was appropriated to new ways of thinking.[4] But we are still far away, it will be seen, from the cherished dream I spoke of earlier, of pictures as a significant visual commentary on a narrative text.

Illustration of English secular narrative texts, of course, lags a long way behind continental practice, and it is not until the early fifteenth century that we begin to get extensively illustrated manuscripts of such texts. The fifteenth century sees the development of programs of illustration for works like Gower's *Confessio Amantis*, Lydgate's *Troy-Book*, *Fall of Princes* and *Life of St Edmund*, and of prose texts like *Mandeville's Travels*, the translation of Deguileville's *Pilgrimage of the Soul*, or the translations of the *Dicts and Sayings of the Philosophers* or of Christine de Pizan's *Epistle of Othea*. The literary interest of the pictures in such manuscripts as visual commentary is for the

---

[3]Lesley Lawton, "The Illustration of Late Medieval Secular Texts, with Special Reference to Lydgate's *Troy-Book*," in Derek Pearsall, ed., *Manuscripts and Readers in Fifteenth-Century England: The Literary Implications of Manuscript Study*, Essays from the 1981 Conference at the University of York (Cambridge [Eng.]: D. S. Brewer; Totowa, NJ: Biblio, 1983), 41–69. For the examples alluded to, see 46, 47.

[4]A classic of the genre is Rosemond Tuve, *Allegorical Imagery: Some Mediaeval Books and Their Posterity* (Princeton: Princeton University Press, 1966).

most part limited. The *Troy-Book*, for instance, has a well-established pictorial program, as Lesley Lawton points out, in the eight out of twenty-three manuscripts that have illustrations, with a set number of pictures designed to mark the major formal divisions of the text, but the episodes chosen for illustration are not particularly significant and seem to have been picked up fairly arbitrarily from a rapid survey of the early part of the text that follows the illustration.[5] In these circumstances the pictures function as little more than the highest member in a general hierarchy of decoration designed to articulate the formal structure of the text.

The illustrations of Gower's *Confessio Amantis* are more interesting: there are a few that have more but most manuscripts that are illustrated have just two pictures, and they are always the same—a picture of the statue that figures in Nebuchadnezzar's dream in the Prologue, and a picture of the lover confessing to the priest Genius at the beginning of Book I.[6] The choice of the two pictures is unexpected enough to make one think that Gower himself did indeed have some part in it. Whether Gower chose the pictures or not, they do reinforce a conceptual scheme for the poem which is of some significance: the visual presentation of the lover's confession draws attention to the structure of a poem that will examine through confession and shrift the disordering power of human love; that disordering power in its turn can be seen as analogous to the disorders and divisions in the world at large, which is the theme of the Prologue and of Gower's account of Nebuchadnezzar's dream. The statue of that dream is an emblem of a mutable world brought to ruin by division. There is here, it will be seen, a clear interpretative value to be attached to the pictures in manuscripts of the *Confessio:*

---

[5]Lawton, "Illustration of Late Medieval Secular Texts," 52.

[6]There is a (now necessarily incomplete) descriptive catalogue of the manuscripts of the *Confessio Amantis* in G. C. Macaulay (ed.), *The English Works of John Gower*, 2 volumes, EETS, ES 81–82 (London: Oxford University Press, 1900), I:cxxxviii-clxvii. There is a more recent listing of the manuscripts of the *Confessio*, though without descriptions, in John H. Fisher, R. Wayne Hamm, Peter G. Beidler, and Robert F. Yeager, "John Gower," Chapter XVII in Volume 7 of Albert E. Hartung, ed., *A Manual of the Writings in Middle English 1050–1500* (New Haven: The Connecticut Academy of Arts and Sciences, 1986), 2408-9. For some discussion of the illustration in manuscripts of the poem, see Jeremy Griffiths, " 'Confessio Amantis': The Poem and its Pictures," in A. J. Minnis, ed., *Gower's Confessio Amantis: Responses and Reassessments* (Cambridge [Eng.]: D. S. Brewer, 1983), 163–78.

they do give a pointer to an important contemporary and maybe authorial reading of the poem. Two other manuscripts of the *Confessio* that are very fully illustrated, the Morgan and New College manuscripts, do not, as far as I have studied them, offer much to the reader of the poem, except a sense of the illustrators' desperation in their search for illustratable scenes and appropriate models. Anyone who wanted to use the pictures as a visual mnemonic for the stories, which seems to be the most current explanation of their function, would need to know the stories very well indeed in order to recognize them in these pictures.

The great disappointment in the period is of course the absence of any extensively illustrated manuscripts of Chaucer.[7] The few that exist are interesting, but they could rarely be said to contribute significantly to our understanding of Chaucer's poetry. The most famous is the Ellesmere manuscript of the *Canterbury Tales*, which has portraits of the pilgrims on horseback set in the manuscript margin, without frame, at the point in the poem where the pilgrim begins his or her tale. The portraits are done with an unusual degree of fidelity to the text (see especially the pictures of the Pardoner and the Cook), even if occasionally the pressure of some traditional iconographic model is too powerful to resist. Such is the case with the rendering of the Doctor of Physic as the satirical stereotype of the physician inspecting urine-samples — which hardly seems appropriate to a pilgrim, especially one on horseback. But, as I say, there is generally a good deal of response to the detail of Chaucer's text, and the placing of the portraits at the appropriate point in the *Tales*, and not beside the portraits of the pilgrims in the General Prologue from which they are actually drawn, shows a keen recognition of the dramatic structure of the *Canterbury Tales* as a whole, and a desire to make it explicit, long before the development of the idea of the "dramatic principle" by modern critics.

The exceptional nature of Ellesmere emerges from a comparison with Cambridge University Library MS Gg.iv.27, which also has a cycle of pilgrim portraits — or once had, since many have been cut

---

[7]For discussion of the illustration in the Chaucer manuscripts, see Margaret Rickert, "Illumination," in John M. Manly and Edith Rickert (eds.), *The Text of the Canterbury Tales, Studied on the Basis of all Known Manuscripts*, 8 vols. (Chicago: University of Chicago Press, 1940), I:561–605.

out—but where fidelity to the text seems to have been sacrificed to ostentation, or has maybe just been lost in the life-and-death struggle of the artist with the representation of the horse.

Aside from Ellesmere and Gg.iv.27 there are the pilgrim pictures in the "Oxford" manuscript and a few initial miniatures for the *Canterbury Tales* which are of passing interest, such as the rather pathetic little picture of Chaucer as narrator in Bodleian Library MS Bodley 686, but no actual illustrations of the narrative of the *Canterbury Tales*, neither the dramatic links nor the tales. There is nothing, for instance, to compare with the lively illustration in British Library MS Royal 18.D.ii (fol. 148), a manuscript of Lydgate's *Siege of Thebes*, of pilgrims leaving Canterbury. This seems the very kind of scene that one would have thought illustrators would be eager to try out for the *Canterbury Tales*. The comparative absence of illustrated manuscripts of the *Canterbury Tales* is indeed something of a puzzle, and I am not sure that the usual explanations—that it was a book that people wanted to read and not to have merely as a coffee-table book; or that it had its own internal system of narrative punctuation—will quite do. Nor do I think the absence of an existing program of illustration would necessarily be quite the deterrent it has been assumed to be, unless English artists were totally lacking in the kind of ingenuity that French illustrators displayed, for instance, in manuscripts of the *Decameron*. The same puzzle arises with *Troilus and Criseyde*, for which there is only the famous frontispiece in Corpus Christi College (Cambridge) MS 61, followed in the manuscript by ninety spaces. There has been plenty of discussion of this frontispiece, and more than enough discussion of the spaces and what would have filled them if the program of illustration had been completed, but the manuscript remains enigmatic.[8]

---

[8]See Derek Pearsall, "The *Troilus* Frontispiece and Chaucer's Audience," *Yearbook of English Studies* 7 (1977): 68–74; M. B. Parkes and Elizabeth Salter, Introduction to *Troilus and Criseyde, Geoffrey Chaucer: A Facsimile of Corpus Christi College Cambridge MS 61* (Cambridge [Eng.]: D. S. Brewer, 1978); Elizabeth Salter and Derek Pearsall, "Pictorial Illustration of Late Medieval Poetic Texts: The Role of the Frontispiece or Prefatory Picture," in Flemming G. Andersen, Esther Nyholm, Marianne Powell and Flemming Talbo Stubkjaer, eds., *Medieval Iconography and Narrative: A Symposium*, Proceedings of the Fourth International Symposium organized by the Centre for the Study of Vernacular Literature in the Middle Ages (Odense: Odense University Press, 1980), 100–23.

Amid all these puzzles and frustrations, it is very gratifying to come upon a manuscript that has been supplied with a large number of competent illustrations that are of considerable interpretative interest. Either the artist himself or the person who gave him his instructions has read the text carefully and, as I shall try to argue, with an unusually sharp eye for expressive detail, and a keen understanding of the poem. I refer to MS Douce 104, a manuscript of the C-Text of *Piers Plowman*, dated 1427, which has seventy-two marginal illustrations, mostly of single figures. The illustrations provide an interesting commentary on the poem and at times what I think of as insights into it.[9]

Sometimes, it is true, we do find pictures based on traditional stereotypes, or pictures done because the subject is intrinsically illustratable, or pictures that pick out some detail from the text on a fairly arbitrary basis because it is illustratable. FORTUNE'S WHEEL (fol. 53, text at C XI.174; Scott #40) finds a way in as a standard attribute even though there is no mention of the Wheel in the text, only Fortune. A picture of a SCHOOLMASTER (fol. 52, XI.124; Scott #38 and fig. 23) in a skull cap, a cloak with a furred neck, wielding a birch cane over a strangely detached bare bottom, refers to Dame Study's remarks about the way she taught Scripture, but does not of course keep to the allegory of female Study and meanwhile picks up "þe bare ers" from the related passage at VI.157 to embroider the rather arbitrarily chosen detail. A HANGED MAN (fol. 79, XVII.138; Scott #58) illustrates the very passing reference to the fate of the thief who had love but hated *leute*.

But more often what one is struck by is the precision with which illustrations follow the detail of the text. The Seven Deadly Sins of passus VI-VII provide a good sequence. There is ENVY (fol. 25, VI.74; Scott #12 and fig. 11), done as a leaping figure in a rough short coat tied at the waist, his mouth twisted, his left hand raised, fist clenched, exactly as the text has it—"A wroth his fust vppon Wrath"

[9]References to the illustrations, of which it is impossible, unfortunately, to reproduce here more than a few, are to folio recto unless verso is specified. I am grateful to the Bodleian Library, and in particular to Mrs. Mary Clapinson, Keeper of Western Manuscripts, for providing me with the photographs for reproduction and giving me permission to use them here. References to the text of *Piers Plowman* are throughout to Derek Pearsall, ed., *Piers Plowman, by William Langland: An Edition of the C-text*, York Medieval Texts, second series (London: Edward Arnold, 1978).

(VI.66). WRATH (fol. 26, VI.143; Scott #13), with ugly face, is dressed in a tight-fitting blue jerkin, his left hand raised to his scalp tearing at his hair, as the text says twice, referring to anger or angry people scratching at others with their nails (VI 140) and tearing at their hair (VI 140 50). COVETOUSNESS (fol. 27, VI.214; Scott #15) has a hood and cloak, an expensive-looking red hat, and there is a faithful effort to represent the "designer stubble" to which the text refers ("as a bondemannes bacoun his berd was yshaue" [VI.201]), though less success with "baburlippid" (VI.198). He has a purse at his belt, but this is plausible enough without being taken to be a mistaken or excessively witty allusion to the leathern purse which his sagging cheeks resembled (VI.199). GLUTTONY (fol. 29, VI.356 [reproduced here as fig. 1]; Scott #16) has his coat thrown open to reveal him apparently pissing, with reference to the text at VI.399 (I take the representation to be of an exposed penis and not an inordinately protuberant navel), at the same time that he "globbes" (VI.397) at a

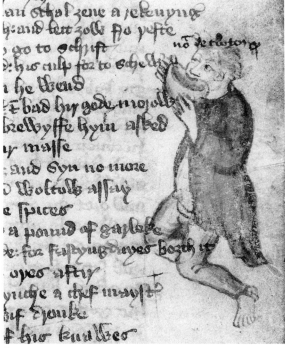

Figure 1.   GLUTTONY

great bowl, his legs staggering under him (VI.403). The portion of
the text to which the illustration so vividly refers is quite a long way
from where the illustration occurs: this is not uncommon.

Another striking though mixed example is the PILGRIM (fol. 33,
VII.165 [fig. 2]; Scott #18). He has on a red cloak not much like a
saracen's garb (VII.161), but his pilgrim's staff is twisted all round
with strips of cloth exactly as in the text (VII.162–63). Furthermore,
these strips of cloth serve in the picture to bind a formalized palm
branch to his staff, which is one of the functions they are presumed
to be a relic of (though not mentioned in the text), the allusion being
to the carrying of palms by pilgrims ("palmers") in token of visit to
the Holy Land. The pilgrim's hat is set with small objects that may
be "aunpolles" or phials (VII.165), and his cloak decorated with vari-

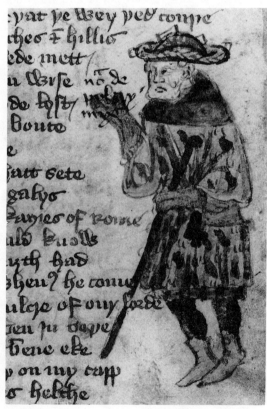

Figure 2. PILGRIM

ous things some of which might possibly be keys (VII.167). He carries a bell, the explanation of which is to be found in the manuscript's reading of VII.164 — "A bolle and a bagge a bar by his syde" — where, instead of *bolle* Douce 101 has *belle*. This is a remarkable testimony to close reading, and a terrible mistake, since it was lepers who carried bells. On the other hand, it would not be wise to assume too readily that the text that the illustrator read, or that the person read who gave him his instructions, was the text of Douce 104 itself. It may well have been, and is perhaps more likely to have been, its exemplar. Support for this view is given by the picture of DEATH (fol. 71, XV.308/XVI.1; Scott #53) as a skeleton, with his arms raised in the air to frighten people, which must refer to a passage in the text (XV.306) which is actually missing in Douce 104.

At other times, I am struck by the illustrator's vivid use of facial expression to convey the sense of the text. There is a very ugly LIAR (fol. 9, II.114; Scott #3 and fig. 3), shown presenting the marriage charter of Meed, as the story has it at II.69–70. The SPADE-WIELDER (fol. 39, VIII.259; Scott #25) of passus VIII has just the right sort of frenzied eagerness in his face of those who in VIII.183 hasten to obey Hunger's command to work or starve to death. There is a bust of a CLERK (fol. 54, XI.236; Scott #42) who is dressed in a richly furred robe and who looks more than slightly discomfited at the accusation in the text that clerks seldom live as they teach. The PENITENT THIEF (fol. 65, XIV.146; Scott #48) in heaven, said in the text to be a little uneasy in his suddenly found new home, certainly does not look too cheerful.

Sometimes it is a vivid use of gesture that contributes most to the effectiveness of a picture. CAIN (fol. 48v, X.212; Scott #35 and fig. 21), "þe corsede creature," in a green coat, has his hands to his head in a gesture of despair as if he recognizes the eternal punishment to which his iniquity has doomed him. The emperor TRAJAN (fol. 56, XII.73; Scott #44 and fig. 25), with a very odd Roman-style helmet on his head, sticks his tongue out into his hand and blows a monstrous raspberry as he exclaims "ȝe? bawe for bokes!"

Sometimes the vivid illustrative detail adds to rather than represents what is said in the text. The LAWYER (fol. 41, IX.50; Scott #27 and fig. 16) of the Pardon passus pleads at the bar in a rich furred robe, using the traditional gesture of logical argumentation, ticking off points on his fingers as he goes along: he is also very open-mouthed, as if to suggest the windiness of legal oratory. The BISHOP (fol. 44, IX.269; Scott #31 and fig. 19) of the same passus, who shirks his pastoral responsibilities, is shown lying with eyes closed (IX.257), his crozier in his hand, and his mitre falling off, whilst in the other corner of the page a wolf tears at the bloodied neck of a sheep (IX.266), symbolizing the danger to the neglected flock. The BRE-TONER (fol. 37v, VIII.157; Scott #23 and fig. 14) of the previous passus is shown in hood and hat, short tunic and hose, sword at his belt, left hand raised as if picking fruit, and with two dead birds slung on a stick over his shoulder, in reference to the stealing of food and poaching boasted of in VIII.153–55. Finally PRIDE (fol. 24, VI.3 [fig. 3]; Scott #11), one of the finest pictures in the series, is done

Figure 3. PRIDE

from the traditional iconography of Pride as a male, and almost entirely without hints from the text, which represents Pride as a woman, "Purnele proude-herte." He is shown as a slender epicene figure, standing in a very jaunty and impudent fashion, in a blue and red parti-colored tight-fitting doublet and hose, with very fancy red gloves, a protruding girdle around his waist hung with pendant baubles, or "folly bells,"[10] and long golden hair hanging in tresses decorated with beads or jewels. There is little or no specific relation to the text, as I say, but the tight doublet and hose would certainly be a very painful garment to wear if it had a hairshirt sewn on the inside, as Purnele Proude-herte proposes for her penance (VI.6).

Allegory of course is a notorious problem for illustrators, and on occasions the illustrator's solutions are no more than perfunctory. TOM TWO-TONGUE (fol. 109, XXII.162; Scott #69) is represented with an odd-looking forked tongue, and the head of ANTICHRIST (fol. 107, XXII.53; Scott #67) in the same passus has only some demonically curly hair to make us think of him as the ultimate evil. One of the most interesting failures is the SHERIFF CARRYING MEED (fol. 10, II.177; Scott #4 and fig. 4). The well-established allegorical motif in which the sins ride upon wicked men is explicitly one in which the wicked men are described as saddled horses: Meed, we are told, is riding "softliche in saunbure" (II.178), comfortably in a saddle, upon the Sheriff. But the illustrator chooses instead to show her being realistically carried on his shoulders, like someone being hoisted aloft after a sporting triumph.

At other times the illustrator seems to have got hold of the allegory quite firmly and to have rendered it with even a touch of sophistication. The picture of MEED (fol. 11, III.13; Scott #5) has her looking innocent and pretty in a close-fitting long white gown and fancy headdress. She is not altogether unlike MERCY (fol. 94, XX.153; Scott #61), who has a completely different role in the poem. It is, however, eminently appropriate to the allegory that Meed should be represented thus as an attractive and sympathetic figure and not as a vice. I am persuaded too that the PARISH PRIEST (fol. 105, XXI.409; Scott #66), the "lewed vicory" of passus XXI, is a sensible-looking fellow, since this is in accord with my interpretation of his

---

[10]"folly bells": I am indebted to Dr. Scott's descriptive catalogue (30) for giving me a name for these things.

rather ambiguous role in the allegory. Extremely interesting is the
picture of ACTIVA VITA (fol. 69, xv.194 [fig. 4]; Scott #51 and fig.
27), shown in a brown coat, green hose and hood, with footwear
with toes poking through, a look of earnestness, a "hopur," or seed-
basket, over his shoulder, and a "plouh-pote," or plough-stick (a
long-handled small-headed spade for clearing thick accumulations of
earth and weeds from the ploughshare), in his hand. There is no
mention of these details at the point in the text where the picture
appears, Activa Vita being represented here as a minstrel and waferer. The illustrator has picked up the idea of Activa Vita as Piers
Plowman's apprentice from the text here at xv.195 and then given
him the attributes of Piers from passus VIII. Quite specifically, the
"hopur" is from VIII.60 and the unmistakable "plouh pote" from
VIII.64. This is an astute piece of cross-referencing that draws out an
important implication of the allegory.

Figure 4.   ACTIVA VITA

This cross-referencing, this use of pictures to structure the text by association, is the last, most important and potentially most controversial of the characteristics that may be ascribed to the illustrator of Douce 104 (or, as one must always remind oneself, the person who gave him his instructions). A simple example is a sequence in passus III-IV, showing first CONSCIENCE (fol. 15, III.285; Scott #7 and fig. 7) as a noble-looking figure, in a blue robe over a white gown, a flowing red hood, and with a double-pointed beard. A little later comes the KING (fol. 18, IV.7; Scott #8 and fig. 8) in ermine cape and royal purple robe, with sceptre and crown and traditional kingly double-pointed beard. Very closely following comes REASON (fol. 19, IV.52; Scott #9 and fig. 9), sitting in judgment, in a red cloak, with an imposing hat, and double-pointed beard. The cross-referencing seems deliberately to underline the allegorical role of Conscience and Reason as the essential advisors or attributes of the King, associating them through the shared dignity of the royal double-pointed beard and, I would suggest tentatively, through the red and blue that combined give the royal purple.

Friars, as is well-known, are one of the recurrent and obsessive themes of the poem, which circles on them ever more narrowly as the embodiment of all that is most corrupt (because of what was once most admirable) in the institutional life of the church. It seems to me no accident that the illustrator spends some effort in giving them a particularly oily and complacent air of self-satisfaction, drawing attention to their insidiousness as much as their downright wickedness. In the picture of MEED AND THE FRIAR (fol. 11v, III.45; Scott #6 and fig. 5), Meed, in a dangerously low-cut gown, kneels excessively close to the friar as she receives absolution, while he is oleaginous in the extreme. A FRANCISCAN FRIAR (fol. 46, X.25; Scott #33) in passus X, in a grey habit, gestures vivaciously as he explains with some satisfaction to the dreamer how Dowel is to be found, above all, among friars. A more obviously FALSE FRIAR (fol. 67v, XV.75; Scott #50) in passus XV has his hands raised in prayer to heaven and a look of unctuous piety on his face as he engages in the false preaching mentioned in the text.

Above all, starting with the illustration of the LUNATYK LOLLARE (fol. 42, IX.110 [fig. 5]; Scott #28 and fig. 17) of passus IX, there seems to me to be a pattern of recurrent reference to one of the most important developing themes of the C-Text, that of beggary and

Figure 5. LUNATYK LOLLARE

poverty.[11] Here a man is shown barefoot and naked except for a
rough ragged dun-colored garment thrown over one shoulder and
descending to the knees. He has straggling tufts of hair here and
there and his arms are raised in gestures that suggest lack of control
or contemptuous dismissal of the world. But it might be a deliber-

---

[11]For the theme of poverty in *Piers Plowman*, see David Aers, *"Piers Plowman* and
Problems in the Perception of Poverty: A Culture in Transition," in Derek Pearsall,
ed., *Essays in Memory of Elizabeth Salter*, Leeds Studies in English, new series 14
(University of Leeds: Department of English, 1983), 5–25; Geoffrey Shepherd,
"Poverty in *Piers Plowman*," in T. H. Aston, P. R. Coss, Christopher Dyer and Joan
Thirsk, eds., *Social Relations and Ideas: Essays in Honour of R. H. Hilton*, Past and
Present Publications (Cambridge [Eng.]: Cambridge University Press, 1983),
169–89; Derek Pearsall, "Poverty and Poor People in *Piers Plowman*," in Edward
Donald Kennedy, Ronald Waldron, and Joseph S. Wittig, eds., *Medieval English
Studies Presented to George Kane* (Cambridge [Eng.]: D. S. Brewer, 1988), 167–85.

ately contorted version of the traditional gestures of the preacher, since these feeble-minded simpletons, these "lunatyk lollares," are said to possess strange gifts of prophecy (IX.114) and to be as it were God's privy disciples (IX.118), The hair might be a version of the tonsure, as if to underline the point made in the text that the truest kind of unworldly spirituality is to be found among these poor outcasts of society—just as Lear found the truest emblem of man in Poor Tom.[12] The picture would be a good one of Poor Tom—or, one might hazard, of Langland himself in some of his self-imagings. Soon after, in the same passus, there is a BLIND BEGGAR (fol. 43, IX.181; Scott #29 and fig. 18), leaning heavily on a stick, head bent and eyes closed in an expressive gesture of infinite weariness, as the illustrator recognizes the compassion in the poem for the traditionally deserving poor, including the blind (IX.177). The WHITE FRIAR (fol. 47, x 89; Scott #34 and fig. 20) preaching in passus x is Dobet, the religious who preaches Paul's words concerning the welcome that should be given to fools. The figure places his hands simply on the ledge of the pulpit and inclines his head to one side in a gesture of pity and sad admonition. It is almost as if he is preaching about the fool or lunatic in the earlier picture, to whom he hears an uncanny kind of resemblance. The poet would not usually be expected to give friars such an unambiguous role, but the illustrator may have recognized the hidden association always immanent in the poem between poor beggars and mendicant friars.

In passus XI the illustrator picks out of Dame Study's speech the POOR BEGGAR (fol. 51, XI.50 [fig. 6]; Scott #37 and fig. 22) and shows him with staff, barefoot, submissive, withdrawing, one of the poor who are neglected and who wait vainly at the gate (XI.42) while the well-fed rich drool on after dinner about fine points of theology (XI.40). A little later in the same passus RECHELESNESSE (fol. 53, XI.196 [fig. 7]; Scott #41) stands forth in ragged clothes, barefoot, snapping his fingers contemptuously at the world in a gesture reminiscent of that of the "lunatyk lollares." The illustrator has clearly seized upon the poem's point about the association among folly,

---

[12]For some discussion of the "lunatyk lollares" and their role in the poem's developing meditation on spiritual poverty, see Derek Pearsall, " 'Lunatyk Lollares' in *Piers Plowman*," in Piero Boitani and Anna Torti, eds., *Religion in the Poetry and Drama of the Late Middle Ages in England: The J. A. W. Bennett Memorial Lectures, Perugia, 1988* (Cambridge [Eng.]: D. S. Brewer, 1990), 163–78.

Figure 6.   POOR BEGGAR

divine carelessness and poverty. Another OLD MAN (fol. 55, XII.10 [fig. 8]; Scott #43 and fig. 24) in passus XII is shown sitting on the ground, enfolded in a brown cloak, with eyes downcast and head resting on hand. There is an echo of the earlier image of old age in the picture of the blind beggar at IX.181 (fol. 43), which is remembered now in the illustration of the passage in the text where Old Age laments that Will is given over to Fortune (XII.1–2). It may be Will himself, grown old in sin; the face is drawn with deep and poignant expressiveness. Finally, in the account of Poverty and its relation to the Seven Deadly Sins, there is a picture of a POOR MAN (fol. 72, XVI.70 [fig. 9]; Scott #54 and fig. 28) sitting with his hands clasped over his knees in an uncomfortable-looking position, head bent, fair hair unkempt. The suggestion is one of patient humility (XVI.70) and perhaps more specifically of the poor man who has no proper bed to go to (XVI.74) and who cannot really enjoy self-indulgence.

The idealization of patient poverty as the epitome of that careless-

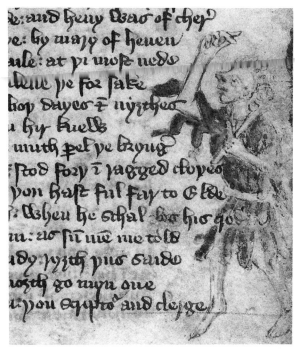

Figure 7.   RECHELESNESSE

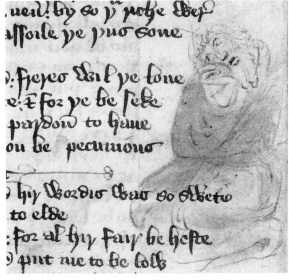

Figure 8.   OLD MAN

Figure 9.   POOR MAN

ness of the world which is the true spiritual life is first strikingly
announced in the portrayal of the "lunatyk lollares" of passus IX and
subsequently developed in a series of important passages, including
many that are added in the C-Text. One of the several indications
that the illustrator of Douce 104 was a thoughtful reader of *Piers
Plowman* is his responsiveness to this theme and his attempt to underline its development in a series of related pictorial ways. The manner
in which he picks up this theme can be associated with scribal or
editorial interventions in the Ilchester manuscript and in Huntington Library MS HM 114, where material on poverty is similarly
given a special prominence in editorial recensions of the text.[13] The
illustrator of Douce 104, or the person who gave him his instructions, is very much a reader of the poem, and one who participates
intelligently in the making of its meaning.

---

[13]See Derek Pearsall, "The 'Ilchester' Manuscript of *Piers Plowman*," *Neuphilologische Mitteilungen* 82 (1981): 181–93; Wendy Scase, "Two *Piers Plowman* C-Text Interpolations: Evidence for a Second Textual Tradition," *Notes and Queries*, new series 34
[232] (1987): 456–63.

MÍĊEÁL F. VAUGHAN

I T PROBABLY DESERVES critical notice when, despite their disagreements on other fundamental matters, the modern editors of
the A-Version of *Piers Plowman* essentially agree about how to end the
poem. In the last lines of A XI, as David C. Fowler has noted, there
is the "brilliance" of an "emphatic conclusion"[1]; and George Kane,

---

[1]See David C. Fowler, *Piers the Plowman: Literary Relations of the A and B Texts* (Seattle:
University of Washington Press, 1961), 39–42; and *Piers the Plowman: A Critical Edition
of the A-Version*, ed. Thomas A. Knott and David C. Fowler (Baltimore: Johns
Hopkins Press, 1952), 169, note to l. 250. Quotations and line-numeration, except as
otherwise noted, are from this edition. Quotations of the B-Version are from the
edition of George Kane and E. Talbot Donaldson (London: Athlone Press, 1975).
Those of the C-Version are from the edition of Derek Pearsall (London: Edward
Arnold, 1978), and I have adopted his numberings of passus and lines rather than
those of W. W. Skeat (*The Vision of William Concerning Piers the Plowman in Three Parallel
Texts*. 2 vols. [London: Oxford University Press, 1886]) and others.

I have throughout this article referred to the manuscripts of the A-Version by
means of the sigla employed in Knott-Fowler (23–25), providing in brackets the
alternates used by Kane (see *A-Version* 1–18).

The principles of the Knott-Fowler edition are critically discussed by Kane in the
introduction to his edition of the A-Version (esp. 53–114), and in *Piers Plowman: The
Evidence for Authorship* (London: Athlone Press, 1965). For critical discussion of the
principles behind Professor Kane's editions, David Fowler's reviews are worth
attention: of Kane's *A-Version*, in *Modern Philology* 58 (1960–61): 212–14; and of
Kane-Donaldson's B-Version, in "A New Edition of the B text of *Piers Plowman*," *The
Yearbook of English Studies* 7 (1977): 23–42. A important reconsideration of Kane's
editing is to be found in Charlotte Brewer, "The Textual Principles of Kane's A
Text," *The Yearbook of Langland Studies* 3 (1989): 67–90. And see also Thorlac
Turville-Petre's review of the Kane-Donaldson B-Text: *Studia Neophilologica* 49
(1977): 153–55.

while acknowledging the tendency of scribes to consider the text incomplete in one way or another, himself grants "a sense of ending" in these final lines of a "distinctive . . . first form of *Piers Plowman*, authorially sanctioned for copying" and consisting of a prologue and eleven passus.[2] Both editions, furthermore, print in an Appendix the problematical passus XII witnessed by three related manuscripts of the A-Version. Nevertheless, John Alford is quite correct when he states that "[m]ost scholars agree that the first version of *Piers Plowman* remained unfinished. The poet had reached an impasse" — an impasse signalled by the fact that "only two dreams are complete."[3] This general consensus, however, rests on fundamental uncertainties, and recent discussion has tended to reflect them.[4] Nevertheless, Father Dunning stands almost alone among critics of *Piers* A in reading it as a complete artistic whole[5] — a view that Professor Fowler forcefully endorses. The editorial agreement about the end of A XI and placement of A XII implies, I believe, a substantive agreement with regard to the *text* of *Piers* A not easily reconciled with the critical consensus. My purpose in this essay is to assess these implications further and to articulate something of the continual uncertainty that has accompanied readings of *Piers* A — and such uncertainty should, perhaps, motivate some of our own.

The minimal consideration accorded the A-Version by most students of *Piers* may in part account for the dismissive quality inherent in the scholarly consensus identified by Alford: critics really want to

---

[2]"The Text," in John A. Alford, ed., *A Companion to Piers Plowman* (Berkeley: University of California Press, 1988), 188–89. Kane's views on the completeness of the A-Version here seem distinctly more restrained than the earlier argumentative assertions of *Evidence*, where he declares: "every indication, to an impartial view, is that *A* is unfinished" (22). We should note, however, that most of his other statements regarding the incompleteness of A in this earlier volume qualify their assertions of incompleteness by reporting them as supported by "strong evidence" (21); or by stating there is "strong contrary evidence" against A's being "finished" (21); or by attributing the poem's incompleteness to the views of scribes, rubricators, or other early readers (47-48; and cf. "The Text" 180-82, 186).

[3]"The Design of the Poem," in *Companion* 46 and 31.

[4]For example, Anne Middleton, "Making a Good End: John But as a Reader of *Piers Plowman*," in *Medieval English Studies Presented to George Kane*, ed. Edward Donald Kennedy, Ronald Waldron, and Joseph S. Wittig (Wolfeboro and Woodbridge: Brewer, 1988), 243–66; and Malcolm Godden, *The Making of Piers Plowman* (London/New York: Longman, 1990), 75–76, and n. 15.

[5]T. P. Dunning, *Piers Plowman: An Interpretation of the A Text*, Second Edition, Revised and Edited by T. P. Dolan (Oxford: Clarendon Press, 1980).

get on with discussing the B- or C-Version.[6] Yet their dissonance
with the A-Version's editors deserves attention. When, despite divergent (even antithetical) views regarding authorship and other textual
matters, Professors Fowler and Kane agree on a fundamental feature of the A-Version — the shape of its text — then we should accord
such agreement serious acknowledgment. The modern editorial
consensus, indeed, has for almost forty years obviated the need for
further sustained attention to the text of the A-Version. However,
given the radical disagreement between the two editors with regard
to the *place* of the A-Version in the history of the *Piers Plowman*
tradition, we ought perhaps re-examine this editorial consensus
about the ending of the A-Version and its significance for critical
reading of the poem.

Two major considerations present themselves. First, elements in
the established text complicate any simple view of its conclusiveness;
and, second, the manuscripts of the A-Version indicate that the
reception of this poem by its earliest readers, its scribes, is quite
mixed. Despite "all the brilliancy of A" and the "imaginative lucidity"
of its final lines,"[7] despite its "emphatic conclusion" and "sense of
ending," one major difficulty with this conclusion of the A-Version
has lessened satisfaction with it as the ending of a completed poem:
the Dreamer is not said explicitly to wake from his dream.[8] While we
may readily grant that lines 250–303 of passus XI are marked by
"exact parallelism" (Fowler, *Literary Relations* 217, n. 46) with those of
VIII.127–81 — a parallelism that gains unavoidable importance once
our attention is drawn to it[9] — yet that same attention also reveals the
inconsistency about the Dreamer's awakening. Although they specifically take note of this discrepancy, both of the modern editions of

---

[6]Consider, for instance, Donaldson, Chambers, Kirk, as cited by Alford 46.

[7]E. Talbot Donaldson, *Piers Plowman: The C-Text and Its Poet* (New Haven: Yale
University Press, 1949), 53.

[8]Kane ("The Text" 188) would seem not entirely to agree that the text lacks
conclusion: "There is a sense of ending in the last lines of A.11, but the same has
been claimed for the end of 8 (Rigg-Brewer 29, 30)." Indeed, both claims *may*
indeed be accurate — and not surprisingly since passus VIII concludes the *Visio* and
passus XI the *Vita* of the A-Version.

[9]Cf. Kane, *Evidence* 21: "The failure to reawaken the Dreamer, and the unfulfilled
promise to consult Reason [as promised in the rubrics to passus IX in eight manu-
scripts] are strong evidence that *A* is an unfinished, or hastily concluded poem." See
also Alford, "Design" 31.

the A-Version substantially agree about the text and form of the ending, and we may well inquire whether the absence of a declared awakening should be so determinative of critical reception — or rejection — of the A-Version. As we shall see, some scribes and later readers were quite willing to accept this as the poem's conclusion without any such awakening.

In the absence of any clear indication that the Dreamer awakes, modern editors have been moved to punctuate the A-Version at A XI.250 to indicate (and support) their readings of the text before them. Even before finally adopting passus XII as for the most part authorial, Skeat assigned A XI.250–303 to Will-the-Dreamer and, placing these lines within quotation marks, so ended the poem.[10] The absence of the Dreamer's awakening did not concern him, and he gave no sure indication — before he adopted the view that passus XII, itself apparently incomplete, continued the A-Version — that he had any suspicion that the poem which ended at A XI was incomplete or unfinished.[11] So if we go back to Skeat's earlier views of the

---

[10]This is the form of the A-Version published in 1867 by EETS (OS 28). He makes no substantial change in the end of A XI between that edition and the *Parallel Texts* of 1886. As the 1867 edition indicates, he was aware of U, and only subsequently informed of the existence of R (pages 137*-144* being inserted in subsequent reissues of EETS, OS 28). These manuscripts, supported by the further addition of I[J], caused him to raise to certainty his earlier views regarding A XII: in 1867 he had found the "supposition. . .very probable" that "the author himself began a continuation which he afterwards abandoned, betaking first himself to an expansion of the part already written, and afterwards adding thereto a continuation different to the one he at first contemplated" (xxvii). But even so, the shape of the *text* is essentially unchanged. In short, even before he had become convinced that there was a "tercius passus de dowel," he was unconcerned by the poem's ending with Will speaking the last lines in a dream: his comments (1867 xlii-xliii) concluding his "ARGUMENT OF THE POEM (TEXT A.)" are perfectly happy to have the debate and the poem end in this way.

[11]The incompletion of the A-Version, its fragmentary condition, is only hinted at by Skeat *after* he is firmly committed to the authorial status of A XII: see, for example, *Parallel Texts* II.ix. I can find no support for Professor Kane's characterization (in "The Text" 177) that Skeat believed in 1867 that "the A text, with only a prologue and eleven sections, had not been completed by the poet (Skeat 1867, xxvi, xxvii)"; I do not find that view expressed on these pages of Skeat, nor anywhere else. In fact, on an immediately previous page (xxv), in discussing the "really *two* poems, each perfectly distinct from the other, with different titles, and separate prologues" that later combine to make up the A-Version, he specifically speaks to the matter of completeness and conclusion: "Each poem is complete in itself, and the concluding passages of each are wrought with peculiar care with a view to giving them such completeness. . . ."

shape of the A-Version — before he adopted A XII as authorial — we can adduce them as support for A XI's conclusiveness: to him the ending of XI had sufficient marks of closure to conclude the poem. Even this firm believer in single authorship did not need to hypothesize the fragmentary incompleteness of A. And Father Dunning, who in 1937 was still very much "inclined to think that B was written by someone other than the A poet," was quite forceful in proclaiming A XI the conclusion of a completed poem.[12] These two scholars, fundamentally in disagreement on substantial matters in *Piers* studies, could also meet upon this significant common ground.

In presenting the ending of A XI, Skeat, like the more recent editors, follows the Trinity manuscript since his favored Vernon manuscript has here lost the folio containing the end of the poem:

> ". . . For, *Michi vindictam, et ego retribuam*;
> I shal punnisshen in purcatory or in the put of helle
> Eche man for his misdede but mercy it make."
> "ȝet am I neuere the ner for nouȝt I haue walkid
> To wyte what is Do-wel witterly in herte; . . . ."
>
> (247a-51)

It is at this point worth noting also that in the appended pages to EETS, OS 28 in which Skeat first edits A XII from MS R, and declares it (143*) to be "Langland's beyond a doubt, every word of it, from line 1 down to the end of line 100" (which he numbers 105 in *Parallel Texts*), he goes on to remark on the last of these lines: "It is obvious that this notice of his own death is a mere flourish, introduced for the sake of winding up the poem at a moment when he had no idea of expanding and rewriting it" (144*). In other words, just as he was willing earlier to consider the A-Version complete at A XI.303, he is now confident that it concludes at XII.105. In neither case does he hold the poem incomplete; that suspicion awaits his *Parallel Texts*, by which point he considers lines 99–103 (recte 105?) "probably spurious" (II.165, note to line 99; and compare the note, II.329 to lines 98–100 — uncorrected from the line-numbering of EETS, OS 28, these correctly refer to lines 103–05 in the new numbering adopted after adding the five lines found in MS I[J]). Our confidence in this last position may be decreased by noticing how he yields to the "autobiographical fallacy," conflating the character of Will the narrator with the author: see George Kane, "The Autobiographical Fallacy in Chaucer and Langland Studies," The Chambers Memorial Lecture (London: H. K. Lewis, 1965).

[12]Quotation is from Dolan's Introduction, xvi. For Dunning's views on the ending, see 140–43. Even the authorial addition of passus XII, he continues, "does little more than reiterate the conclusions arrived at in the end of the second passus" (A XI) and "emphasizes the fact that the poem is at an end" (143).

Skeat concludes this speech, in Will's voice (presumably), at 303a
with the Latin line from C (XI.298a), which for him concludes A XI:
Breuis oracio penetrat celum.[13]

In addition to rejecting Skeat's quotation marks surrounding
250–303a (and his borrowing of the Latin verse), Knott-Fowler and
Kane relegate to Appendices the twelfth passus Skeat appends as an
authorial continuation of his A-Version. However, though Knott
and Fowler forcefully argue the formal completion of the A-Version
and Kane (at about the time of his edition) holds the "impartial view"
that A was unfinished, their texts at this point are remarkably congruent. Even their approaches to punctuating A XI.250 are similar.
Knott-Fowler's version of XI.247a–51 is:

> ". . . For, *Michi vindictam, et ego retribuam.*
> 'I shal punisshen in purcatory, or in the put of helle,
> Eche man for his misdede, but mercy it make.' "

> Yet am I nevere the ner, for nought I have walkid,
> To wyte what is Do-wel witterly in herte; . . . .

In Kane's text, these lines (255–59 in his version) read:

> ". . . For *Michi vindictam et ego retribuam.*
> I shal punisshen in purcatory or in þe put of helle
> Eche man for his misdede but mercy it make."
> —ȝet am I neuere þe ner for nouȝt I haue walkid
> To wyte what is dowel witterly in herte, ...

Though their methods of marking the break differ, the effects are
quite similar — and quite different from Skeat's. Knott and Fowler
explain their blank lines and indentation at line 250 as follows:
"Although nothing specific is said about an end to the dream (which
began at 9.58), we can assume that the dreamer awakens at this

---

[13]I quote the text from the 1886 *Parallel Texts*. In his 1867 edition he frankly
admits the Latin verse "does *not* strictly belong to the A-class of manuscripts, but to
the C-Class. But I have introduced it for two reasons: (1) because it is very appropriate and makes an excellent concluding line, and is closely connected with the
sense of the lines before it. . ." (154).

point. In the remainder of this passus he sums up his thinking concerning the search for Do-wel, etc." (169).

Kane has nowhere articulated the rationale for his punctuation in such detail, nor is it easy to identify his assumptions, but the force of his dash is consistent with attributing the following words to a speaker other than the dreamed "I"—which may be identified as either the waking Dreamer in the narrated past or the present Narrator. The present-tense verb of XI.250 may suggest the latter, and so a reading of Kane's punctuation produces an attribution not substantially different from that specifically articulated by Knott and Fowler. The ambiguous nature of the dash and its unspecified significance may, of course, allow it other (though to my mind less likely) interpretations. It may well be that the indefinite quality of the dash recommended itself to Kane, since it allowed him to leave the voicing of these words unspecified, subject to interpretative rather than editorial determination. Despite his own more definitely expressed later views, he did not alter the punctuation of this line in his revised edition of the text—even though "repunctuation" is one of the few revisions he allowed himself in the 1988 edition (ix).[14] We may safely infer, then, that Kane's dash marks an unspecified break in the dreamed dialogue. Whether the "I" of 250 is the Dreamer (still sleeping or awake) or the Narrator is indeterminate—and probably should remain so. This voice exists somewhere in or between Skeat's still-dreamed Will and Knott and Fowler's decisively awakened Dreamer/Narrator.

The nuances of such editorial disagreements may clarify a fundamental problem with these lines: given the expected closure and the apparent need for some authoritative position to end the continuing argument over the importance of learning—absent the lack of any decisive narrative or syntactic markings—the text cries out for some form of punctuation to mark what the words themselves cannot on their own make clear. And this is true whether one takes the remaining lines of XI as part of a dreamed discussion which continues in another passus, or as the conclusive summing-up of the *Vita*'s second dream. Some sort of editorial intervention is required to mark the

---

[14]See Kathleen M. Hewett-Smith, "Revisions in the Athlone Editions of the A and B Versions of *Piers Plowman*," *Yearbook of Langland Studies* 4 (1990): 151–54.

shift to an authoritative speaker.[15] It is, perhaps, finally indifferent whether the punctuation takes the form of quotation marks, a dash, or a visual break in lineation: all are similarly intrusive and dependent on interpretation. Skeat's choice of punctuation well articulates his view of the text's meaning; Knott and Fowler have explicated the interpretation signalled by theirs. Since it remains arguable in which voice, ultimately, authority may reside, it may be that Kane's dash, in not being either fully determinate or accompanied by explanation of its significance, is an attractive editorial intrusion: its unspecified significance forces readers themselves to make the necessary choice among competing possibilities. And, absent their accompanying footnote, the Knott-Fowler text would have similar effect.

Similar concerns as these clearly exercised scribes and early readers of the A-Version, and they were no more unanimous in their views than the most recent editors. Some took it as a completed poem; others supplemented it in various ways. However, since "it is known that scribes corrupted texts,"[16] it would seem foolhardy for scholars to align themselves too easily with even a majority of those scribes. The very arguments that Kane makes in support of minor details of his text can as justly be adduced regarding larger matters, such as that text's state of completeness. Simply because many (or even most) scribes felt the poem was unfinished ought not to force us to agree. Perhaps we should credit those few scribes who were willing to offer a "complete" short text as much as we credit those who sought deliberately to extend or supplement one they considered partial, incomplete, or even superseded by a revised edition.

---

[15]The poem evidences a number of unmarked changes of speech, but in most cases context makes the choice of speaker quite clear. There are, basically, three main ways of signalling change of speaker in *Piers*: 1) an introductory formula (e.g., running from a simple "N seide" to a more extended syntactic pattern which implies introduction); 2) an intrusive (or concluding) formula (predominantly "quod N"); and 3) a change unmarked by other than subject/point-of-view (e.g., a question followed by an answer, or a reactive remark). Of the 197 instances I have inventoried in A (Pro-XI), 76 (or 39.5%) are in the first group; by far the largest number (104 or 54%) are in the second; and only 12 (7%) are unmarked. These do not include cases where there is a shift from dramatized speaker to narrator, which would all fit in my category III; I have, however, included instances of quotation within other speeches, instances where a speaker directly invokes an authority. In A XII the ratios are roughly comparable: 1) 4 (25%); 2) 10 (62.5%); and 3) 2 (12.5%).

[16]Kane, "The Text" 189.

The scribes of the extant texts of the A-Version are indeed more evenly divided on the question of its being a whole, complete poem than are modern critics. It remains to determine whether the inconsistencies among the manuscripts are relatively insignificant, perhaps attributable to scribal error. Or are they more significant than that, details to which a careful reader should give further serious attention? Minor divergences may be easily dismissed or ignored, but they may also direct our attention to more fundamental matters, and cause us to examine textual and interpretative issues we have for more than a generation left resting quietly. Since we presently may find it difficult to separate the text of the A-Version from those of the other versions, and since hypotheses about authorship will directly implicate one's definition and expectations regarding any one of these texts, we should reflect on our own assumptions as we examine this textual geography. If, for instance, we accept the theory of single authorship, then we will expect consistencies and compatibilities among the texts and will give them priority over any noted inconsistencies. On the other hand, if we remain open to the possibility of multiple texts — or even multiple authors — then we will realize that even the very same words can be spoken by different voices and articulate quite differently intended meanings.

I do not expect to deal directly and fully with these larger issues here; rather, I wish to locate a place for discussing the text of *Piers* A, a place where we might concentrate as much as possible on the manuscript record of the poem's reception by its earliest readers and copyists. Does the *text* of the A-Version of *Piers* warrant modern scholars' accepting or endorsing the views of those who "in the fourteenth and fifteenth centuries . . . regarded" the A-Version as "incomplete" or who believed its "incompleteness . . . was evident" (Kane, *Evidence* 47, 48)? Or should we take more seriously the integrity of the text as recent editors have given it to us? Matured theses (about authorship or texts or completeness) attract, and deserve, periodic reconsideration: that is one of the principles by which our knowledge and understanding advance. When a seemingly insignificant loose thread shows itself at the end of a finely worked tapestry, a simple tug may reveal it to be truly insignificant; alternatively, such a slight effort may begin to unravel a fundamentally flawed or incomplete structure and reveal the work as less finished than it previously appeared.

II

Whether we hold the view that the various versions of *Piers* are
elements in a literary "tradition" or stages in a single author's poem,
the ending of the A-Version must challenge our understanding of the
differing meanings (in addition to the differing texts, of course) that
mark the three (or more) versions; and even a brief examination of
Skeat's parallel edition of the three versions will begin to reveal the
substantial nature of the revisions that the B- and C-Versions make
of A XI. What (in the texts of both Knott-Fowler and Kane) seems to
be the voice of the awakened narrator (or poet) in lines XI.250–303 is
presented clearly in the B-Version as a speech of Will within the
dream of B X; in the C-Version we stand at one further step from the
poet/narrator: the lines are delivered there by Rechelesnesse, spoken
within the (relocated) inner dream in C XII.

Rechelesnesse, a minor character with only three (or at most
eight) lines at the beginning of B XI (34–36/41), takes over C
XI.196–305 (which is, to take the ordinary critical view, C's rewriting of B's version of A's ending), and continues to play a significant
role up to C XIII.127.[17] Because of these reassignments, what may
appear in modern editions as the narrator's final, waking comments
in A, and as Will-the-Dreamer's argument with Scripture within the
analogous dream in B (and in Skeat's A), becomes in C the substance of a speech assigned to a character with the very untrustworthy name of Rechelesnesse. All three of these characters and
their fictional levels in the poems are radically different and offer
substantially differing claims as authorities. Their positions do not,
further, easily concord with a single consistent view. When words
that may be taken at one point by editors and readers as presented in
the voice of the author — *in propria persona* more or less — become
specifically enunciated in the voice of a personified dream-character

---

[17]Skeat holds off the close of his speech to 309 [= Pearsall's 311]. Pearsall supplies
very useful comments on these matters in his notes: especially at XI.196, 306,
XII.87, 98, and XIII.128.

There are useful discussions of these and related issues in Donaldson 170-75; in
C. David Benson, "An Augustinian Irony in 'Piers Plowman'," *Notes and Queries* 221
(1976): 51–54; and in David F. Johnson, " 'Persen with a Pater-Noster Paradys
Oþer Hevene': *Piers Plowman* C.11.296-98a," *Yearbook of Langland Studies* 5 (1991):
77–89.

named Rechelesnesse, we must acknowledge ourselves in the presence of something closer to revolution rather than to merely modest adjustments of textual attribution. Such a revolution demands more sophisticated justification and interpretation than can be accomplished by adding quotation marks or other punctuation. Are the ideas expressed in these virtually unchanged words in three versions of the poem so fluid that we can take them as both the author's own authoritative conclusion to his poem and the dismissed ravings of an intermediate, and dreamed, Rechelesnesse?

The B-Version, for all its divergences from A earlier in this passus, follows (as we shall see) the pattern of certain other readers of the earlier version and introduces "quod I" at x.372 (its equivalent to A xi.250), thereby marking the speaker as the disputatious Will. And at the beginning of its next passus, B xi — in a situation parallel to that found in the appendicular A xii (which begins with direct address to the dreamer: " 'Crist wot,' quod Clergie, 'knowe hit yif the lyke, / I have do my dever the Do-wel to teche; . . .' ")—we find further corroboration that the B-Version assumes Will speaks until the end of B x:

> Thanne Scripture scorned me and a skile tolde,
> And lakked me in latyn and liȝt by me sette,
> And seide *"Multi multa sciunt et seipsos nesciunt."*
>
> (B xi.1–3)

Other, seemingly minor discrepancies in detail — such as where one passus ends and another begins — tend to confuse the rhythm and structure of this stage of the debate, and obscure relationships with the earlier and later versions of these passages. To take one instance: the final line of A (xi.303) parallels B x.469–70 and C xi.298; B ends its passus x at 481 and the first 36 lines of B xi parallel C xi.163–198; the subsequent lines of B (xi.37–43) have their parallels in the final lines of C xi (306–315); and the opening lines of C xii then reproduce B xi.44ff. As these details suggest, there are major formal reconsiderations or revisions occurring at this point, the immediate successor to A's conclusion; they suggest a wrestling with A's ending that may be evidenced already at earlier points in this text of that ending. All of this *could* reinforce a view of the A-Version as unconcluded, or poorly concluded, or unacceptably

concluded. When we add in the reattribution of texts to newly identified speakers—such as Rechelesnesse—we can readily agree that B
and C do not simply provide a previously elided full stop, or supply
a half-line notice of the Dreamer's awakening (such as we find in the
concluding lines of B and C). Rather, we find ourselves considering
substantial revision and argumentative alteration of the A-Version,
not modest correction or emendation. But thoroughgoing analyses
of the revisions of A XI in B and C, important as they would be, will
not detain us here; their relevance to larger questions about the
status and reception of A XI, however, should be evident. What we
probably need—and what neither Fowler nor Kane could safely
claim has already occurred—is more sustained comparison of these
passus in A, B, and C, both as textual and conceptual constructs; the
closest we have come to *explaining* these changes is probably that
offered by Donaldson (70–75); now more than forty years ago.

The competing hypotheses regarding authorship can at best be
characterized as "not proven," Kane's widely quoted monograph
notwithstanding. Any real advances in that discussion, upon which
subsequent literary analysis should rightly depend, can only come
from careful attention to the sorts of questions I am touching upon
here. Perhaps others will be stimulated to do more than touch upon
them, and such examination will ultimately affect the larger contexts
of discussion of *Piers Plowman*. Whatever we might finally say of the
shape given the end of the A-Version in B and C, such revisions do
not necessitate our reading lines 250–303 of A XI as emphatically
inconclusive; and, furthermore, they cannot easily be adduced as
evidence that the authors of B and C thought A unfinished, "at an
impasse," or incomplete. Nor, on the other hand, is it logically necessary that one who harbors doubts about the existence of some ideal,
unitary poem called *Piers Plowman*, or about its being the work of a
single author, must take A's ending as firmly concluded: the assertion in A XII that Wille—the author of what "here is wryten, and
other werkes bothe, / Of Peres the plowman" (101–2)—is dead and
buried, offers at least one genuine option. In other words, critical
views regarding the integrity of the poem—or the lack thereof—do
not automatically implicate us in literary-historical or interpretative
conclusions. Text and reading are separable.

In the face of textual, interpretative, or other uncertainties, the
absence of explicit waking at the end of the A-Version might signify

either some uncertainty about that text — on the part of its author, its scribes, or its early readers; *or* alternatively, the fragmentariness of the surviving text; *or even* the arguable hypothesis that A XI.250–303 (or even XI.250–XII.00) is a sketch of a conclusion, one produced by the author before he died (as reported at the end of A XII) or by one particularly astute early reader who felt the poem did not otherwise conclude satisfactorily. Does the lack of exactness in the parallels with VIII.127–81 point to authorial inconsistency or lack of finish, or does it point to an editorial attempt at concluding "in the style of" the original?[18] Of course, the surviving manuscripts will dictate no clear or certain answers to these difficult questions, and we may have further reason to lament the loss of the folio containing the poem's ending in the Vernon manuscript; but the multiple, though not exhaustive, possibilities given above should stimulate thoughts about our modern reception of the A-Version. Even if the last lines of A XI as they now stand were demonstrably their author's conclusion, the question would remain whether they provide readers with convincing closure to the poem they are reading. The strength of Professor Fowler's remarks about an "emphatic conclusion" attests to his clear sense of the questions (and answers) provided by earlier critics; and these critics must include, as we know, the scribes to whom we owe the survival of the poem in its various versions.[19]

Some of our critical difficulties issue from our confusing the written text with its varied reception. Does a subsequent view that an earlier conclusion is problematic or unsatisfying necessitate its having been originally a recognized "impasse"? I think not. Is the reassignment (if that is what occurs) of A's concluding lines in B — and again in C — compatible with ordinary adjustments in a single author's mind? Do they demand an hypothesis of conversion or

---

[18]Similar questions could be raised about the bulk of A XII, which even a cautious scholar like Kane states "may be wholly or partly authentic, representing wholly or partly an imperfect or abortive continuation of the poem by the author" (*A-Version* 51). For recent, very stimulating discussion of the attribution of this text, see Middleton.

[19]See Kane, *Evidence* 48: "those who concerned themselves with the poem in the fourteenth and fifteenth centuries . . . distinguished between a short and a fuller form of the poem, that is to say between *A* and the other versions, because the incompleteness of the former was evident to them."

revolution in that author's thinking? Or do they warrant an hypothesis of multiple authors? If they signal a moment of crisis on the part of the author, an "impasse" sufficient to cause the abandonment of the A-Version, they may as easily support a claim for another person's being involved in rewriting. And we must consider the doubleness of this revision: the solution of the "impasse" in B is itself only partial and temporary since the C-Version even more fundamentally alters this crucial passage in the poem. Consistency, then, might demand we abandon any further independent consideration of B, in favor of C's revision — and carry it out with something like the alacrity (and near irreversibility) that has in recent years greeted the A-Version. But those of us who have now put away the things of a child will have little difficulty conceiving how one might subsequently grow uncertain about earlier certainties. It follows, then, that to read the text of A as concluded does not necessarily prevent its being subsequently revised — nor that revision's being itself later substantially reworked. If we resist personifying the versions and treat them as independent texts, these matters will begin to appear differently. An author's change of mind or heart may not effect a similar change in his audience's — especially if his earlier versions are not systematically suppressed or corrected. There is an important principle behind the New Criticism's insistence that we read the poem in itself, freed from biography, history, and intention. If the text of *Piers* A has been received and circulated in its own independent form, then (no matter what we conclude about the author) we owe that text a considered analysis and understanding — in and of itself. Perhaps too many of us have simply avoided doing this for too long.

To re-open discussion of these issues, then, let us go behind the nearly unanimous judgment of present critics of *Piers* and concentrate on the less unanimous opinions and uncertainties we find among the earliest known readers of the A-Version, and particularly on those details that bear upon the text's conclusion. Though the most recent editors may substantially agree upon the shape and significant details of the text, there is considerably less consensus among the manuscripts. The manuscript endings for A XI warrant fuller consideration, not least for the help they can give us in determining how the A-Version was received and understood by some of its earliest readers.

III

Study of the A-Version of *Piers Plowman* as a poem with its own integrity and appeal continues to be retarded by the general critical consensus that the A-Version is an abandoned early fragment of a work carried to conclusion by its author in the B- and C-Versions. This is not, of course, a view shared by Professor Fowler, who reveals himself thereby an heir of two doubting Thomases: Thomas A. Knott and Thomas P. Dunning. And while I found myself earlier giving full assent to the more widely held view, I now confess myself more doubtful, unpersuaded that there is sufficient evidence for me to accept the view fully and without question. The conjunction of Knott-Fowler and Kane on the matter of the authoritative shape of the text of the A-Version reinforces me in withholding my assent. But regardless (I hope) of my own convictions, or lack thereof, I find that, no matter what view one holds on the difficult matter of authorship, the textual record surrounding the end of the A-Version may be adduced to support either hypothesis—or neither of them. The manuscript record is divided and does not unambiguously resolve the matter of the A-Version's integrity.

Examining the extant A-Version manuscripts, however, helps refine these questions and their implications and, by doing so, makes clear which questions might reward further attention. There are, after all, a number of possible solutions to the "problem" of the ending of the A-Version, and early readers of the text may be found to have dealt with it as modern editors have—or, alternatively, produced other reasonable solutions that we might ourselves consider. If we exclude the four manuscripts that are structurally incomplete (T_2[E], L, V, H) and a fifth (N), which ends at the conclusion of passus VIII and is continued from that point with a C text, and if we likewise exclude the problematic Z-Text (Bodley 851),[20] then there remain four distinct types of conclusions for *Piers Plowman* A. Since important manuscripts such as V and H are among those structurally incomplete, we unfortunately cannot consult or reconstruct the original endings for a crucial branch of the text. Indeed, aside from

---

[20]See A. G. Rigg and Charlotte Brewer, eds. *Piers Plowman: The Z Version* (Toronto: Pontifical Institute of Medieval Studies, 1983); and George Kane, "The 'Z Version' of *Piers Plowman*," *Speculum* 60 (1985): 910–30.

V, none of the five incomplete manuscripts takes us past the end of
the Visio: three of them conclude at (N) or very near (L and H) the
end of passus VIII.[21]

Classified with respect to their types of ending, the remaining
twelve manuscripts of the A-Version of *Piers Plowman* may be arranged as follows[22]:

I. Completed at A XI.303: A and (originally) Di[K].
II. Completed (essentially at A XI.303) with some individual
scribal lines: H₃, D, and M.
III. Continued after A XI.303 by the "John But" passus: U, I[J],
and R.
IV. Continued after A XI.303 by C-Version (usually beginning
with C XI.299): T, Ch, H₂, W, and (as an afterthought)
Di[K].

In what follows, our attention will rest primarily on various features of A XI.250–303, even though these lines prove in many important respects to be quite the least substantially revised section of
this much-altered passus as it passes from A into B and C. When we
leave behind the revisions of these fifty-plus lines (and of those preceding them) in the B- and C-Versions, we can easily detect in the A-
Version manuscripts efforts by many of the scribes to supply a more
satisfactory, more conclusive ending to this version of *Piers Plowman*

---

[21]L breaks off at VIII.152, and H at VIII.139; T₂[E] ends at VII.44, with a mis-
placed VII.70–213. Knott and Fowler take it that N continues as A up to IX.13, but
since the first thirteen lines of IX offer little to differentiate A from B/C, the point
remains arguable. Kane concludes that N ceases to be an A text with the end of
passus VIII (Kane's VIII.184 equals Knott-Fowler's VIII.181). Nevertheless, in his
remarks on the possible length of the text in H, L, and T₂[E] he makes no reference
to N. This is perhaps a little surprising, since its concluding (by his account) at the
passus division may put it forward as offering something very close to the missing
"perfect specimen of a form of the poem ending with VIII" (40). He had earlier (36)
referred to "N's very faithful attestation of distinctive *A* lines and passages to the end
of *A* VIII. . . ." And one might also factor in N's curious (and unique) rubric that
provides the transition from A to C: "Passus nonus de visione & vltimus & hic
desinit / Et decetero tangit auctor de inquisicionibus de Dowel / Do bettre & Dobest
sicut patebit speculantibus. Inquisicio prima" (Knott-Fowler 240).
[22]My groups, because of their emphasis on the shape of the *endings*, will be found
to differ from the eight groups identified by Kane, in his discussion of the "shape" of
the A-Version (*A-Version* 20–21, 42ff). The most noticeable variation appears in my
rearranging manuscripts in his groups 4 and 5 into my groups I and II.

that ends at A xi.303 — and, concomitantly, a more forceful marking of those lines as being the conclusion of that poem.

If manuscripts of a "complete" A-Version circulated independently — and for a considerable period as the manuscripts in my first two groups would suggest, many other manuscripts offer evidence of its early having attracted either of two alternative endings: a C-Supplement or an additional, twelfth passus for the A-Version (which subsequently plays no part in the evolution of B and C). In all, three manuscripts (Group iii above) contain the added twelfth passus, while five (Group iv) provide a continuation from the C-Version. If the manuscripts in my groups i and ii — whatever importance one might assign their minor differences — may confirm the completeness of the A-Version and their scribes' satisfaction with its ending, these other two groups raise fundamental questions about its contemporary reception as a complete poem in anything like that form. And can we, by looking at these, determine what there was about the A-Version ending that invited, at a relatively early stage, new attempts at closure, attempts that generated substantial additions or supplements beyond the end of xi.303? And if we acknowledge these as substantial changes to the original, can we remain altogether confident that the A-Version really warranted independent circulation as a coherent, concluded whole? Do the four manuscripts that actually conclude the poem in the vicinity of xi.303 deserve the textual authority they have in attesting to an independent A-Version of *Piers Plowman*? What can we learn from those that continue the poem beyond this point?

Three manuscripts follow A xi.303 with a twelfth passus, rubricated as "Passus tercius de dowel ₇c' " in U (likewise in I and R, absent the "₇c' "). In R, the only "complete" manuscript, the new passus opens:

> Crist wot quod clergie knowe hit ʒif þe lyke
> I haue do my deuer þe Dowel to teche . . . .

The imprecation "Crist wot," and the following "quod clergie" mark this as the beginning of a new speech. The double direct address ("ʒif þe lyke / . . . þe . . . to teche") suggests that Clergie (a speaker who appeared earlier) is now responding to another speaker within the format of a continuing, dreamed debate. This would seem to deny

the immediately preceding lines any status as narratorial or authorial summation; rather, the twelfth passus implies that these lines are
"in character." Like Skeat, who introduced quotation marks, or those
A manuscripts that insert "quod I" at 250 (discussed below, pp.
231), the author of this twelfth passus takes the concluding words of A XI
as enunciated still in the world of dreamed debate, with their speaker
being Will, the dreamed persona of the Dreamer/Narrator. The
twelfth passus, in this regard, conforms to a view held by manuscripts in my three other groups: namely M, W, and Di[K], the
three manuscripts that have "quod I" in XI.250. It is, therefore,
hardly surprising that Skeat, when he included passus XII in his
edition of the A-Version (or all but its final twelve lines), retained the
quotation marks he had previously introduced at 250.

The manuscripts in my Group IV resolve the apparent openness
of A XI in a different way: by appending a "supplement" from the C-
Version. While I do not propose here to extend the brief remarks
above regarding the C-Version's revising what it inherited from the
ending of the A-Version — with its concomitant reassignment of the
concluding lines to Rechelesnesse — a substantially different solution
(even one inconsistent with the revision of A XI in the C-Version) is
offered by these five manuscripts. They do not engage in any substantial revision of A XI, but close it with an addendum from the C-
Version, often quite awkwardly connected to the the preceding text.
Four of these manuscripts follow A XI.303 with a passus break, and
commence a new passus with the equivalent the last 18 lines of C XI
(lines 298a-315). In MS T, for instance, the passage reads:

> Passus _tercius_ de dowel Breuis _oracio_ penetrat celum
> Selde falliþ þe _seruaunt_ so depe in arerage
> As doþ þe reue ⁊ þe countrollo_ur_ þat rekne mote ⁊ acompte
> Of alle þat þei han had of hym þat is here maist_er_
> Ac lewide labo_ur_eris of litel vndirstonde
> Selde falliþ so foule ⁊ so depe in synne
> As clerkis of holy chirche þat kepe shulde ⁊ saue
> Lewide men in good beleue ⁊ lene hem at h_er_e wille
> Homo _pro_ponit qu_od_ a poete þo and plato he hi3te
> _Et deus disponit_ quod he let god do his wille
> Alle þat treuþe techiþ ⁊ testifieþ for goode
> þei3 þei folewe þat fortune no foly ich it holde

Ne concupiscencia carnis ⁊ cetera
Ne shal not greue þe gretly ne begile þe but þou wille
Tho fare wel fippe quod fauntelot and forþ gan me drawe
Til <u>concupiscencia carnis</u> accordite til al my werkin
Of Dowel ne of Dibut no ueynte me ne thouhte
Ne Clergie ne his conseile y counted hit ful litel.[23]

The parallels among the four manuscripts that do this are not exact, and there is one obvious difficulty with T's weaving together of the two versions. At the end of the above passage the following occurs: Passus secu*n*dus de dobet / Allas ey qu*o*d elde ⁊ holynesse boþe (i.e., C XII.1). Clearly this rubric is unexpected, both in regard to its place — a eighteen-line passus is unusual — and in its denomination of the passus as "de dobet."[24]

Two other manuscripts (Ch and H₂) correspond with T in beginning "Passus tercius de dowel" at C XI.298a (Ch after the Latin tag; H₂ before); however, unlike T they do not begin another passus at C XII.1. A fourth manuscript, Di[K], offers additional complications. In its present, final form it does not begin a new passus after A XI.303; instead it emulates the pattern of most C-Version manuscripts and postpones the break until after C XI.315, when it writes "finis." However, this was not the original shape of the manuscript. The scribe first wrote "Amen" at the end of XI.303; subsequently this was crossed through in the same ink and a following, marginal "ffinis de dowell" was erased.[25] Only after (presumably) both these "corrections" were made did the scribe continue (with what appears to be a

---

[23]I provide these transcriptions, as I do others, from photographic copies of the A-Version's manuscripts available in David Fowler's papers in the University of Washington's Archives. I have not supplied punctuation from the manuscript. (The text of the last two lines, not available in the photographs, is borrowed from Pearsall's edition.)

[24]Subsequent passus (C XV, XVII, XVIII) revert to "de dowel." I have not been able to determine if any other C-Version manuscripts have this same variant.

[25]The text here erased, it should be noted, is not the simple "finis" found at the end of its other passus: in all cases, indeed, except the "Explicit visio" at the end of A VIII, and the "finis totaliter" at the end of C XXII. For other details, see Knott-Fowler 252; Kane 10, 42. Di[K] begins the next passus with "Passus quartus de dowell," a numbering which is consistent only with that of the rubricator's guide at this point in MS W (Kane, *A-Version* 18). The competing numbering systems of A and C show up quite clearly in these manuscripts with the C-Supplement: C XII is in other C manuscripts usually "Passus secundus"; in these A manuscripts the earlier system of the A-Version clearly dominates: see Kane, *A-Version* 40–42.

slightly different, darker, ink); the text starts, like the others we have just been considering, with C XI.298a.

My final witness to the C-Supplement, W, provides a further variation in grafting C to A: it begins a new passus (with C XII.1) here, omitting entirely the last eighteen lines of C XI.[26] In doing so, it sustains the possibility that Elde and Holynesse's "Allas" at the beginning of C XII reacts to the preceding words as an expression issuing from a "Wil" who "hath al his wille." In the context of A XI the "me" comforted by "Couetyse-of-yes" (at C XII.3) must here be identified with the past Dreamer (as it will be in B), not with the C-Version's Rechelesnesse. In the manuscripts that provide a C-Supplement, whether they heard in the last lines of A XI the words of Will asleep or the Dreamer (or Narrator) awake, the scribes — aside from Di[K], of course — were confident with marking a firm passus break, and avoided any explicit marking of a change in voice. This *may* suggest the scribes' mechanical transcription of their exemplars, or their unwillingness to employ any critical judgment in the face of ambiguity or lack of clarity. (And the eighteen-line passus of T is certainly consistent with a quite mechanical copying of its exemplar[s].) It may be unfair to generalize on the basis of the little evidence I have provided regarding these manuscripts, but (with the possible exception of T, whose double passus marking may suggest he is adding the supplement on his own) we can infer very little from these manuscripts about their scribes' reception of A XI as a conclusion. Their awareness of a "continuation" is patent, and to that extent their manuscripts will invite less consciousness of any ending at this point; it will also have the corollary that their involvement with that ending will be unlikely to be marked by direct intervention of an editorial sort. In other words, these manuscripts *could* be taken as confirming the original shape and quality of the A ending, a view

---

[26]We can only guess whether the blank line at the bottom of its fol. 31r would have been filled by the passus-title alone, as the marginal rubricator's guide would suggest, or accompanied by the Latin tag. The regular presence of such guides and the absence of supplied rubrics from the spaces provided for them in the C-Version portion of this manuscript would suggest that some significant delay interposed after the completion of the A-Version, which is consistently supplied with rubrics, and free of such marginal guides. This is further suggested by the fact that fol. 31 would be the seventh folio of a quire of eight, and presumably such rubrication was, minimally, carried out by quires.

consistent with both Knott-Fowler and Kane, who trusted one of these, T, as their base manuscript.

While the manuscripts in my groups III and IV, then, may suggest some scribal dissatisfaction with the ending of the A-Version, consistent with reacting to the absence of waking, that dissatisfaction is moderated by their knowledge of a continuation of the text — in the form of the longer C-Version or of the briefer passus XII. In any event, these scribes would, in light of their knowledge of a longer poem, be unlikely to emend the ending of A XI in any substantial way so as to effect closure. Among them, MSS W and Di[K] supply "quod I" at XI.250 and thereby reinforce the attribution of the following lines to the dreamed Will. All eight manuscripts in these groups, however, because of their confidence about the poem's continuing, do not provoke any serious challenge to accepting XI.250–303 as the end of an independent version of *Piers Plowman*. For them, any closural tendencies are simply temporary, marking the end of a stage or episode in a continuing debate, a continuing poem.

Like W and Di[K], MS M also reads "quod I" in XI.250, a reading that modern editors have rejected, even though it parallels the B-Version's "solution" to the absence of any awakening: that is, the dream does not end here and the remaining lines continue as part of the dreamed debate. M, however, unlike the other manuscripts (or versions) we have been considering so far, does not continue the poem beyond the end of A XI. This scribe's accepting such an ending leaves us with an important question: Is the Dreamer's awaking formally required at the end of a literary dream vision?

In MS M, lines 247–51 (at the very top of p. 548) read:

No vindicabis q*uia* m*ihi* vind*i*ctam ⁊ ego ret*r*ibuam
I schal punischi*n* in purgatorie or in the pet of helle
Ich man for his misdede but ȝif m*er*cy lette
ȝit am I q*uo*d I neu*er*e ner for nouth þat I haue walkyd
to weti*n* what is dowel witt*er*ly in herte.[27]

---

[27]At line 250 MS Di[K] reads "Yett ame I neu*er* the nere q*uo*d I though I haue Iwalked" and W has "ȝit am neuere þe ner*e* q*uo*d I for oght I hawed." Though the two manuscripts are in frequent agreement, Kane was perhaps correct to ignore this as a point of correspondence (*A-Version* 76, 113).

The modern editors' typographical markings to indicate a shift of voice are, to my mind, no less intrusive than MWDi[K]'s "quod I." Though the latter may conflict with metrical patterns, it is hardly more intrusive. The various location of "quod I" in these manuscripts may further attest to its being introduced independently by these scribal editors (or their ancestors) for punctuation—much as Knott-Fowler and Kane mark their texts. The texts of these three manuscripts record one readily available solution to the passage's perceived ambiguities. Along with the B-Version, which also has "quod I" in its rewriting of the analogous line, these manuscripts attest to relatively early attempts to identify the speaker of the received text. Independently, perhaps, they present one mildly intrusive emendation to resolve that difficulty, to indicate the speaker, and to define the text's local shape. We may, however, be no closer to determining what they felt with respect to the poem's conclusion: the beginning of a quotation necessitates our locating its end. But even the conclusion of this dreamed dialogue need not automatically close the dream or the poem.

Though rejected by Knott-Fowler and by Kane, the texts of these three manuscripts at A XI.250 are congruent with that of Skeat, who, as we saw above, introduced quotation marks to accommodate the lack of any verbal (or other) marker in his exemplar. (And he, also, appears not to have been unduly concerned by the omitted awakening of the Dreamer.) Though different, the solution of our more recent editors is no less intrusive: their interruptive punctuation is more intent on marking the dream's (and the poem's) closure. But can so much be left to depend on what modern conventions of

---

M, along with the B-Version and certain other manuscripts of the A-Version, intrudes a similarly definitive "quod sche" at A I.83. Closer to the text at hand, while A, Di[K] and W add "quod I" at A XI.216, M agrees with the majority which omits it; in this case the similarity with the B-Version is obscured by the substantial revision of the lines involved: B X.328 does contain "quod I" in the analogous line. But none emulates the B-Version (X.158) by inserting "quod I" at A XI.112.

For comparative purposes, these are the cases I have noted in which "quod I" (or other "quod N" variant) appeared in A-Version manuscripts, but has been rejected by Knott-Fowler and Kane: I.59: H and V; I.83: H, H_2, M, R, and W; II.5: H, H_2, I[J], U, V, and W; V.70: H; VII.9: W; VIII.116: H, W; XI.216: A, Di[K], W; XI.250: Di[K], M, and W. In only two cases have I found Knott-Fowler and Kane disagreeing: the former includes "quath she" (witnessed in MSS H, H_2, M, and V) at II.16, and "quod I" (favoring the reading of I[J] over that of R) at XII.67. (At XII.88, both editions omit the "quod he" in the last extant line of I[J].)

punctuation may be induced to make clear? To concentrate on deciding which of these editorial intrusions is correct, or even acceptable, may distract us from more important questions. Do these two options, indeed, exhaust the possibilities? Do any of the other manuscripts point toward better, or different, readings?

If these (and other) insertions of "quod I" stand as examples of early scribal attempts to give greater clarity to, or remedy difficulties they perceived in, their texts of the A-Version — and modern editors' unanimous rejection of most of these attempts would point toward such a judgment — we might usefully examine the work of other scribes to determine if the difficulties are accurately perceived (and remedied) by their colleagues in MWDi[K]. Are there alternative readings of the text, other responses to the same perceived difficulties? Nothing that I have seen directly signals a break or shift of speaker at XI.250, except perhaps the unusual line inserted in MS H$_3$ immediately before it: "Reddam vnicuique iuxta op*era* sua."[28] But it might be going too far to take this as a sophisticated act of punctuation.

However, another significantly different solution to the difficulty raised in these lines may perhaps be detected in the Ashmole manuscript. This scribe introduces a preliminary "And" at the beginning of 250: "And ʒit am I neuyr þe ner for out I haue walkyd." Far from emphasizing a break in the narrative level of the text, this instead erases any potential ambiguity about who is speaking by insisting on continuity: the conjunction presumably implies assignment of 250ff. to Scripture.[29] Its equivalent of line 267 offers a likely candidate for the conclusion of Scripture's speech, with an unmarked shift of voice in the next line: here, the *omission* of a conjunctive "And" (which appears in all but MSS A and W) could sustain a reading of XI.268

---

[28]This text (in which I am unable to detect Kane's "extra minim" [*A-Version* 48] in the "vnicuique") conflates a number of biblical phrases (for example, Prov. 24:29; Ps. 61[62]:13; Matt. 16:27; Rev. 22:12; etc.), and does not appear in the A-Version anywhere else. Neither does it show up in B or C at this point, though with slightly different wording it does appear at B XII.216a, C V.32a, and C XIV.152a.

[29]The insertion of "And" at 250 may gain particular weight when one notices how many times the scribe of MS A omits an initial "And": see, for instance, 256, 264, 267, 268, 273, 283, 288, 296 — but retained, significantly perhaps, at 285: another "And ʒit. . . ."

as Will's reaction to the immediately preceding advice from Scripture:

". . . Was neuyr in þis [werld] to wysere clerkis;
ffor alle connyng clerkis syn god went on erde   265
Takyn example of here sawis in sermonys þat þei makyn,
Be here werkis and wordis wyssyn vs to do wel."
"ʒif I schal werche here werkis [to] wynne me heuyn,   268
And I with here werkis ⁊ witte wynne me pyne,
Than wrouth I vnwysely with alle þe wittis þat I lere. . . ."³⁰

The sentiments of the subsequent lines are strongly opposed to "clergie" and the benefits of learning, as Will has shown himself earlier. He cites the counter-authority of the gospels ("A Good Friday, I fynde, a feloun was saved" [271]) against Dame Scripture; and his invocation of "austyn þe elde" as the "doutiest doctor" may be read ironically, since the text he authorizes — "Ecce ipsi indocti rapiunt celum vbi nos / sapientes in infernum margimur" (295a) — lowers the status of "nos sapientes" below that of "indocti," such as the Dreamer. The ironic color subtly reminds us of the Dreamer's more overt clerkly "Contra," earlier delivered against both the two friars (IX.16) and Scripture (XI.228).

Although I am not aware of anyone arguing that lines 250–67 continue Scripture's speech — the sense of these lines in the modern critical editions would make it difficult to sustain such a view — there is, certainly, an acceptably "scriptural" cast to the points raised here, with their emphasis on biblical characters and events, as well as other examples of book-learning. And other variants in this passage of MS A (for example, the reading of 256: "leue it wel be oure lord no lettere betere") might further support such an attribution. The scribe-editor of Ashmole, at least, may have read the lines in Scripture's voice. But such speculations with regard to a scribe's interpretations and intentions do not easily admit of persuasive demonstra-

---

³⁰I have punctuated the Ashmole text to reflect the hypothetical shift of speakers at this point; likewise, I have supplied "werld," omitted from 264, and substituted "to" for the manuscript's "⁊" in 268. Kane (A-Version 144) speaks of "the generally slovenly character of the copy in a manuscript like A."

The intensive rewriting that occurs in the B-Version does not substantially change 250–70, but extensive interpolations appear in what follows, after lines 270, 284, and 293.

tion; at best they can be suggestive, perhaps plausible, justifications of the logic behind a single manuscript's variant readings. But then any argument of this sort is an attempt to reveal and explain pat terns and coherences in a text, whether one grants priority to local textual details or to larger ideal structures will of course affect the kind of coherence one perceives. Any certain and easy access to such ideal structures must remain in doubt when the complexities of local textual matters are less well understood. If we could deny scribes any editorial interests, or skills, life might be much easier for modern readers. Luckily for us we cannot.

In any case, even when we grant lines XI.250–303 the authority of the A-Version poet, we find that a number of early, not demonstrably unintelligent readers of this ending have evidenced difficulties akin to those many of us, including the poem's modern editors, have felt at this point: who is speaking these words, and if this is the poem's end why does the text not explicitly mark the Dreamer's waking? Other, less crucial shifts of speakers have been more clearly marked. Where does Scripture stop speaking and another begin? And who *is* that other? In the absence of clear marking, through narrative or syntax, what does (or can) the text mean? Previous critics have been able to overlook or downplay these matters, to accept as decisive a reasonable editorial solution to the problems, and to get on with their reading. Perhaps they were correct in this, emulating as they did the solutions evidenced in the work of their ancestors, the early scribal editors.

But the difficulties these manuscripts raise are not limited to matters of word choice and phrasing in and around lines 250 and 285, and they are, arguably, symptomatic of substantial and unresolved problems in the A-Version's ending. When we examine such difficulties, we repeatedly discover the long history behind our own modern uncertainties. And while these uncertainties are not, of course, necessarily the author's, being only demonstrably those of the early readers and transmitters of the text, yet since we are constrained to discover the author's text through theirs, we should give more attention to their difficulties and uncertainties. For instance, the Ashmole manuscript — whose intention and interpretation of the voices in this ending we have just been speculating about — *alone* of the surviving manuscripts of the A-Version of *Piers Plowman*, actually ends its text of the poem with lines closely parallelling those at which modern

editors have printed as the end of theirs. Following the equivalent of
A XI.303 — I with oute penauns at here partyng into þe blisse of
heuyn — the Ashmole scribe writes "Amen" (at the beginning of the
next line). Though the text lacks a colophon more firmly indicating
closure, this conclusive Amen provides sufficient warrant of this
text's ending. The warrant is further confirmed by the blank remainder of this verso page (378), which is subsequently filled with Latin
texts, culled for the most part from the preceding text of *Piers*.
Support for this reception of the A-Version as a complete text and of
this being its ending is, of course, to be found elsewhere — though in
no case is that support uncomplicated by other editorial interventions by the scribe. As we saw above, Di[K] at one time also concluded with a scribal "Amen" at the same point as MS A, but it was
subsequently cancelled and supplanted by a C-Supplement.

Like A and Di[K], the three manuscripts in my Group II (H₃, D,
and M) also punctuate the ending in the vicinity of XI.303, and so
sustain the modern editors' views that one self-contained version of
Piers Plowman comes to an end at this point. However individual they
may be in their treatment of the ending, these three manuscripts
confirm their scribes' confidence in a conclusion of the A-Version at
XI.303. Their various treatments of this A-Version ending are worth
at least brief examination here. In their probable order of composition, they conclude as follows.[31]

MS H₃ (Knott-Fowler 24: "About 1420"; Kane 8: "third quarter of
the fifteenth century. Doyle prefers 1425–1450") closes with:

Sawerys ⁊ sowerys ⁊ sweche leude Iottys   (= XI.301)
ffor þei leuyn as þei be leryd ⁊ oþer wyse nouth

---

[31]Transcriptions of H₃ and M are printed in Kane, *A-Version* 48–49; while providing the text of the Latin *explicit*, Kane does not record the English couplet. The
textual notes in Knott-Fowler do not record the added lines in M and H₃ but do
provide the rubrics and the two additional lines in D (252).

I omit from consideration the "seven closing lines to the A text in the Westminster
manuscript" discussed by Middleton (245–46). Kane's discussion of these lines
("The Text" 182) cites them as lines supplied by a "marginal commentator" who is
adding "a pious ending in the poet's voice." This ending, however, does not appear
alongside the ending of the A-Version, but is appended to the conclusion of the C-
Text. The A-Text portion of the Wesminster MS concludes on fol. 31; these lines "in
a later hand, of no value" (Skeat, EETS, OS 81, 853) appear on fol. 76r. (I am
indebted to Professor Kane for confirming the location of these lines.).

Musyn *in* no materes but holdy*n* þe ryth be leue.
He þat redyth þis book ⁊ ryth haue it *in* mende.
Preyit for pers þe plowma*n*s soule.
W*ith* a pat*er* n*ost*er to þe paleys of heuene   (= XI.302)
W*ith* outy*n* gr*et* pe*n*ans at hys p*ar*tyng to comy*n* to blys.   (= XI.303)
Explicit tractus de perys plowman. q*uod* . heru*n*.
Qui cu*m* patre ⁊ sp*iri*tu s*an*cto viuit ⁊ regnat p*er* o*m*nia s*e*c*u*la s*e*c*u*loru*m*
Ame*n*.[32]

The ending of MS M (Knott-Fowler 24: "End of fifteenth century
(?)"; Kane 12: "about 1425") reads:

Wit outy*n* penau*n*ce at her*e* p*ar*tynge in to þe heye blisse
ffor þey I rede alle men þat on crist be leuyn
Asken m*er*cy of god for her*e* misdedes
And coueiten no*n* clergie ne catel on þis erþe
But alwey to s*er*uen god ⁊ hendy*n* in hise werkys
And þat he grau*n*te vs þe Ioie þat euer*e* schal lastyn
W*ith* pers þe plowma*n* to wonyn in his blysse Amen Amen
Explicit prologus de dowel dobet ⁊ dobest[33]

MS D (Knott-Fowler 23: "second half of fifteenth century"; Kane
3: "late fifteenth century") concludes as follows:

with oute penau*n*ce at here partyng in to heye blysse
Now of þis litel book y haue makyd an ende
Goddis blessyng mote he haue þat drinke wil me sende

                    E x p l i c i t   l i
                    b e r   p e t r i   pl
                    o u m a n   ƒ

---

[32]This apparently ends the manuscript: the remaining two-thirds of this verso is
blank — except for the later British Museum stamp. There is what appears to be a
pious three lines in the same scribe's hand in the middle of the next recto [= fol.
124], some marginal rulings, and, in a later hand, a version of the last line above,
written in a narrow column.
[33]The text ends at the bottom of the recto — the *explicit* takes the scribe one line
further into the lower margin than on other pages. (The rubrics are in the main
scribe's hand.) Two sets of wavy lines run across the bottom of the page, marking it
presumably as completing the work of the manuscript's main scribe; the verso is
blank except for three lines at top, repeating (a later hand imitating?) IV.15–17,
which are at the top of 495, the beginning of an earlier quire, number xxii.

Together with MS A and (presumably) the lost exemplar of the A-Version for Di[K][34] (which has no particular affiliation with MS A), these manuscripts attest to the poem's having ended at XI.303 in the version they were copying. Each is followed originally by blank space on the remainder of the folio. All, in other words, are comfortable with the poem's ending here. Their comfort perhaps should prompt us to question our own.

The changes and additions in D, M, and H₃ are, effectively, little more than extended, free-form but determinately conclusive scribal punctuation. In the case of H₃ and M, the additional lines may have been inspired by the completion of their commissions: the "tractus de perys plowman" ends H₃, and the end of this "prologus" concludes the work of the main scribe of M (what follows is in a different hand). The fact that in both these cases the text of *Piers* concludes the scribes' work on these manuscripts may account for the expansiveness of these two conclusions, and of both the general similarities and the specific divergences between them. But while they differ from one another, neither evidences any dissatisfaction with the poem's ending; their added lines essentially confirm and reinforce their exemplar's version of this ending. In the case of M, the finality of the ending may be in some doubt: his terming the completed text as "prologus" certainly leaves us with questions about the original plan of the work, and of this scribe's enterprise: Can the denominated end of a "prologue" be taken as the ending of an entire work? But this scribe, at least, did not proceed further. To him, either the duty of following his exemplar was paramount, or else the "ending" of the A-Version at A XI.303 suggested that its author, for all his brilliance and emphasis, has not yet concluded; this is but prologue.[35]

---

[34]Kane is right, I believe, in his view regarding the composition of Digby (*A-Version* 41–42): its C-Supplement is decidedly an afterthought, and a single exemplar for the two parts is extremely unlikely.

[35]Only W, aside from M, titles the beginning of passus IX "prologus" of Dowel, Dobet and Dobest; M, furthermore, provides no breaks or rubrics for the concluding two passus, which his *explicit* suggests he took as a single prologue, begun at A IX. (The rubrics of M are in the hand of the main scribe.) Other manuscripts introduce passus IX with the title "vita," or simply (as V does) "Incipit hic Dowel Dobet and Dobest." N, uniquely, titles it "Inquisicio prima [de Dowel]"; what follows, however, is C X — not A IX — and C XI is titled "Primus Passus de Dowel." Transcriptions of all the rubrics can be consulted in Knott-Fowler (171ff), and in Kane (1–18).

All in all, however, these manuscripts confirm the end (of something) by way of pious closings. Thus they parallel in spirit, if not in exact detail, the "Amen" of MS A. In the case of D, admittedly, the piety is mixed with the scribe's highly secular request for drink (instigated, perhaps, by the prospect of his now having to copy *The Charter of the Abbey of the Holy Ghost*). To emphasize the closure of the prologue, M offers a fairly simple and straightforward addition of six lines, while H_3 ends his "tractus" by inserting four lines between 301 and 302, thereby instigating more intrusive syntactic and phrasal changes in his version of 302-3. Two of the manuscripts (H_3 and D) confirm that the poem ("tractus" or "liber") at some point ended here and that their scribes were satisfied with that completeness; with the possible exception of M, they evidence no consciousness of continuation, alternative ending, or other version of *Piers Plowman*.[36] And we are left in the dark as to the character of the work to which M has concluded a "prologus." None of this group, furthermore, shows much concern with the lack of waking by the dreamer/narrator: of the three, M again is odd-man-out and (as we have already seen) inserted "quod I" at A XI.250. In view of his text's being rubricated as "prologus" we may assume that the lack of clearly marked closure can be accepted because its need is postponed. To the scribes of H_3 and D, the absence of "quod I" marking the last lines as Will's in a dream, or of any overt signal of waking, appears of little moment; they are satisfied the poem is ended, and their scribal additions and firm *explicit*s confirm that.

We can now recognize in the above four groups of A-Version manuscripts signs of the variant reception of this poem; it would be an oversimplification to say that their treatments of the latter stages of the A-Version produce anything like a consistent response, or that they attest to unambiguous closure. Some scribes, conscious of continuations of one sort or another, behaved accordingly at the end of A XI; others, thinking this the end of a complete poem, accepted the fact and marked it in diverse fashion. That in all these cases the text remains essentially the same ought perhaps to stimulate us to reflect more fully on and attempt to clarify more completely the various

---

[36]H_3 is, of course, B-Version before v.106, and in the remainder of passus V (and in a few cases in later passus) shares a number of B-Version insertions with M. D shows almost no sign of contamination from either the B- or C-Version.

options it makes available to readers. If the earliest readers did not do so, must we insist on the Dreamer's waking up, or assume the work incomplete because he does not?

How we choose to regard the ending of the A-Version — completed or fragmentary — obviously depends on how prominent our awareness of longer versions of *Piers Plowman* is — and on the degree to which we have come to accept those longer versions as later (and therefore definitive) in evolutionary progress. Such awareness cannot help but affect our reception of an earlier, shorter text, as it did that of at least some scribes. But it ought not to lead us to reject the A-Version as some lower form of poem unworthy of careful attention and preservation: some earlier scribes also resisted such a conclusion. In any event we cannot assert uncritically that the shorter version is *in itself* incomplete since other readers have accepted it as complete. There is a distinct possibility that it was complete, that it achieved closure in its own terms; and we might do well to recover those terms rather than insist on our own. We would certainly not be the first to address these problems: the scribes of the A-Version give ample, and substantially varied, evidence of alternative understandings of the form and meaning of this text, and their readings challenge an easy acceptance of any modern editorial or critical consensus regarding the voicing of the words that make up the ending of this poem.

My remarks above will reveal continuing uncertainties about the closure of the A-Version — and at this point I depart from Professor Fowler's confidently expressed views — but it is past time that someone from among those who hold the poem unconcluded and incomplete argued as confidently and sustainedly in favor of that position. That view needs fuller argument and defense to warrant retaining its place as the almost-universal view of critics and scholars. In the absence of any clear certainty in the manuscripts and versions, let me register mine as one voice calling for fuller examination of richer issues that have been simplified or passed over in our haste to resolve ideological conflicts about matters external to the text of *Piers* A, such as authorship and unity. After all, the George Kane "[m]ost scholars" appeal to in support of their facile consensus regarding the unfinished state of the A-Version has in his own writings shown himself to be of two minds about the "ending" of that poem, and we ought to take seriously his honest, and instructive, vacillation. It is the product of a long-standing and widely shared uncertainty that deserves a better critical fate than being relegated to the status of an ideological Shibboleth, or being filed away with other uninteresting questions we don't need to think about any more. The widespread critical consensus for single authorship is a useful, and plausible, fiction, but it cannot pass for established, demonstrable fact. Even if it were to, it could not obscure the individuality and integrity of the three (or four) versions of that poem "qui vocatur Perys ploughman."[37] These distinct versions of *Piers Plowman* deserve better, and if we set aside authorship and authorial intention as primary concerns about which we are willing to make large assumptions we will discover that David Fowler's vision of the literary relations between the two versions he has so carefully examined deserves more engaged response than it has received heretofore. The challenges he has raised transcend debates about the poet's identity; they speak eloquently to the distinctiveness of a number of great Middle English poems, which we call *Piers Plowman*.

---

[37]From the "Memorandum" in Trinity College, Dublin, MS D.4.1., fol. 89v.

David C. Fowler

CAROLINE FOWLER AARON

DAVID COVINGTON FOWLER was born January 3, 1921, in Louisville, Kentucky, the second son of Susan Amelia Covington and Earle Broadus Fowler. David's father was head of the English Department at the University of Louisville and, subsequently, Dean of the Humanities; David's mother, who described herself as neither "an Ibsen doll nor a Dickens Dora," pursued advanced studies at the University and assisted her husband with translations of German literary criticism. Their four children (Earle, David, William, and Caroline) were taught at an early age to respect the closed study door and urged to take advantage of the wooded acres surrounding their home for unsupervised exploration.

David entered the first grade at Beechmont Elementary School, Louisville, and the following year was assigned to third grade at Auburndale School, where he completed his elementary education. At twelve, he missed an entire year of school bedridden with rheumatic fever; he did, however, complete the seventh grade at home and was not held back. He remembers it as a year in a dark room listening to a small crystal radio that brought to life Buck Rodgers and The Shadow. When his health returned, David resumed old activities with renewed energy: a favorite was spelunking in and around Otter Creek State Park, where he often tempted fate by swimming from one unfamiliar cave to another, or by tiptoeing along sharp rock walls, water up to his chin, clasping a flashlight in his mouth.

For ninth grade he transferred to Louisville's Southern Junior

High, where, in addition to the standard curriculum, he studied Latin and trombone. During that year, after a brief and sudden illness, his father died. At fifteen, David enrolled in Louisville Male High and in his senior year he joined the Hallack Literary Society, a group that met off-campus to discuss poetry and other literature.

David's maternal aunts, Mary Covington (law librarian at Duke University) and Evabelle Covington (economics instructor at Salem College, North Carolina), undertook to offset the costs of his college education — if he would agree to a warm climate. (They were obviously concerned that rheumatic fever had left his heart weak and felt that sun would assure his return to good health.) He gratefully accepted their offer, and enrolled on a music scholarship at the University of Florida, where he pursued studies which included languages and literatures — English, German, Spanish, French, and Greek — in addition to music. He played trombone in the marching band during football season (a sport for which he remains an avid fan) and also performed with a swing band, in light operatic productions, and occasionally on campus radio. For a time, he held a job in the English Department giving eye exams to incoming freshmen: as it turned out, many of those students needed remedial glasses rather than remedial classes.

During his senior year at the University of Florida, Pearl Harbor was bombed, and David promptly signed up for the Naval Officers' Training Program. Graduating with his BA in English in 1942, he returned to Louisville where, on June 7th, he joined the Navy. In September of that year he went to Notre Dame to attend Naval Officers' Training School, graduating January 28, 1943. On that same day he married Mary Gene Stith. They returned together to Miami, where David attended subchaser school, graduating in November to leave for the Pacific aboard a ship used primarily for communications' operations and to facilitate landings in the Marianas and the Philippines. At the end of the war, David was assigned the task of generating the paperwork that enabled sailors to separate from the Navy at Great Lakes Naval Station, Lake Forest, Illinois.

Contemplating his own separation from the Navy, he began to plan for graduate school and applied to the University of Chicago, where his father had received his Ph.D. and where his uncle, David Covington (for whom he had been named), had been a brilliant student in Classics, who died suddenly in his mid-twenties. David's

aunts and his mother, who took much interest in his continued
education and hoped he would follow a career in the diplomatic
service, were delighted to see him follow in his father's and uncle's
footsteps. Accepted into the English Department for fall of 1946, he
completed his Master's degree in 1947 and his Ph.D. in 1949. His
original plan was to focus on the Renaissance, but (as he describes
it) "One of my professors nudged me in another direction. He said to
understand the Renaissance you'd better have a good background in
Medieval; so I walked back, reached the fourteenth century, and
never returned. I became fascinated by the medieval world picture.
It sets up an interesting tension between a point of view from the
past, which you respect, yet you can't bring back, and the twentieth
century you're living in." This professor, James R. Hulbert, served
as advisor for his dissertation, an edition of the *Vita* of the A-Text of
Piers Plowman.

Ph.D. in hand, David accepted a teaching position at the University of Pennsylvania, and while there was awarded an ACLS Fellow-
ship. (He subsequently, in 1962 and in 1975, received Guggenheim
Fellowships, both of which he spent in Oxford.) Approached, in
1951, with appointments from both the University of Washington
(at Professor Hulbert's recommendation) and Queen's College, New
York, he chose Washington — despite being told by his friends at
Penn: "if you go to Seattle you'll see nothing but rain and Indians."
Arriving in Seattle for autumn quarter of 1952, he was appointed as
an Instructor in the English Department; in the following year, with
the publication of his first book, *Piers the Plowman: A Critical Edition of
the A Version*, he was promoted to Assistant Professor. His courses for
the Department included undergradute courses on Arthurian literature and graduate courses on *Piers* and Chaucer, courses he has
taught regularly for more than forty years at the University of Washington.

Established in the Department, David focused on his family — his
two daughters were born: Sandra in 1953 and Caroline in 1954 —
and on his bibliography (a full account of which is provided by Paul
Remley elsewhere in this volume). In 1959 he published *Prowess and
Charity in the Perceval of Chrétien de Troyes*, and David (not satisfied
within the confines of well-known English and French narrative
poetry) embarked on a six-month trip to Cornwall to study the
Cornish language and medieval drama. After he published his arti-

cle on the dating of the Cornish *Ordinalia*, the Cornish Gorseth declared him a Bard of Cornwall, enabling him to attend a subsequent International Celtic Congress as an honorary Cornishman.

In the course of his Cornish studies, he discovered connections between *Piers* and the works of the Cornishman John Trevisa, which he decribes as follows: "between the lines I began to see the portrait of a man that led me to think the B-Text might have been composed by John Trevisa, an Oxford scholar and translator. The moment at which this dawned on me — that I was dealing with an absolutely new idea — was indeed a moment I'll never forget. Even if it turns out not to be true. It's one of those imponderable things that, when it first hits you, really makes you pound the table!" It was this discovery that sparked a more-than-thirty-year-long quest for a comprehensive catalogue of John Trevisa's contributions to Medieval English literature. This quest led to David's conviction that Trevisa was the author of the B-Text of *Piers*, an argument put forth in *Piers the Plowman: Literary Relations of the A and B Texts* (1961). In more recent years these studies have been bearing mature fruit in the forthcoming literary biography of John Trevisa.

Besides *Piers* and Trevisa, other areas of study have also been rewarding and important to David: for example, the Bible and literature, which led to the publication of two books, *The Bible in Early English Literature* (1976) and *The Bible in Middle English Literature* (1984). In the mid-sixties the University of Washington's right to offer a "Bible as Literature" course was challenged by two fundamentalist ministers. Since David's *Outline for the Study of the Bible as Literature* was being used as the course study-guide at the time, he became the central witness on behalf of the University and helped defend, up to the level of the State Supreme Court, the University's academic freedom and scholarly integrity. From this, he emerged as something of a folk hero locally.

Another of David's life-long interests was in the study of ballads, the subject of numerous articles and a book, *A Literary History of the Popular Ballad* (1968). Merely listing David's publications would document only partly the energy that he has for research and writing, for lecturing and exchanging ideas with colleagues and students alike. To see him at work stimulates one to envision every footnote, manuscript, rare-book room, or library as the locale for *the great adventure*: scholarship is not conducted because it is required or expected, but because there is such satisfaction to be gleaned when the pursuit of information leads to the joy of discovery. He once said that he could not imagine any system of education that would fail the interested student: if there is a library and a will, there is a way.

David's contributions to his University extend beyond his scholarship, teaching, and giving testimony in state courts; he has served effectively in various administrative positions: as Associate Dean of the Graduate School, as Chairman of the Faculty Senate, as Director of Graduate Studies in English. He has also been an active participant on various committees, such as those charged with fostering Medieval and Renaissance Studies, Folklore Research, Linguistics, and Religion; and others dealing with the Humanities Program Review, English Department Placement, University Curriculum, Faculty Development, and the University Press. He has been president of the Medieval Association of the Pacific and of the Northwest section of the American Association of Religion/ Society for Biblical Literature; and he has chaired program committees for the Modern Language Association, the Medieval Association of the Pacific, and an International Arthurian Congress. In 1985 he directed a National Endowment for the Humanities Summer Seminar for School Teachers on *Piers Plowman* at Exeter College, Oxford.

These activities of the public man are matched by his more private and personal contributions. A huge of volume of correspondence — all catalogued and neatly filed away in the University of Washington's Archives — is a testament to his dedication to scholarly exchange. Not a letter goes unanswered, nor any request for information or advice unheeded. Having always been eager to steer students towards projects of scope and substance, he is ever willing to be on hand when they need assistance, advice, encouragement, or critical response. Though he officially retired from full-time teaching at the University in 1986, he has continued to teach and guide students' and colleagues' projects ever since — and no doubt will continue to so, however and whenever he can.

David's private life has been a story of success and commitment. In January 1993, he and Mary Gene celebrated their fiftieth anniversary. He has been quick to acknowledge a continuing debt to her, and she has been unfailing in her support and eager with her help, whether proofreading galleys or offering critical suggestions. They have been partners on repeated trips to England, and their shared and diverse interests have broadened them both, and made them rich in good friends, both at home and abroad. David has enjoyed good health and stamina, which until recently allowed him to continue to play tennis and golf. He maintains his interest in music, frequently playing guitar and recently reacquiring the trombone of his youth. His has been a full and active life, marked by one real tragedy: Sandra's death in 1986, aged 33, as a result of a brain tumor. He remains a hero to two grandchildren, Nicola and John, and a cherished member of both his immediate and extended family.

This brief inventory of his life would be incomplete if it closed without my acknowledging more personally my own appreciation of David Fowler. For me, he has been both father and teacher: from him I have learned the value of books, a sound forehand in tennis, and the merits of looking up "big" words before using them in conversation. When I was eight he took time out from a research project of his own to illustrate *my* attempt at book-production. He read stories about knights of the Round Table to my sister and me, and comforted us when we discovered that Lancelot was only a literary figure. He saw to it that we travelled to interesting places, and met fascinating people — not that we didn't cry out in exasperation on occasion: Not *another* medieval ruin! He guided us through plays and operas, escorted us to museums and libraries, and always with that irrepressible sense of adventure. Who else could convince us that a secondhand bookstore was every bit as wonderful as a cave? My debts and my appreciation are endless, and my love and respect deep. His public life has garnered many honors, and his private life equally gives cause for celebration.

A Chronology of the Scholarship of David C. Fowler

PAUL G. REMLEY

T HE CHRONOLOGY PRINTED BELOW lists references to more than two hundred scholarly publications by and about Professor David C. Fowler. These have been supplemented with references to related items ranging from complete, unpublished fair-copy manuscripts preserved among the collection of Fowler's papers in the University of Washington Libraries to televised lectures and sound recordings. In total, the list comprises more than 250 numbered items issued over a period of forty-five years. Grouping these materials under such traditional headings as "note" or "review article" would only serve to obscure the coordination of effort to which Fowler's publication-history bears witness. Rather, the chronological arrangement adopted here is intended to enable readers to follow the concurrent development of Fowler's work in several related areas — say, *Piers Plowman*, the Bible, and Old Cornish drama — during any given period and may also serve to illuminate some of the high-water marks of his career. To cite but one example of the latter: from 1958 to 1961 Fowler published two books (one on Chrétien de Troyes, the other on *Piers Plowman*), three major articles (on John Trevisa, Geoffrey of Monmouth, and the Cornish *Ordinalia*), three notes (on the ballad tradition and *Pearl*), and five reviews (on Chrétien, *Piers*, and folklore studies). Both books issued during these years attracted the attention of the international scholarly community, the study of Chrétien alone generating review copy equivalent to the better part of its page-count. Fowler also found time during this period to complete a television series on medieval romance, to prepare and oversee the publication of a substantial, 141-page viewer's guide, and to read a paper before the Celtic Group of the Modern Language Association.

While he has maintained a similarly energetic schedule throughout his career, the quantitative assessment of Fowler's scholarship is only of secondary concern here. The present chronology is intended above all to provide a reliable guide to the complex yet judiciously conceived program of research according to which Fowler has addressed the subjects within his purview. Fowler has published studies of texts composed in many of the languages of medieval Europe, but most frequently those in Middle English, Old French, and Old Cornish. In other words, he has maintained a concentration in his work on primary sources on one major vernacular from each of the Germanic, Romance, and Celtic language groups, supported by a strong command of medieval Latin. Fowler's broad critical interests also resolve themselves into fairly well-defined categories: ballad and folklore, the scriptural tradition, and Arthurian literature, among others; one is struck, moreover, by how early on in the record of his publications each of these areas receives attention. The threefold system of indexing employed below offers multiple lines of approach to this body of work. A summary of Fowler's major publications, arranged according to subject matter, serves to introduce the main list of publications, which is arranged chronologically; a more detailed subject index, whose entries are subdivided into familiar bibliographic categories ("book," "article," etc.), concludes the apparatus. These resources help to trace each of Fowler's major projects from conference paper to journal article and, in almost every instance, through the completion of at least one book — two each in the cases of *Piers Plowman* and the Bible. (The most conspicuous remaining *desideratum*, a separate monograph by Fowler on the life and writings of John Trevisa, is in fact now in the press.) Entries listing Fowler's reviews of books by his contemporaries document his continual exchange of ideas with scholars throughout the world, and these are complemented here by newly compiled summaries of reviews and notices of Fowler's six books, which augment by dozens the references previously accessible in standard indexes of reviews. Wherever possible, information about conference papers, early drafts, lectures, and the like is presented within the main entry treating the final, published version of a particular project and, where precise dates are available, cross-referenced in the chronology. The decision to include information about some of Fowler's unpublished studies was motivated both by their frequent availability among the Fowler Papers and also by the possibility that Fowler himself, who corresponds regularly with scholars in many fields, might well supply additional details about the content or disposition of a particular project.

Taken together, the references listed here span more than four decades of research by David C. Fowler. Given Fowler's continuing vigor as an author and educator, however, as well as the availability of many boxes of unconsulted archival material among the Fowler Papers, they surely provide no more than a preliminary indication of the full range of his scholarship.[1]

I. Summary of Major Publications.

a. *Piers Plowman*
    Piers the Plowman: A Critical Edition of the A-Version, ed. Knott and Fowler **(1952)**.
    Piers the Plowman: Literary Relations of the A and B Texts **(1961)**.
    "Contamination in Manuscripts of the A-Text of *Piers the Plowman*" **(1951)**.
    "The Relationship of the Three Texts of *Piers the Plowman*" **(1952–53)**.
    "Poetry and the Liberal Arts: The Oxford Background of *Piers the Plowman*" **(1969)**.
    "Piers Plowman," in *Recent Middle English Scholarship and Criticism* **(1971a)**.

---

[1] I would like to express my gratitude to Naomi B. Pascal, Editor-in-Chief at the University of Washington Press, for generously providing information about works by Fowler published at the Press; to many members of the staff of the University Libraries for help with specific references, especially Madeline A. Copp, Gary L. Menges, and the entire personnel of the Manuscripts and University Archives Division; and to Mícheál F. Vaughan for valuable editorial advice and meticulous proofreading of drafts. Finally, I would like thank David C. Fowler himself for his friendship and collegiality over the past five years. I could hardly have foreseen this happy circumstance when I started to collect his books as an undergraduate in the 1970s.

"A New Interpretation of the A and B Texts of *Piers Plowman*" **(1973–74)**.

"A New Edition of the B Text of *Piers Plowman*" **(1977)**.

"Editorial 'Jamming': Two New Editions of *Piers Plowman*" **(1980)**.

"*Piers Plowman:* In Search of an Author" **(1988a)**.

b. Bible and Scriptural Tradition

The Bible in Early English Literature **(1976)**.

The Bible in Middle English Literature **(1984)**.

"Some Biblical Influences on Geoffrey of Monmouth's Historiography" **(1958)**.

"The Date of the Cornish 'Ordinalia' " **(1961a)**.

"A Middle English Bible Commentary (Oxford: Trinity College, MS 93)" **(1968b)**.

"The Middle English *Gospel of Nicodemus* in Winchester MS 33" **(1988)**.

c. John Trevisa

"John Trevisa and the English Bible" **(1960–61)**.

"New Light on John Trevisa" **(1962)**.

"John Trevisa: Scholar and Translator" **(1970a)**.

"More About John Trevisa" **(1971)**.

John Trevisa **(1993)**.

The Life and Times of John Trevisa **(1993a)**.

"*The Governance of Kings and Princes*": *John Trevisa's Middle English Translation of the* De Regimine Principum *of Aegidius Romanus* **(forthcoming)**.

d. Ballad and Folklore

A Literary History of the Popular Ballad **(1968)**.

"Toward a Literary History of the Popular Ballad" **(1965)**.

" 'The Hunting of the Cheviot' and 'The Battle of Otterburn' " **(1966)**.

"The Gosport Tragedy: Story of a Ballad" **(1979)**.

"Ballads," in *A Manual of the Writings in Middle English, 1050–1500* **(1980a)**.

e. Arthurian Romance

Prowess and Charity in the Perceval of Chrétien de Troyes **(1959)**.

"L'Amour dans le *Lancelot* de Chrétien" **(1970)**.

"*Le Conte du Graal* and *Sir Perceval of Galles*" **(1975)**.

"The Quest of Balin and the Mark of Cain" **(1984a)**.

II. A Chronology of the Scholarship of David C. Fowler.

1. **1948**. "Piers Plowman." *Times Literary Supplement* 47 (13 March 1948): 149. Author's query.

2. **1948a**. "A Bibliography of *Piers Plowman* to 1948." Chicago: [n.p.], 1948. Lithographically reproduced typescript.
   Bibliography:
   (1) *National Union Catalog* [hereafter *NUC*]. Pre-1956 Imprints. Vol. 179: 445.
   (2) Fowler Papers. See item **1971-**. Accession 1696-2-74-2. Box 4, folder 24.

3. **1949**. "A Critical Text of *Piers Plowman* A-2." Ph.D. dissertation. University of Chicago. September 1949.
   Bibliography:
   (1) "Research in Progress-1949." *PMLA* 64.2 (1949): 123 (no. 888).
   (2) *NUC*. Pre-1956 Imprints. Vol. 315: 246.

4. **1950**. "More Kentucky Superstitions." *Southern Folklore Quarterly* 14 (1950): 170–76. [With Mary Gene Fowler.]

5. **1951**. "Contamination in Manuscripts of the A-Text of *Piers the Plowman*." *PMLA* 66 (1951): 495–504.

6. **1951a**. Review. *JEGP* 50 (1951): 257–58.
   Philologica: The Malone Anniversary Studies. Ed. Thomas Austin Kirby and Henry Bosley Woolf. Baltimore: Johns Hopkins Press, 1949.

7. **1951-**. Biographical notice. "Fowler, David Covington." *Directory of American Scholars: A Biographical Directory*. Ed. Jacques Cattell, et al. 2nd ed. (1951) to 8th ed. (1982) [most recent to date]. Lancaster, Pa.: Science Press, etc., 1951-.

8. **1952**. *Piers the Plowman: A Critical Edition of the A-Version*. Ed. Thomas Albert Knott and David C. Fowler. (Baltimore: Johns Hopkins Press, 1952).
   Related items:
   (1) Knott. "An Essay toward the Critical Text of the A-Version of *Piers the Plowman*." *Modern Philology* 12 (1914–15): 389–421.
   (2) "*Piers Plowman*: A Critical Text of the A Version." Ed. Knott. Chicago: University of Chicago Library, [n.p.].

Typescript. Bibliography: *NUC*. Pre-1956 Imprints. Suppl. vol. 742: 2.

(3) Knott. Glossary and historical sketch for edition of A-version. University of Chicago Library. These items and Fowler's early plans for the present edition are described in a letter of 17 December 1947 from David C. Fowler to Myra P. Knott. Bibliography: Fowler Papers. See item 1971-. Accession 1696-2-1974-2. Box 1, folders 1–2.

(4) Knott. Materials for edition of B-text. *Ibid.* Box 12. Manuscript. [Twenty-two envelopes containing thousands of collation slips.]

(5) Fowler. "A Bibliography of *Piers Plowman* to 1948." Lithographically reproduced typescript. See item **1948a**.

(6) Fowler. "A Critical Text of *Piers Plowman* A-2." Dissertation. See item **1949**.

(7) Fowler. Introduction, text, textual notes, scriptural index, glossary. Manuscript and typescript: Fowler Papers. See item **1971-**. Accession 1696-2-74-2. Box 4, folders 1–2; box 6, folder 14; box 7, folders 13–62; box 8, folder 1.

Reviews and notices:

(1) J. A. W. Bennett. *Modern Language Review* 50 (1955): 193–94.

(2) Stella Brook. *Review of English Studies* ns 6 (1955): 179–80.

(3) Norman E. Eliason. *Modern Language Notes* 69 (1954): 191–92.

(4) Robert Worth Frank, Jr. *Modern Language Quarterly* 16 (1955): 85.

(5) Gordon H. Gerould. *Speculum* 28 (1953): 180–81.

(6) Thomas A. Kirby. *English Studies* 35 (1954): 129–32.

(7) Hans Marcus. *Archiv für das Studium der neueren Sprachen und Literaturen* 190 (1954): 135–36.

(8) *Times Literary Supplement* 52 (11 Sept. 1953): 576. "Medieval Literature."

(9) Bogislov von Lindheim. *Anglia* 71 (1952–53): 495–97

(10) Gladys D. Willcock. *Year's Work in English Studies* 33 (1952): 73–74.

9. **1952a**. "The 'Forgotten' Pilgrimage in *Piers the Plowman*." *Modern Language Notes* 67 (1952): 524–26.

10. **1952b**. Review. *Modern Language Notes* 67 (1952): 350–51. *Ag-*

nus Castus: A Middle English Herbal, Reconstructed from Various Manuscripts. Ed. Gösta Brodin. Essays and Studies on English Language and Literature 6. Uppsala: Lundequist, 1950.

11. **1952c.** Gladys D Willoock. Review of *Piers the Plowman*, ed. Knott and Fowler. See item **1952**.

12. **1952–53.** "The Relationship of the Three Texts of *Piers the Plowman*." *Modern Philology* 50 (1952–53): 5–22.

13. **1952–53a.** "*The Waste Land*: Mr. Eliot's 'Fragments.'" *College English* 14 (1952-53): 234–35. Reprinted as: "What the Thunder Said." *A Collection of Critical Essays on The Waste Land*. Ed. Jay Martin. Twentieth Century Interpretations. Englewood Cliffs, N.J.: Prentice-Hall, 1968. 34–36.

14. **1952–53b.** Bogislov von Lindheim. Review of *Piers the Plowman*, ed. Knott and Fowler. See item **1952**.

15. **1953.** Review. *Modern Language Notes* 68 (1953): 131–33. *The Good Wife Taught Her Daughter, The Good Wyfe Wold a Pylgremage, The Thewis of Gud Women.* Ed. Tauno F. Mustanoja. Annales Academiae Scientiarum Fennicae B61.2. Helsinki: Suomalaisen Kirjallisuuden Seuran, 1948.

16. **1953a.** "Narrative Genius and Literary Form in Chaucer's Early Poetry." Conference paper. Modern Language Association, Medieval Section, Chicago, 30 December 1953. Manuscript and typescript: Fowler Papers. See item **1971-**. Accession 1696-2-74-2. Box 6, folder 20.

17. **1953b.** Gordon H. Gerould. Review of *Piers the Plowman*, ed. Knott and Fowler. See item **1952**.

18. **1953c.** *Times Literary Supplement.* Review of *ibid.*

19. **1953–60.** Bibliographical notices. "Fowler, David C." *Progress of Medieval and Renaissance Studies in the United States and Canada.* Ed. S. Harrison Thompson. Vols. 22 (1953) to 25 (1960) [no more published].

20. **1954.** "An Unusual Meaning of 'Win' in Chaucer's *Troilus and Criseyde*." *Modern Language Notes* 69 (1954): 313–15.

21. **1954a.** Review. *Modern Language Notes* 69 (1954): 289–91. Morton W. Bloomfield. *The Seven Deadly Sins: An Introduction to the History of a Religious Concept, with Special Reference to Medieval English Literature.* East Lansing, Michigan: Michigan State College Press, 1952.

22. **1954b.** Norman E. Eliason. Review of *Piers the Plowman*, ed. Knott and Fowler. See item **1952**.
23. **1954c.** Thomas A. Kirby. Review of *ibid.*
24. **1954d.** Hans Marcus. Review of *ibid.*
25. **1955.** Review. *Modern Language Quarterly* 16 (1955): 360–62. Richard Foster Jones. *The Triumph of the English Language: A Survey of Opinions Concerning the Vernacular from the Introduction of Printing to the Restoration.* Stanford: Stanford University Press, 1953.
26. **1955a.** "The Bible." Telecourse. See item **1956**.
27. **1955b.** "Literary Tradition in Arthurian Romance." Conference paper. Modern Language Association, Comparative Literature Section, Arthurian Group, Chicago, 28 December 1955. Manuscript: Fowler Papers. See item **1971-**. Accession 1696-2-74-2. Box 6, folder 22.
28. **1955c.** J. A. W. Bennett. Review of *Piers the Plowman*, ed. Knott and Fowler. See item **1952**.
29. **1955d.** Stella Brook. Review of *ibid.*
30. **1955e.** Robert Worth Frank, Jr. Review of *ibid.*
31. **1956.** *Outlines for the Study of the Bible as Literature.* Seattle: distributed by University of Washington Press, 1956.
    Bibliography:
    (1) *NUC* 1953–57 Imprints. Vol. 8: 150.
    (2) *NUC* 1956–67 Imprints. Vol. 37: 390.
    Related items:
    (1) "The Bible." Telecourse. Seattle: KOMO-TV, 1955.
    (2) "The Bible at Court." Conference paper. American Association of Religion and Society of Biblical Literature, Missoula, Mo., 3 May 1974.
    (3) "The Bible as Literature." Sound recording. Eleven 7" reels, 3 ¾ ips, four-track, monophonic. Seattle: University of Washington Libraries, 1978.
    Review:
    Earl B. Robinson, *Gordon Review* [Wenham, Mass. Gordon College and Divinity School] 4 (Fall 1958): 148.
    "Bible as Literature" Controversy:
    Fowler's *Outlines* and an unsuccessful legal challenge raised against the University of Washington course "The Bible as Literature" (English 390), taught by Fowler and others,

have been discussed many times by scholars of constitutional law. See in particular:

(1) William F. Caldwell. "The Bible as Literature: A Constitutional Controversy." *Research Studies* [Pullman, Wash. Washington State University] 39 (1971): 96–118.

(2) Robert S. Michaelsen. "Constitutions, Courts and the Study of Religion." *Journal of the American Academy of Religion* 45 (1977): 291–308.

(3) Fowler Papers. See item **1971-**. Accession 1696-71-15. Box 1, folders 9–14, and 1696-2-74-2; box 4, folders 1–3 and 24; box 8, folder 23, and box 9, folders 13–14.

Case citation:

Calvary Bible Presbyterian Church; Tacoma Bible Presbyterian Church; Rev. Thomas W. Miller and Rev. Harold Webb vs. Regents of the University of Washington (1966–68).

Legal bibliography:

(1) Washington, King County Superior Court. Civil case no. 657 671. "Deposition Upon Oral Examination of Harold Leland Webb, Jr." 1 June 1966.

(2) *Ibid.* "Statement of Facts." 6 June 1966 to 14 June 1966. 3 vols. [Trial transcript.]

(3) *Ibid.* "Defendant's Proposed Findings of Fact and Conclusion of Law." June 1966.

(4) Supreme Court of the State of Washington. Briefs for Appellants and Respondent. Case no. 39226 and 436 P. 2d 189 (1967).

(5) Supreme Court of the United States. Brief in Support of a Petition for a Writ of Certiorari 165 (October 1967); Brief in Opposition to the Petition 1503 (October 1967), and 393 U.S. 960 (1968). Certiorari denied.

32. **1957**. Review. *Journal of American Folklore* 70 (1957): 293.

(1) *English Drinking Songs.* Sung by A. L. Lloyd. Ed. Kenneth S. Goldstein. 12" LP. Cat. no. RLP12-618. New York: Riverside Records, 1956.

(2) *Irish Humor Songs.* Sung by Patrick Galvin. Ed. Kenneth S. Goldstein. 12" LP. Cat. no. RLP12-616. New York: Riverside Records, 1956.

33. **1957a**. *Piers Plowman: A Modern English Translation.* [Prologue and Confession of Seven Deadly Sins.] Draft. Manuscript:

Fowler Papers. See item **1971-**. Accession 1696-2-74-2. Box 6, folder 23. c. 1957.

34. **1958**. "Some Biblical Influences on Geoffrey of Monmouth's Historiography." *Traditio* 14 (1958): 378-85.

35. **1958a**. "An Accused Queen in 'The Lass of Roch Royal' (Child 76)." *Journal of American Folklore* 71 (1958): 553-63.

36. **1958b**. *A Viewer's Guide to Medieval Romance*. Telecourse viewer's guide. Seattle: University of Washington Adult Education and Extension Services, 1958.

Bibliography:

NUC. 1956-67 Imprints. Vol. 37: 390.

Related items:

(1) "Medieval Romance." Telecourse. Seattle: KCTS-TV, 1958.

(2) Manuscript: Fowler Papers. See item **1971-**. Accession 1696-3-79-14. Box 2, folders 4-5.

37. **1958c**. Review. *Modern Language Quarterly* 19 (1958): 91-92.

Jean Frappier. *Chrétien de Troyes. L'Homme et l'oeuvre*. Connaissance des lettres 50. Paris: Hatier-Boivin, 1957.

38. **1958d**. "Medieval Romance." Telecourse. See item **1958b**.

39. **1958e**. Earl B. Robinson. Review of *Outlines for the Study of the Bible as Literature*. See item **1956**.

40. **1959**. *Prowess and Charity in the Perceval of Chrétien de Troyes*. University of Washington Publications in Language and Literature 14. Seattle: University of Washington Press, 1959.

Related item:

Manuscript and corrected proofs: Fowler Papers. See item **1971-**. Accession 1696-2-74-2. Box 5, folders 5-6.

Reviews and notices:

(1) Robert W. Ackerman. *Bulletin bibliographique de la Société Internationale Arthurienne* 12 (1960): 28-29.

(2) *Book Exchange* April 1962: 13.

(3) Gerald Bordman. *Journal of American Folklore* 74 (1961): 81-82.

(4) R. Bossuat. *Moyen Âge* 67 (1961): 184-89.

(5) James F. Burks. *Modern Language Journal* 44 (1960): 189-90.

(6) *Cahiers de civilisation médiévale* 3 (1960): 412 (no. 1716).

(7) Sergio Cigada. *Studi Francesi* 4 (1960): 316-17.

(8) M.-M. Dubois. *Études anglaises* 13 (1960): 52.

(9) Jean Frappier. "Le Graal et ses feux divergents." *Romance Philology* 24 (1970-71): 373-440, at 374-81.

(10) *French News* 10 (Fall 1960): 7.

(11) L. Geschiere. *Het Fnnuu Duel* [Amsterdam] January 1961: 5-7.

(12) Mary Hackett. *Year's Work in Modern Language Studies* 21 (1959): 44.

(13) Edward B. Ham. *Modern Language Quarterly* 21 (1960): 276-78.

(14) Urban T. Holmes, Jr. *Books Abroad* 34 (1960): 177-78.

(15) George Fenwick Jones. *Comparative Literature* 12 (1960): 166-69.

(16) Elspeth Kennedy. *Medium Ævum* 30 (1961): 52-55.

(17) Erich Köhler. *Zeitschrift für romanische Philologie* 75 (1959): 551-55.

(18) Hanne Lange. *Cahiers de civilisation médiévale* 4 (1961): 194-95.

(19) *Literature of Medieval History*. Ed. Gray Cowan Boyce. 5 continuously paginated vols. Suppl. to Louis John Paetow. *A Guide to the Study of Medieval History*. Millwood, N.Y.: Kraus, 1981: 2142.

(20) Faith Lyons. *French Studies* 14 (1960): 352.

(21) John F. Mahoney. *Speculum* 37 (1962): 277-78.

(22) J. Mitchell Morse. *College English* 21 (1959-60): 507.

(23) Helaine Newstead. *JEGP* 60 (1961): 162-65.

(24) E. Ploss. *Deutsches Archiv für Erforschung des Mittelalters* 18 (1962): 634.

(25) "M. T." *Personalist* 41 (1960): 525-27.

(26) *Unitarian Register*, Mid-Summer 1960: 23.

(27) E. T. Verhoeff-Schot. *Regesten van de aanwisten van het Instituut voor vergelijkend Literatuur-Onderzoek* [Utrecht. Rijksuniversiteit] 5 (1960): 5-6.

(28) F. J. Warne. *Modern Language Review* 55 (1960): 281-82.

41. **1959a**. *"Pearl* 558: 'Waning.' " *Modern Language Notes* 74 (1959): 581-84.

42. **1959b**. Review. *Modern Language Quarterly* 20 (1959): 285-87.

(1) Robert Worth Frank, Jr. *Piers Plowman and the Scheme of Salvation: An Interpretation of Dowel, Dobet, and Dobest*. Yale

Studies in English 136. New Haven: Yale University Press, 1957.

(2) Willi Erzgräber. *William Langlands Piers Plowman: Eine Interpretation des C-Textes.* Frankfurter Arbeiten aus dem Gebiete der Anglistik und der Amerika-Studien 3. Heidelberg: Winter, 1957.

43. **1959c.** Review. *Modern Language Quarterly* 20 (1959): 388–91. Urban T. Holmes, Jr. and M. Amelia Klenke. *Chrétien, Troyes, and the Grail.* Chapel Hill: University of North Carolina Press, 1959.

44. **1959d.** Review. *Journal of American Folklore* 72 (1959): 270. J. R. W. Coxhead. *Old Devon Customs.* Exmouth: Raleigh Press, 1957.

45. **1959e.** "*Piers Plowman* and the Cornish *Ordinalia.*" Conference paper. Modern Language Association, Celtic Group, Chicago, 28 December 1959. Typescript: Fowler Papers. See item **1971-.** Accession 1696-2-74-2, box 7, folder 6.

46. **1959f.** "An Interpretation of the *Vita* in *Piers Plowman.*" Manuscript. See item 1961.

47. **1959g.** W. Mary Hackett. Review of *Prowess and Charity in the Perceval.* See item **1959.**

48. **1959h.** Erich Köhler. Review of *ibid.*

49. **1959–60.** J. Mitchell Morse. Review of *ibid.*

50. **1960.** "On the Meaning of *Pearl,* 139–140." *Modern Language Quarterly* 21 (1960): 27–29.

51. **1960a.** Robert W. Ackerman. Review of *Prowess and Charity in the Perceval.* See item **1959.**

52. **1960b.** James F. Burks. Review of *ibid.*

53. **1960c.** Sergio Cigada. Review of *ibid.*

54. **1960d.** M.-M. Dubois. Review of *ibid.*

55. **1960e.** Edward B. Ham. Review of *ibid.*

56. **1960f.** Urban T. Holmes, Jr. Review of *ibid.*

57. **1960g.** George Fenwick Jones. Review of *ibid.*

58. **1960h.** Faith Lyons. Review of *ibid.*

59. **1960i.** "M. T." Review of *ibid.*

60. **1960j.** *Unitarian Register.* Review of *ibid.*

61. **1960k.** E. T. Verhoeff-Schot. Review of *ibid.*

62. **1960l.** F. J. Warne. Review of *ibid.*

63. **1960m.** *Cahiers de civilisation médiévale.* Notice of *ibid.*

64. **1960n**. *French News*. Notice of *ibid.*
65. **1960–61**. "John Trevisa and the English Bible." *Modern Philology* 58 (1960–61): 81–98.
66. **1960–61a**. Review, *Modern Philology* 58 (1960–61): 212–14. *Piers Plowman: The A Version. Will's Visions of Piers Plowman and Do-Well. An Edition in the Form of Trinity College Cambridge MS R. 3. 14, Corrected from Other Manuscripts, with Variant Readings*. Ed. George Kane. London: Athlone Press, 1960.
67. **1961**. *Piers the Plowman: Literary Relations of the A and B Texts*. University of Washington Publications in Language and Literature 16. Seattle: University of Washington Press, 1961.
   Related items:
   (1) "An Interpretation of the *Vita* in *Piers Plowman*." Manuscript with extensive notes and revisions. c. 1959. Fowler Papers. See item **1971-**. Accession 1696-2-74-2. Box 6, folder 36. Expanded version in Chapter One.
   (2) Manuscript and typescript. *Ibid.* Box 5, folders 7–10, and box 8, folder 11.
   Reviews and notices:
   (1) Morton W. Bloomfield. *Speculum* 37 (1962): 120–23.
   (2) G. Bourquin. *Études anglaises* 15 (1962): 277–78.
   (3) M. Camillus. *Globe* [Sioux City, Iowa] 3 August 1961.
   (4) S. S. Hussey. *Review of English Studies* 14 (1963): 177–79.
   (5) George Kane. *Medium Ævum* 33 (1964): 230–31.
   (6) Robert E. Kaske. *JEGP* 62 (1963): 208–13.
   (7) Stephen J. Laut. *Thought* 37 (1962): 621–22.
   (8) Angus MacDonald and Betty Hill. *Year's Work in English Studies* 42 (1961): 68.
   (9) Paule Mertens-Fonck. *Moyen Âge* 70 (1964): 590–91.
   (10) *Publishers' Weekly* 180.11 (11 Sept. 1961): 70.
   (11) D. W. Robertson, Jr. *Modern Language Quarterly* 23 (1962): 84–85
   (12) *Weekly List of New Catholic Books* [Washington, D.C. Catholic University of America] 27 March 1961.
   (13) R. M. Wilson. *Modern Language Review* 57 (1962): 627.
68. **1961a**. "The Date of the Cornish 'Ordinalia.'" *Mediaeval Studies* 23 (1961): 91–125.
69. **1961b**. Gerald Bordman. Review of *Prowess and Charity in the Perceval*. See item **1959**.

70. **1961c**. R. Bossuat. Review of *ibid*.
71. **1961d**. L. Geschiere. Review of *ibid*.
72. **1961e**. Elspeth Kennedy. Review of *ibid*.
73. **1961f**. Hanne Lange. Review of *ibid*.
74. **1961g**. Helaine Newstead. Review of *ibid*.
75. **1961h**. M. Camillus. Review of *Piers the Plowman: Literary Relations*. See item **1961**.
76. **1961i**. Angus MacDonald and Betty Hill. Review of *ibid*.
77. **1961j**. *Publishers' Weekly*. Notice of *ibid*.
78. **1961k**. *Weekly List of New Catholic Books*. Notice of *ibid*.
79. **1962**. "New Light on John Trevisa." *Traditio* 18 (1962): 289–317.
80. **1962a**. *Book Exchange*. Review of *Prowess and Charity in the Perceval*. See item **1959**.
81. **1962b**. John F. Mahoney. Review of *ibid*.
82. **1962c**. E. Ploss. Review of *ibid*.
83. **1962d**. Morton W. Bloomfield. Review of *Piers the Plowman: Literary Relations*. See item **1961**.
84. **1962e**. G. Bourquin. Review of *ibid*.
85. **1962f**. Stephen J. Laut. Review of *ibid*.
86. **1962g**. D. W. Robertson, Jr. Review of *ibid*.
87. **1962h**. R. M. Wilson. Review of *ibid*.
88. **1962–67**. Biographical notice. "Fowler, David Covington. 1921-." *Contemporary Authors*. Ed. James M. Ethridge and Barbara Kopala. First revision. Vols. 1-4. Detroit: Gale, 1962–67. 328.
89. **1963**. Review. *Modern Language Quarterly* 24 (1963): 410–13. Morton W. Bloomfield. *Piers Plowman as a Fourteenth-Century Apocalypse*. New Brunswick, N.J.: Rutgers University Press, 1962.
90. **1963a**. "Hierarchy and Conflict in Middle English Verse." Conference paper. Modern Language Association, Middle English Section, Chicago, 28 December 1963.
91. **1963b**. S. S. Hussey. Review of *Piers the Plowman: Literary Relations*. See item **1961**.
92. **1963c**. Robert E. Kaske. Review of *ibid*.
93. **1964**. Review. *Western Folklore* 23 (1964): 209–13.
    (1) *Pammelia Deuteromelia Melismata*. Ed. Thomas Ravenscroft.

Bibliographical and Special Series 12. Philadelphia: American Folklore Society, 1961.

(2) *Loose and Humorous Songs from Bishop Percy's Folio Manuscript.* Ed. Frederick J. Furnivall. Hatboro, Pa.: Folklore Associates, 1963.

(3) *Ancient Ballads Traditionally Sung in New England.* Vol. 3. Ed. Helen Hartness Flanders. Philadelphia: University of Pennsylvania Press, 1963.

(4) *Reprints from Sing Out!: the Folk Song Magazine.* Vol. 5. New York: Oak Publications, 1963.

(5) *The Viking Book of Folk Ballads of the English-Speaking World.* Ed. Albert B. Friedman. New York: Viking Press, 1963.

94. **1964a.** Review. *Romanic Review* 55 (1964): 112–14.

(1) William Matthews. *The Tragedy of Arthur: A Study of the Alliterative Morte Arthure.* Berkeley: University of California Press, 1960.

(2) Helen Adolf. *Visio Pacis: Holy City, and Grail: An Attempt at an Inner History of the Grail Legend.* University Park, Pa.: Pennsylvania State University Press, 1960.

95. **1964b.** Review. *Modern Language Quarterly* 25 (1964): 117–20. D. W. Robertson, Jr. *A Preface to Chaucer: Studies in Medieval Perspectives.* Princeton, N.J.: Princeton University Press, 1962.

96. **1964c.** "Toward a Literary History of the Ballad." Conference paper. See item **1965**.

97. **1964d.** George Kane. Review of *Piers the Plowman: Literary Relations.* See item **1961**.

98. **1964e.** Paule Mertens-Fonck. Review of *ibid.*

99. **1965.** "Toward a Literary History of the Popular Ballad." *New York Folklore Quarterly* 21 (1965): 123–41. Read as paper: "Toward a Literary History of the Ballad." American Folklore Society, Regional Meeting, Durham, N.C., Duke University, 23 April 1964. See also item **1968**.

100. **1965a.** *A Viewer's Guide to the Folk Ballad.* Telecourse viewer's guide. See item **1968**.

101. **1965b.** "A Sixteenth-Century Minstrel's Book." Conference paper. California Folklore Society, University of California at Los Angeles, 9 April 1965. Partial typescript: Fowler Papers. See item **1971-**. Accession 1696-2-74-2. Box 7, folder 3.

102. **1965–66.** Review. *English Language Notes* 3 (1965–66):

295–300. George Kane. *Piers Plowman: The Evidence for Authorship*. London: Athlone Press, 1965.

103. **1965–66a.** "The Folk Ballad." Telecourse. See item **1968**.

104. **1965-.** Biographical and bibliographical notice. "Fowler, David Covington." *Répertoire international des médiévistes*. Ed. Pierre Gallais, et al. 1st ed. (1965) through 5th ed. (1979) [last seen]. Poitiers: University of Poitiers, et al., 1965-.

105. **1966.** " 'The Hunting of the Cheviot' and 'The Battle of Otterburn.' " *Western Folklore* 25 (1966): 165–71.

106. **1966–67.** Review. *Modern Philology* 64 (1966–67): 70–71. Wolfgang Clemen. *Chaucer's Early Poetry*. Tr. C. A. M. Sym. London: Methuen, 1963.

107. **1966–68.** *Miller and Webb vs. Regents of the University of Washington*. See item **1956**.

108. **1967.** "Lesser on Yeats's 'Sailing to Byzantium.' " *College English* 28 (1967): 614.

109. **1967a.** "Poetry and the Liberal Arts: The Oxford Background of *Piers Plowman*." Conference paper. See item **1969**.

110. **1968.** *A Literary History of the Popular Ballad*. Durham, N.C.: Duke University Press, 1968.

Related items:

(1) Manuscript and typescript: Fowler Papers. See item **1971-**. Accession 1696-2-74-2. Box 5, folder 11, and box 6, folder 7.

(2) *A Viewer's Guide to the Folk Ballad*. Telecourse viewer's guide. Seattle: University of Washington, 1965.

(3) "The Folk Ballad." Telecourse. Seattle: KCTS-TV, 1965–66.

(4) Manuscript notes for preceding. Fowler Papers. See item **1971-**. Accession 1696-3-79-14. Box 2, folder 3.

(5) "Toward a Literary History of the Popular Ballad." See item **1965**.

Reviews and notices:

(1) *Book Review Digest* 65 (1969–70): 446.

(2) Bertrand H. Bronson. *Western Folklore* 28 (1969): 280–86.

(3) *Cahiers de civilisation médiévale* 13 (1970): 26* (no. 401).

(4) *Choice* 6 (1969): 354.

(5) Tristram P. Coffin. *Modern Language Quarterly* 30 (1969): 148–49.

(6) T. S. Dorsch. *Year's Work in English Studies* 49 (1968): 20.

(7) Edith Fowke. *Journal of American Folklore* 83 (1970): 90–91.

(8) Albert B. Friedman. *Speculum* 45 (1970): 127–29.

(9) Lillian Herlands Hornstein. *English Language Notes* 7.1 (1969–70): 73–77.

(10) Patricia Ingham. *Medium Ævum* 39 (1970): 66–68.

(11) *Literature of Medieval History.* Ed. Gray Cowan Boyce. 5 continuously paginated vols. Suppl. to Louis John Paetow, *A Guide to the Study of Medieval History.* Millwood, N.Y.: Kraus, 1981: 2108.

(12) Andrew B. Meyers. *Library Journal* 93 (1968): 4559–60

(13) *Ibid. Library Journal Book Review* (1969 for 1968): 342.

(14) J. H. P. Pafford. *Modern Language Review* 65 (1970): 131–32.

(15) W. Edson Richmond. Review article. "The Development of the Ballad: A New Theory." *Genre* 3 (1970): 198–204.

(16) Bruce A. Rosenberg. *Modern Philology* 67 (1969–70): 301–2.

(17) P. M. Tilling. *English Studies* 54 (1973): 80–82.

(18) *Times Literary Supplement* 3 Oct. 1968: 1098. "Mainstream Minstrelsy."

(19) *Virginia Quarterly Review* 45 (Spring 1969): lvi.

(20) Natascha Würzbach. *Anglia* 90 (1972): 393–96.

111. **1968a.** Johannes C. H. R. Steenstrup. *The Medieval Popular Ballad.* Tr. Edward Godfrey Cox. Boston: Ginn, 1914. Reprinted with a foreword by David C. Fowler and a bibliographic essay by Karl-Ivar Hildeman. Seattle: University of Washington Press, 1968.

112. **1968b.** "A Middle English Bible Commentary (Oxford: Trinity College, MS 93)." *Manuscripta* 12 (1968): 67–78. Read as paper: "A Middle English Bible Commentary (Trinity College Oxford MS 93)." Conference on Medieval Studies, Kalamazoo, Mich., Western Michigan University, 14 March 1968. See also item **1976.**

113. **1968c.** Review. *Scandinavian Studies* 40 (1968): 166–69. *Danish Ballads and Folk Songs.* Ed. Erik Dal. Tr. Henry Meyer. Copenhagen: Rosenkilde, 1967.

114. **1968d.** "The Man of Law's Tale." Written for: *The Art of Geoffrey Chaucer: A Collaborative Study.* Proposed ed. Edmund

Reiss. Book as a whole never published. c.1968. Manuscript and typescript: Fowler Papers. See item **1971-**. Accession 1696-3-79-14. Box 1, folder 54.

115. **1968e.** "What the Thunder Said." See item **1952–53a**.

116. **1968f.** Lucy McEligot. "Faculty Portrait: David Fowler." *Alumnus* [Seattle. University of Washington. Alumni Association] 58.4 (Summer 1968): 26–27. [Includes full-page photographic portrait of Fowler playing guitar.]

117. **1968g.** "*Piers Plowman* Scholarship since 1940." Conference paper. Modern Language Association, Middle English Section, New York, 27 December 1968. Manuscript: Fowler Papers. See item **1971-**. Accession 1696-2-74-2. Box 6, folder 32.

118. **1968h.** "A Middle English Bible Commentary (Trinity College Oxford MS 93)." Conference paper. See item **1968b**.

119. **1968i.** T. S. Dorsch. Review of *A Literary History of the Popular Ballad*. See item **1968**.

120. **1968j.** Andrew B. Meyers. Review of *ibid*.

121. **1968k.** *Times Literary Supplement*. Review of *ibid*.

122. **1969**. "Poetry and the Liberal Arts: The Oxford Background of *Piers the Plowman*." *Arts libéraux et philosophie au moyen âge*. Actes du Quatrième Congrès International de Philosophie Médiévale. Montreal: Institute d'études médiévales, 1969. 715–19. Read as paper: Montreal, 31 August 1967. Also in: *Medieval Drama: A Collection of Festival Papers*. Ed. William A. Selz. Festival papers 3. Vermillion, S. D.: Dakota Press, 1969. 78–83.

123. **1969a**. Review. *Speculum* 44 (1969): 308–10. Robert Longsworth. *The Cornish Ordinalia: Religion and Dramaturgy*. Cambridge, Mass.: Harvard University Press, 1967.

124. **1969b**. "Poetry and the Liberal Arts: The Oxford Background of *Piers the Plowman*." *Medieval Drama: A Collection of Festival Papers*. See item **1969**.

125. **1969c**. "Love in Chrétien's *Lancelot*." Conference paper. See item **1970**.

126. **1969d**. Bertrand H. Bronson. Review of *A Literary History of the Popular Ballad*. See item **1968**.

127. **1969e**. Tristram P. Coffin. Review of *ibid*.

128. **1969f**. Andrew B. Meyers. Review of *ibid*.

129. **1969g**. *Choice*. Review of *ibid*.

130. **1969h**. *Virginia Quarterly Review*. Notice of *ibid*.
131. **1969-70**. Lillian Herlands Hornstein. Review of *ibid*.
132. **1969-70a**. Bruce A. Rosenberg. Review of *ibid*.
133. **1969-70b**. *Book Review Digest* Notice of *ibid*.
134. **1970**. "L'Amour dans le *Lancelot* de Chrétien." *Romania* 91 (1970): 378-91. English version: "Love in Chrétien's *Lancelot*." *Romanic Review* 63 (1972): 5-14. Read as paper: International Arthurian Congress, Ninth, Cardiff, 8 August 1969.
135. **1970a**. "John Trevisa: Scholar and Translator." *Transactions of the Bristol and Gloucestershire Archeological Society* 89 (1970): 99-108.
136. **1970b**. W. Edson Richmond. "The Development of the Ballad: A New Theory." Review article on *A Literary History of the Popular Ballad*. See item **1968**.
137. **1970c**. Edith Fowke. Review of *ibid*.
138. **1970d**. Albert B. Friedman. Review of *ibid*.
139. **1970e**. Patricia Ingham. Review of *ibid*.
140. **1970f**. J. H. P. Pafford. Review of *ibid*.
141. **1970g**. *Cahiers de civilisation médiévale*. Notice of *ibid*.
142. **1970-71**. Review. *Modern Philology* 68 (1970-71): 405-8. *The Oxford Book of Ballads*. Ed. James Kinsley. New ed. Oxford: Clarendon Press, 1969.
143. **1970-71a**. Jean Frappier. Review of *Prowess and Charity in the Perceval*. See item **1959**.
144. **1971**. "More About John Trevisa." *Modern Language Quarterly* 32 (1971): 243-54.
145. **1971a**. "Piers Plowman." *Recent Middle English Scholarship and Criticism: Survey and Desiderata*. Ed. J. Burke Severs. Pittsburgh: Duquesne University Press, 1971. 9-27.
146. **1971b**. "The Reunion of Historical and Literary Study." *The Discovery of English*. NCTE 1971 Distinguished Lectures. Urbana, Illinois: National Council of Teachers of English, 1971. 69-78.
147. **1971c**. Review. *Romanic Review* 62 (1971): 291-93. Peter Haidu. *Aesthetic Distance in Chrétien de Troyes: Irony and Comedy in Cligès and Perceval*. Histoire des idées et critique littéraire. Geneva: Droz, 1968.
148. **1971d**. "Gregory's *Morals on Job* and Modern Exegesis." Conference paper. See item **1976**.

149. **1971e**. William F. Caldwell. "The Bible as Literature: A Constitutional Controversy." See item **1956**.

150. **1971-**. "David C. Fowler: Papers." Seattle: University of Washington Libraries, Manuscripts and Archives Division, 1971-. Five accessions to date: (1) 1696-71-15; (2) 1696-2-74-2; (3) 1696-3-79-14; (4) 1696-4-82-54, and (5) 1696-5-87-16. Cited as "Fowler Papers" by box, folder, and item numbers.

151. **1972**. "Love in Chrétien's *Lancelot*." See item **1970**.

152. **1972a**. "The Meaning of 'Touch Me Not' in John 20:17." Conference paper. See item **1975a**.

153. **1972b**. Natascha Würzbach. Review of *A Literary History of the Popular Ballad*. See item **1968**.

154. **1972–73**. "Cruxes in *Cleanness*." *Modern Philology* 70 (1972–73): 331–36.

155. **1973**. P. M. Tilling. Review of *A Literary History of the Popular Ballad*. See item **1968**.

156. **1973–74**. Review article. "A New Interpretation of the A and B Texts of *Piers Plowman*." *Modern Philology* 71 (1973–74): 393–404. Elizabeth D. Kirk. *The Dream Thought of Piers Plowman*. Yale Studies in English, 178. New Haven, Conn.: Yale University Press, 1972.

157. **1974**. "The Bible at Court." Conference paper. See item **1956**.

158. **1975**. "*Le Conte du Graal* and *Sir Perceval of Galles*." *Comparative Literature Studies* 12 (1975): 5–20. Read as paper: International Arthurian Society, Exeter, 12–20 August 1975.

159. **1975a**. "The Meaning of 'Touch Me Not' in John 20:17." *Evangelical Quarterly* 47 (1975): 16–25. Read as paper: Society of Biblical Literature, Northwest Meeting, Vancouver, B.C., 5 May 1972.

160. **1975b**. "The Rediscovery of the Cornish Drama." Conference paper. University of Victoria, 14 March 1975.

161. **1975c**. "*Le Conte du Graal* and *Sir Perceval of Galles*." Conference paper. See item **1975**.

162. **1976**. *The Bible in Early English Literature*. Seattle: University of Washington Press, 1976.

    Related items:

    (1) "Gregory's *Morals on Job* and Modern Exegesis." Conference paper. Society of Biblical Literature, Northwest

Meeting, Portland, Ore., 24 April 1971. Expanded version in Chapter Two.

(2) Library exhibition. " 'The Bible in Early English Literature' by David C. Fowler, with Early Bibles from the Beals Collection." Seattle, University of Washington, Suzzallo Library. March-April 1977.

Reviews and notices:

(1) Lawrence L. Besserman. *Speculum* 53 (1978): 572-73.

(2) Elizabeth Biemens. *Religious Studies Review* 4 (1978): 78.

(3) *Book Review Digest* 73 (1977-78): 447.

(4) Beverly Boyd. *JEGP* 76 (1977): 441-42.

(5) *British Studies Monitor* 8.1 (Winter 1978): 76.

(6) *Cahiers de civilisation médiévale* 29 (1986): 24* (no. 434).

(7) Daniel G. Calder. *Modern Language Quarterly* 39 (1978): 71-73.

(8) *Choice* 14 (1977): 199.

(9) T. P. Dolan, L. E. Mitchell, and R. W. McTurk. *Year's Work in English Studies* 58 (1977): 71.

(10) P. Ellingworth. *Bible Translator* [Ashforth, Kent] 29 (1978): 144-45.

(11) W. Ward Gasque and Carl Edwin Armerding. *Christianity Today* 22 (1977-78): 701.

(12) Joseph A. Grispino. "Western Medieval Religious Studies." *Journal of the American Academy of Religion* 45 (1977): 374-75.

(13) Frederick Hockey. *Revue d'histoire ecclésiastique* 74 (1979): 807.

(14) H. T. Keenan. *Library Journal* 102 (1977): 811

(15) *Ibid. Library Journal Book Review* (1978 for 1977): 313.

(16) Alvin A. Lee. *Modern Philology* 77 (1978-79): 81-84.

(17) *New Testament Abstracts* 22 (1978): 81.

(18) *News Tribune* [Waltham, Mass.] 1 July 1977.

(19) *New York Times Book Review* 12 June 1977: 28. "University Presses: They Pick Their Best."

(20) Lister M. Matheson. *Tennessee Studies in Literature* 24 (1979): 134-37.

(21) O. S. Pickering. *Archiv für das Studium der neueren Sprachen und Literaturen* 215 (1978): 400-3.

(22) *Seattle Times.* 19 December 1976. [Includes black-and-white photograph of Fowler.]

(23) Beryl Smalley. *Journal of Ecclesiastical History* 29 (1978): 118-19.

(24) Carroll Stuhlmueller. *Bible Today* 94 (February 1978): 1514.

(25) Donald Tinder. *Christianity Today* 21 (1976-77): 1243.

163. **1976a.** "An Eighteenth-Century Ballad and Its Connection with Hambledon." *Hampshire Field Club and Archaeological Society Newsletter* 4 (1976): 11-12.

164. **1976b.** *Seattle Times.* Review of *The Bible in Early English Literature.* See item **1976.**

165. **1976-77.** Donald Tinder. Notice of *ibid.*

166. **1977.** Review article. "A New Edition of the B Text of *Piers Plowman.*" *Yearbook of English Studies* 7 (1977): 23-42.
Piers Plowman: The B Version. Will's Visions of Piers Plowman, Do-Well, Do-Better, and Do-Best. An Edition in the Form of Trinity College Cambridge MS. B. 15. 17, Corrected and Restored from the Known Evidence, with Variant Readings. Ed. George Kane and E. Talbot Donaldson. London: Athlone Press, 1975.

167. **1977a.** Beverly Boyd. Review of *The Bible in Early English Literature.* See item **1976.**

168. **1977b.** Joseph A. Grispino. Review of *ibid.*

169. **1977c.** H. T. Keenan. Review of *ibid.*

170. **1977d.** T. P. Dolan, L. E. Mitchell, and R. W. McTurk. Review of *ibid.*

171. **1977e.** *Choice.* Review of *ibid.*

172. **1977f.** *News Tribune.* Review of *ibid.*

173. **1977g.** *New York Times Book Review.* Notice of *ibid.*

174. **1977h.** Robert S. Michaelsen. "Constitutions, Courts and the Study of Religion." See item **1956.**

175. **1977i.** Library exhibition. " 'The Bible in Early English Literature' by David C. Fowler." See item **1976.**

176. **1977-78.** *Book Review Digest.* Notice of *The Bible in Early English Literature.* See item **1976.**

177. **1977-78a.** W. Ward Gasque and Carl Edwin Armerding. Notice of *ibid.*

178. **1978.** Review. *Allegorica* 3.2 (Winter 1978): 204-6. Charlotte

C. Morse. *The Pattern of Judgment in the Queste and Cleanness.* Columbia, Mo.: University of Missouri Press, 1978.

179. **1978a**. "The Bible as Literature." Sound recording. See item **1956**.

180. **1978b**. "Medieval Lyrics and the Church Calendar." Paper. See item **1984**.

181. **1978c**. "The Crucifixion Harp in the Ballad of 'The Two Sisters.'" Conference paper. American Association of Religion and Society of Biblical Literature, Pacific Northwest Region Annual Meeting, Portland, Ore., 21 April 1978.

182. **1978d**. Lawrence L. Besserman. Review of *The Bible in Early English Literature*. See item **1976**.

183. **1978e**. Elizabeth Biemens. Review of *ibid.*

184. **1978f**. Daniel G. Calder. Review of *ibid.*

185. **1978g**. P. Ellingworth. Review of *ibid.*

186. **1978h**. H. T. Keenan. Review of *ibid.*

187. **1978i**. O. S. Pickering. Review of *ibid.*

188. **1978j**. Beryl Smalley. Review of *ibid.*

189. **1978k**. Carroll Stuhlmueller. Review of *ibid.*

190. **1978l**. *New Testament Abstracts*. Abstract of *ibid.*

191. **1978m**. *British Studies Monitor*. Notice of *ibid.*

192. **1978–79**. Alvin A. Lee. Review of *ibid.*

193. **1979**. "The Gosport Tragedy: Story of a Ballad." *Southern Folklore Quarterly* 43 (1979): 157–96.

Related item:
"Lecture on the Gosport Tragedy Ballad." Sound recording. One 7" reel, 3 3/4 ips, four-track, stereophonic. Seattle: University of Washington Libraries, 1979.

194. **1979a**. Review. *Christianity and Literature* 28 (Summer 1979): 57–60. Daniel Maher Murtaugh. *Piers Plowman and the Image of God*. Gainesville, Fla.: University Presses of Florida, 1978.

195. **1979b**. "Lecture on the Gosport Tragedy Ballad." Sound recording. See item 1979.

196. **1979c**. "Mary Magdalene in Popular Tradition." Conference paper. Medieval Association of the Pacific, San Francisco, 24 February 1979. Manuscript: Fowler Papers. See item **1971-**. Accession 1696-3-79-14. Box 1, folder 55.

197. **1979d**. Frederick Hockey. Review of *The Bible in Early English Literature*. See item **1976**.

198. **1979e.** Lister M. Matheson. Review of *ibid.*

199. **1979–80.** "A Pointed Personal Allusion in *Piers the Plowman.*" *Modern Philology* 77 (1979–80): 158–59.

200. **1980.** Review article. "Editorial 'Jamming': Two New Editions of *Piers Plowman.*" *Review* [Blacksburg, Va. University of Virginia] 2 (1980): 211–69.
    (1) *The Vision of Piers Plowman: A Critical Edition of the B-Text Based on Trinity College Cambridge MS B. 15. 17.* Ed. A. V. C. Schmidt. Everyman's University Library. London: Dent, 1978.
    (2) *Piers Plowman: An Edition of the C-Text.* Ed. Derek A. Pearsall. York Medieval Texts, 2nd ser. London: Arnold, 1978.

201. **1980a.** "Ballads." *A Manual of the Writings in Middle English, 1050–1500.* Ed. Albert E. Hartung. Vol. 6. New Haven: Connecticut Academy of Arts and Sciences, 1980. 1753–1808 and 2019–70.

202. **1981.** Review. *Yearbook of English Studies* 11 (1981): 224–26.
    (1) *The Vision of Piers Plowman*, ed. Schmidt. See item **1980**.
    (2) *Piers Plowman*, ed. Pearsall. See item **1980**.

203. **1981a.** Review. *Medium Ævum* 50 (1981): 174–76. *Three Lives from the Gilte Legende, ed. from MS B. L. Egerton 876.* Ed. Richard Hamer. Middle English Texts 9. Heidelberg: Winter, 1978.

204. **1981b.** "Recent Editions of *Piers the Plowman*: Dangerous Tendencies." Conference paper. Society for Textual Scholarship, New York, City University of New York Graduate School, 11 April 1981.

205. **1981c.** "In Quest of John Trevisa." Conference paper. International Congress on Medieval Studies, Kalamazoo, Mich., Western Michigan University, 9 May 1981.

206. **1981d.** *Literature of Medieval History.* Notice of *Prowess and Charity in the Perceval.* See item **1959**.

207. **1981e.** *Literature of Medieval History.* Notice of *A Literary History of the Popular Ballad.* See item **1968**.

208. **1982.** "Chaucer's Creation Poem." Conference paper. See item **1984**.

209. **1983.** Review article. *Analytical and Enumerative Bibliography* 7 (1983): 137–55. Vincent DiMarco. *Piers Plowman, A Reference Guide.* Hall Reference Guides to Literature. Boston: Hall, 1982.

210. **1983a.** "Ballads, Middle English." *Dictionary of the Middle Ages.* Ed. Joseph Reese Strayer. Vol. 2. New York: Scribner, 1983. 59–60.

211. **1983b.** "Bible, Old and Middle English." *Dictionary of the Middle Ages.* Ed. Joseph Reese Strayer. Vol. 2. New York: Scribner, 1983. 220–22.

212. **1983c.** *"Piers the Plowman* as History." Conference paper. See item **1984.**

213. **1983–84.** Review article. "Additions to the Golden Mountain: Four Recent Books on Chaucer." *Modern Philology* 81 (1983–84): 407–14.

(1) *Signs and Symbols in Chaucer's Poetry.* Ed. John P. Hermann and John J. Burke. University, Ala.: University of Alabama Press, 1981.

(2) Henrik Specht. *Chaucer's Franklin in the Canterbury Tales: The Social and Literary Background of a Chaucerian Character.* Publications of the Department of English [University of Copenhagen] 10. Copenhagen: Akademisk Forlag, 1981.

(3) Gregory H. Roscow. *Syntax and Style in Chaucer's Poetry.* Chaucer Studies 6. Cambridge: Brewer, 1981.

(4) *New Perspectives in Chaucer Criticism.* Ed. Donald M. Rose. Norman, Okla.: Pilgrim Books, 1981.

214. **1984.** *The Bible in Middle English Literature.* Seattle: University of Washington Press, 1984.

Related items:

(1) "Medieval Lyrics and the Church Calendar." Paper. University of Wisconsin, 5 April 1978. Expanded version in Chapter Two.

(2) "Chaucer's Creation Poem." Conference paper. Conference on Christianity and Literature, Seattle, 22 January 1982. Expanded version in Chapter Three.

(3) *"Piers the Plowman* as History." Conference paper. St. Cross, University of Oxford, 8 March 1983. Expanded version in Chapter Five.

Reviews and notices:

(1) *Book Review Digest* 82 (1986): 544.

(2) Phillip C. Broadman. *Christianity and Literature* 35 (1985–86): 37–38.

(3) Richard W. Clancey. *Theological Studies* 46 (1985): 718–19.

(4) T. P. Dolan, A. J. Fletcher, and S. Powell. *Year's Work in English Studies* 66 (1985): 137.
(5) Martha H. Fleming. *Church History* 54 (1985): 397-98.
(6) Milton McC. Gatch. *Speculum* 63 (1988): 659-61.
(7) L. B. Hall. *Choice* 22 (1985): 1331.
(8) W. Charles Heiser. *Theology Digest* 33 (1986): 171.
(9) Anne Hudson. *Journal of Theological Studies* ns 37 (1986): 307-8.
(10) S. S. Hussey. *Religion* [London] 17 (1987): 85-87.
(11) David L. Jeffrey. *English Studies in Canada* 12 (1986): 452-54.
(12) *Journal of the History of Ideas* 47 (1986): 167.
(13) Marie Anne Mayeski. *Horizons* [Villanova, Pa. College Theological Society] 13 (1986): 166.
(14) Marc A. Meyer. *Catholic Historical Review* 74 (1988): 472-73.
(15) A. J. Minnis. "Devotional Readings." *Times Literary Supplement* 9 August 1985: 884.
(16) *New Testament Abstracts* 29 (1985): 198.
(17) William James O'Brien. *Religious Studies Review* 12 (1986): 58.
(18) Patti Quattrin. *Religion and Literature* 19 (1987): 99-100.
(19) G. H. Russell. *Studies in the Age of Chaucer* 8 (1986): 185-88.
(20) Carroll Stuhlmueller. *Bible Today* 23 (1985): 200.
(21) Donald Sullivan. *Journal of the Rocky Mountain Medieval and Renaissance Association* [Flagstaff, Ariz.] 7 (1986): 156-57.
(22) Hamish F. G. Swanston. *Scottish Journal of Theology* 39 (1986): 253-55.
(23) Georgiana Warden. *Studia Mystica* 9.1 (1986): 75-77.
215. **1984a**. "The Quest of Balin and the Mark of Cain." *Interpretations* 15.2 (Spring 1984): 70-74.
216. **1984b**. "Iconography of the Singing Bone Motif in 'The Two Sisters.'" Conference paper. International Congress on Medieval Studies, Kalamazoo, Mich., Western Michigan University, 12 May 1984.
217. **1985**. Richard W. Clancey. Review of *The Bible in Middle English Literature*. See item **1984**.
218. **1985a**. Martha H. Fleming. Review of *ibid*.
219. **1985b**. L. B. Hall. Review of *ibid*.

220. **1985c.** A. J. Minnis. Review of *ibid.*
221. **1985d.** T. P. Dolan, A. J. Fletcher, and S. Powell. Review of *ibid.*
222. **1985e.** Carroll Stuhlmueller. Review of *ibid.*
223. **1985f.** *New Testament Abstracts.* Abstract of *ibid.*
224. **1985–86.** Phillip C. Broadman. Review of *ibid.*
225. **1986.** Review. *Studies in the Age of Chaucer* 8 (1986): 203–9. *Chaucer and Scriptural Tradition.* Ed. David Lyle Jeffrey. Ottawa: University of Ottawa Press, 1984.
226. **1986a.** *Cahiers de civilisation médiévale.* Notice of *The Bible in Early English Literature.* See item **1976**.
227. **1986b.** W. Charles Heiser. Review of *The Bible in Middle English Literature.* See item **1984**.
228. **1986c.** Anne Hudson. Review of *ibid.*
229. **1986d.** David L. Jeffrey. Review of *ibid.*
230. **1986e.** Marie Anne Mayeski. Review of *ibid.*
231. **1986f.** William James O'Brien. Review of *ibid.*
232. **1986g.** G. H. Russell. Review of *ibid.*
233. **1986h.** Donald Sullivan. Review of *ibid.*
234. **1986i.** Hamish F. G. Swanston. Review of *ibid.*
235. **1986j.** Georgiana Warden. Review of *ibid.*
236. **1986k.** *Book Review Digest.* Notice of *ibid.*
237. **1986l.** *Journal of the History of Ideas.* Notice of *ibid.*
238. **1987.** Review. *Modern Language Quarterly* 48 (1987): 378–85. *The Literary Guide to the Bible.* Ed. Robert Alter and Frank Kermode. Cambridge: Belknap Press, 1987.
239. **1987a.** S. S. Hussey. Review of *The Bible in Middle English Literature.* See item **1984**.
240. **1987b.** Patti Quattrin. Review of *ibid.*
241. **1987–88.** Review. *English Language Notes* 25.2 (1987–88): 80–82. Michael D. Cherniss. *Boethian Apocalypse: Studies in Middle English Vision Poetry.* Norman, Okla.: Pilgrim Books, 1987.
242. **1988.** "The Middle English *Gospel of Nicodemus* in Winchester MS 33." *Leeds Studies in English* ns 19 (1988): 67–83.
243. **1988a.** "*Piers Plowman*: In Search of an Author." *Essays in Medieval Studies* [Chicago. Illinois Medieval Association] 5 (1988): 1–16.
244. **1988b.** Milton McC. Gatch. Review of *The Bible in Middle English Literature.* See item **1984**.

245. **1988c.** Marc A. Meyer. Review of *ibid.*
246. **1989–90.** Review. *Modern Philology* 87 (1989–90): 391–96. *A Companion to Piers Plowman.* Ed. John A. Alford. Berkeley: University of California Press, 1988.
247. **1990.** Review. *Studies in the Age of Chaucer* 12 (1990): 296–305. Anne Hudson. *The Premature Reformation: Wycliffite Texts and Lollard History.* Oxford: Clarendon Press, 1988.
248. **1990a.** Biographical notice. "Fowler, David Covington. 1921-." *Contemporary Authors.* Ed. Hal May and James G. Lesniak. New Revision Series 28. Detroit: Gale, 1990. 181.
249. **1990–91.** Review. *Christianity and Literature* 40 (1990–91): 175–77. Ann W. Astell. *The Song of Songs in the Middle Ages.* Ithaca: Cornell University Press, 1990.
250. **1990–91a.** Review. *Christianity and Literature* 40 (1990–91): 303–6. Susan K. Hagen. *Allegorical Remembrance: A Study of the Pilgrimage of the Life of Man as a Medieval Treatise on Seeing and Remembering.* Athens: University of Georgia Press, 1990.
251. **1992.** Francis Dolores Covella, S.C. *Piers Plowman: The A-Text. An Alliterative Verse Translation.* Introduction and notes by David C. Fowler. Medieval and Renaissance Texts and Studies. Binghamton, N.Y.: CEMERS, 1992.
252. **1992a.** "Harp" (with John Spencer Hill). *A Dictionary of Biblical Tradition in English Literature.* Gen. ed. David L. Jeffrey. Grand Rapids: Eerdmans, 1992. 330–32.
253. **1993.** *John Trevisa.* Aldershot: Variorum Press, 1993.
254. **1993a.** (*The Life and Times of John Trevisa*). Seattle: University of Washington Press, 1993 (forthcoming).
255. **199x.** *"The Governance of Kings and Princes": John Trevisa's Middle English Translation of the* De Regimine Principum *of Aegidius Romanus.* Ed. David C. Fowler and Charles F. Briggs. 2 vols. New York: Garland, 199x (forthcoming).

III. Subject Index.

Arthurian Literature.
Book: 1959. Articles: 1958, 1970, 1975, and 1984a. Paper: 1955b. Reviews: 1958c, 1959c, 1964a, 1971c, and 1978. Paper: 1955b. Telecourse: 1958d. Course booklet: 1958b.

Ballad and folklore.
  Book: 1968. Contributions to books: 1968a, 1980a, and 1983a.
  Articles: 1965, 1966, and 1979. Notes: 1950, 1958a, and 1976a.
  Reviews: 1957, 1959d, 1964 1968n, and 1970-71. Papers:
  1903U, 1978c, 1979c, and 1984b. Telecourse: 1965-66a. Course
  guide: 1965a.
Bible and scriptural tradition.
  Books: 1976 and 1984. Contributions to books: 1983b and 1992a.
  Articles: 1958, 1960-61, 1968b, 1975a, and 1988. Reviews:
  1954a, 1987, 1990, and 1990-91. Paper: 1978c. Telecourse:
  1955a. Course guide: 1956.
"Bible as Literature" controversy.
  1956, 1966-68, 1971e, and 1977h.
Chaucer, Geoffrey.
  Note: 1954. Review article: 1983-84. Reviews: 1964b and
  1966-67. Papers: 1953a, 1968d, and 1986.
Cleanness.
  Article: 1972-73. Review: 1978.
Cornish Ordinalia.
  Article: 1961a. Papers: 1959e and 1975b. Review: 1969a.
Eliot, T. S.
  Note: 1952-53a.
English literature and language before 1500 (specific texts).
  Reviews: 1951a, 1952b, 1953, 1954a, 1978, 1981a, 1987-88, and
  1990-91a. Papers: 1963a and 1979c.
English literature and language (general subjects).
  Article: 1971b. Review: 1955.
Evangelium Nicodemi (Middle English).
  Article: 1988.
Fowler biography and bibliography.
  1951-, 1953-60, 1962-67, 1965-, 1968f, 1971-, and 1990a.
Pearl.
  Notes: 1959a and 1960.
Piers Plowman.
  Edition: 1952. Book: 1961. Contributions to books: 1971a and
  1992. Articles: 1951, 1952-53, 1969, and 1988a. Notes: 1952a
  and 1979-80. Review articles: 1973-74, 1977, 1980, and 1983.
  Reviews: 1959b, 1960-61a, 1963, 1965-66, 1979a, 1981, and
  1989-90. Author's query: 1948. Dissertation: 1949. Papers:

1959e, 1967a, 1968g, and 1981b. Bibliography (lithograph): 1948a. Translation (draft): 1957a.

Trevisa, John.

Edition: 199x. Books: 1993 and 1993a. Articles: 1960–61, 1962, 1970a, and 1971. Paper: 1981c.

Yeats, W. B.

Note: 1967.

TABULA GRATULATORUM

Edward and Leah Alexander
John A. Alford
Joanne Altieri
Nola Jean Bamberry
Kathleen Blake
Dorothee N. Bowie
Paul S. Burtness
Joseph Butwin
Linda Clifton
Georgia R. Crampton
Eric Dahl
Stanley J. Damberger
Sheila Delany
Sheila C. Dietrich
Vincent DiMarco
T. P. Dolan
Anne E. Doyle
Richard J. Dunn
A. S. G. Edwards
Richard K. Emmerson
John H. Fisher
Arthur H. Frietzsche
Donna Gerstenberger
Joan Graham
Malcolm Griffith
Mary Hamel
Ralph Hanna III
Elaine T. Hansen
Markham Harris
Robert B. Heilman
Constance Hieatt

Elton D. Higgs
Ann McCall Hutchinson
Ellin Kelly
Richard L. Kenney and Mary
    F. Hedberg
Sherry M. Laing
David Lawton
Juris G. Lidaka
Christopher R. and Jeanne G.
    Longyear
Charles D. Ludlum
Priscilla Martin
David and Marcia McCracken
Derek Pearsall
Esther C. Quinn
Otto Reinert
Paul and Fiona Robertson
    Remley
Velma Bourgeois Richmond
Florence H. Ridley
Sandra Silberstein
Elizabeth Simmons-O'Neill
James Hinton Sledd
Martin Stevens
William R. and Elaine
    Streitberger
M. Teresa Tavormina
James W. Tollefson
Míceál F. Vaughan
Christina von Nolcken
Ron and Mary Waldron

INDEX